CHARLES BOI

CHARLES BORROMEO

SELECTED ORATIONS, HOMILIES AND WRITINGS

Edited by
John R. Cihak

Translated by
Ansgar Santogrossi O.S.B

Bloomsbury T&T Clark
An imprint of Bloomsbury Publishing Plc

B L O O M S B U R Y
LONDON · OXFORD · NEW YORK · NEW DELHI · SYDNEY

Bloomsbury T&T Clark
An imprint of Bloomsbury Publishing Plc

Imprint previously known as T&T Clark

50 Bedford Square   1385 Broadway
London   New York
WC1B 3DP   NY 10018
UK   USA

www.bloomsbury.com

**BLOOMSBURY, T&T CLARK and the Diana logo are trademarks
of Bloomsbury Publishing Plc**

First published 2017

© John R. Cihak and Ansgar Santogrossi, 2017

John R. Cihak and Ansgar Santogrossi have asserted their right under the Copyright,
Designs and Patents Act, 1988, to be identified as Author of this work.

British Library Cataloguing-in-Publication Data
A catalogue record for this book is available from the British Library.

ISBN: HB: 978-0-5676-7026-7
          PB: 978-0-5676-7025-0
          ePDF: 978-0-5676-7028-1
          ePub: 978-0-5676-7027-4

Library of Congress Cataloging-in-Publication Data
A catalog record for this book is available from the Library of Congress

Cover image © Orazio Borgianni, St Carlo Borromeo,
between 1610–1616. Wikimedia Commons

Typeset by Integra Software Services Pvt. Ltd.

In Remembrance of
Father Jerome Young, O.S.B.
(1958–2012)
Faithful monk, dedicated priest and dear friend

CONTENTS

Contents

FOREWORD

Where lies the secret of Catholic vitality and renewal? Why has the Church grown from a tiny Jewish community 2000 years ago to become a vast international body of more than one billion members today? Why is Catholicism spreading in sub-Saharan Africa, South Korea and China, while we find decline in many countries of the Western world and Japan? What makes the difference? What would St. Charles Borromeo say today?

It is strange that so little of his writings have been translated into English, as he is, after all, one of the most outstanding bishop reformers in the history of the Church.

The Catholic world then was very different from ours, more faithful, pious and more corrupt. Columbus had discovered the New World of the Americas in 1492, forty-six years before Charles' birth to a noble Milanese family in 1538. Luther had sparked the Protestant Reformation in 1517, and some parts of the Catholic Church, such as Milan, were in a disgraceful state, while the faith was spreading in Asia and the New World of the Americas.

Charles' uncle, Pope Pius IV, made him a cardinal at the age of twenty-one before he was ordained a priest and a year later appointed him to a position akin to that of Vatican Secretary of State today. He was an effective administrator of the Papal States with many other responsibilities as well, who organized the construction of the beautiful Casina Pio IV, a Renaissance masterpiece in the Vatican Gardens and now home to the Pontifical Academies of Sciences.

He came from a family of genuine piety and, especially after the death of his brother, was caught up in the Catholic reform movement, which we often call the Counter Reformation. Against the inclinations of his uncle, the Pope, he received permission to live in his archdiocese of Milan, where no archbishop had resided for eighty years. Every area of catholic life there was in disarray. The priests were badly educated and many lived in open concubinage. A contemporary saying captured one response: "If you want to go to hell, become a priest."

Religious life, including the convents, was similarly decadent, and ignorance and superstition were rampant among the laity, despite or perhaps, because of the activity of the 3,000 priests in the archdiocese.

The renewal prompted by the Council of Trent is often passed over in silence today, but it was a remarkable achievement, which preserved the Church in central and southern Europe.

The heart of Borromeo's reforming ideal is well caught in his speech to his fellow bishops during their first provincial council after the Council of Trent: "This is the task: to seek the things which are of God, not our own," and "we too, in the reform and restoration of discipline, should begin with ourselves." Unlike some today, St. Charles realized that renewal can only come from personally answering Christ's call to conversion, from recognizing the sacrifices this endeavor entails and protecting these treasures with vigilance and discipline. Any authentic reform of the Church would begin with the reform of oneself, and the texts that follow show how every member of Christ bears responsibility in this endeavor.

St. Charles is no St. Augustine nor St. John Chrysostom, as his sermons and writings exhibit few flights of imagination and few unexpected psychological insights, but they are packed full of content, ordered very logically in a northern Italian fashion and draw regularly from the Old Testament and the examples and writings of the Church Fathers. Given his tireless insistence on the preaching of bishops and the sheer amount of his own preaching, it was a surprise to learn that Borromeo was by nature reserved and timid, with something of a speech impediment. Life is depicted as a struggle between good and evil, where the rewards of heaven and the punishments of hell are presented vividly. These were the concerns at the heart of his preaching, much more than theological controversies, and this clarity and practicality still provoke his readers to face the stark challenge of the Gospel.

St. Charles Borromeo's life and work transcends his time, with much to say to us who are concerned by today's decline of faith and practice. It is my hope that this book will help foster a renewal in our Western world, similar to the Catholic revival promoted by the Counter Reformation martyrs and preachers, and that the reader will discover in these texts much wisdom and inspiration for their own personal lives.

George Cardinal Pell
Prefect for the Secretariat for the Economy of the Holy See
and Archbishop Emeritus of Melbourne and Sydney

INTRODUCTION: REFORM FROM WITHIN

John R. Cihak

Charles Borromeo (1538–84) should have been part of the problem. Born into privilege as the second son of a noble Milanese family, Charles' father Gilbert was a Count of the Spanish Crown, which at the time ruled that part of northern Italy, and his mother Margaret was from the powerful Medici family. His uncle, John Angelo Medici, would become Pope. As the second son, Charles was destined for an ecclesiastical career, so at nineteen years of age he was given the abbey of Saints Gratinian and Felinus in his hometown of Arona as a benefice and made titular abbot.[1] At twenty-one he graduated from the University of Pavia as a Doctor in Canon and Civil Law. Soon after, his uncle John was elected Pope and took the name Pius IV (1559–65). The new Pontiff, who appreciated Charles' evident talent and integrity, made him a Cardinal in January of 1560, even before his nephew had received Holy Orders. One week later, he was named what today would be the equivalent of the Secretary of State of the Vatican. He was also made administrator of the Archdiocese of Milan; administrator of the Papal States; the Protector of Portugal, Belgium, lower Germany and the Catholic cantons of Switzerland; and Papal Legate to Bologna, Romagna and the March of Ancona, among other duties. Charles was young and powerful. A clearer example of ecclesiastical nepotism would have been difficult to find. Like many ecclesiastics of the late Renaissance, he could have carved out a life of ease and relative luxury in the Church. Many had done it before him; many were doing it around him. The times were decadent, both inside and outside the Church, and it had been that way for a long time.

However, the young man with dark hair, blue eyes and prominently aquiline nose, from the western shore of Lago Maggiore was different. The origins of this difference may be traced to his parents. Gilbert and Margaret were of the nobility, well connected and wealthy, and they were also

---

[1] A cleric receiving a salary is a relatively new phenomenon in the history of the Church. For centuries a cleric or community received economic sustenance from a "benefice," some sort of income-producing property, tied to the parish or office being held.

devoutly Catholic. Gilbert was a weekly communicant—unusually frequent for that time—and was a ruler who governed well and showed particular solicitude toward the poor. They raised their children to believe in and to love Jesus and the Church. Charles was known to be virtuous and devout in his youth, as well as reserved and timid, laboring over some sort of speech impediment, a remarkable fact given that he would become the champion of frequent episcopal preaching. Though the future saint was born into wealth and power both in the Church and in the world, the formation and example he received from his parents helped him decide upon a different path than many of his peers. This difference was already emerging when he, as a nineteen-year-old titular abbot, insisted that the monks under his charge live with greater faithfulness to their rule, and he dedicated all the revenue from this benefice to the poor.

It is difficult to appreciate how challenging the times were during Charles' life and how badly the Church was in need of reform and renewal, especially among her bishops and clergy. We may take the diocese of Milan as an example since the state of the Church there was more or less indicative of most other places. For various reasons, there had crept up within the Church the lamentable practice of a single bishop being named to more than one diocese. Since the bishop is constituted in a spousal relationship to his diocese, signified by the conferral of the episcopal ring, this bad habit of collecting dioceses was a kind of spiritual polygamy. Moreover, bishops rarely resided in their diocese and, often, did not offer Holy Mass or preach. In like manner, many priests did not reside in their parishes. When Charles was named Archbishop of Milan in 1564, no Archbishop of Milan had resided in the diocese for over eighty years. His immediate predecessor never resided in Milan, preferring to live the substantially pagan life of a Renaissance prince rather than that of a spiritual father. According to one Church historian, the previous two Archbishops of Milan had effectively "ungoverned" the diocese.[2]

The diocese of Milan was itself large, both in population and in territory, with about 3,000 priests and 600,000 faithful and encompassing much of Lombardy and extending north into Switzerland. Many priests demonstrated little zeal for the Gospel or for the salvation of souls. The priesthood for them had become more or less a comfortable job. Many dressed in secular clothes and even carried weapons in public. For example,

---

[2]Cf. Marco Navoni, *Carlo Borromeo: Profilo di un vescovo santo* (Milan: Centro Ambrosiano, 2010), 16.

the canons in nearby Pontirolo went around armed and "committing terrible acts," living like brigands and thieves.[3] Many priests lived in open concubinage, some luring their mistresses away from their husbands. The clergy as a whole was so badly educated that many priests did not even know the sacramental form of confession, and many had the mistaken idea that they themselves were exempt from going to confession. Even financially well-endowed churches lacked proper vestments and sacred vessels, the revenue being spent on other things. Priests were so disdained by the people that in Lombardy there was a common saying: "If you want to go to hell, become a priest."

Many of the religious orders in Milan had fallen into laxity, no longer following the original spirit or keeping their particular rule of life. Many communities of women no longer abided by the cloister, and convents became places for balls and festivals instead. The Benedictine nuns of one monastery were simply called "prostitutes." In 1541 the situation was severe enough that the civil authorities in Milan decreed the death penalty for whomever had carnal relations with a nun.[4]

The state of the laity was equally deplorable. Many no longer frequented the Sacraments, and those who did often did so out of routine. Religious ignorance was widespread, so superstition was rampant. Churches became more of a meeting hall than places for recollection and prayer. Holy days had devolved into revelries rather than days of prayer. Adultery and concubinage was commonplace among the laity. Such was the consequence of tolerating the nonresidence of the Church's pastors and of allowing ecclesiastical office to pass into the hands of unspiritual men who were not terribly interested in living a life for Jesus Christ. Underneath all these abuses was a desacralizing current of Church life and society in general.

But not all was lamentation and woe. Others resisted the decadence and one finds a resurgence of Christian asceticism in some quarters. Charles' own personal excesses in this regard should be read in light of this resurgence. In 1527 the Franciscan Antonio Belloti had brought the "Forty Hours" devotion of Eucharistic Adoration to the city. Marian piety was still relatively strong among the Lombards. Pious confraternities promoting prayer and the works of mercy had sprung up among the laity, and some

---

[3] Cf. Federico A. Rossi di Margnano, *Carlo Borromeo: un uomo, una vita, un secolo* (Milan: Mondatori, 2010), 43.
[4] Cf. Rossi di Margnano, *Carlo Borromeo*, 45.

of the new and vibrant religious orders, like the Jesuits and Barnabites, had already established themselves in Milan.

The Council of Trent (1545–63) was envisioned from the outset not only to respond to Protestant objections to Catholic doctrine but also to tackle the thorny problem of internal reform. Its completion was no easy task. Because of conflicts between the Pope and the Holy Roman Emperor—not to mention various wars and the plague—the Council Fathers were unable to meet on a consistent basis, and the Council dragged on for almost twenty years. Although the Council was called to open in 1542, it did not have its first session until 1545. It was suspended in 1552 because of war and remained that way for ten years. Though reform was desired by many, it did not seem that anyone had the political will to see it completed. Many bishops simply did not want to see reforms enacted since it would mean their comfortable lifestyles would have to change. When Pope Pius IV was elected, he was determined to finish the Council of Trent, and he charged his nephew to see it done. Although Charles was not physically present at these final sessions of the Council because of his duties in Rome, he had a prodigious, even daily, correspondence with the Council Fathers. The Council was a success on many levels, but the fear remained that the hard-fought reforms would be ignored and left as an unrealized lofty ideal. The implementation and realization of the Council's reforms at the local level of diocese and parishes became a particular mission for Borromeo.

In order to enter more deeply into Borromeo's own words that follow, it is helpful to consider what made him such an effective reformer in the face of the herculean undertaking of the reforms of the Council of Trent against great odds, such that he would become one of the most prominent Catholic reformers in the history of the Church. Among the many natural talents and supernatural graces of this man, three outstanding qualities bear highlighting: his personal holiness, his ability to forge lasting friendships and his impressive practical intelligence.[5]

---

[5] The complete details of his life can be found in the two classic biographies on the saint, both written by men who personally knew him. The first was written in 1592 by Charles Bascapé, a Barnabite priest and aide to St. Charles (Carlo Bascapé, *Vita e opera di Carlo arcivescovo di Milano cardinale di S. Prassede* [Milan: Veneranda Fabbrica del Duomo, 1965]). This is a translation of an early authoritative Latin biography, accompanied by a congratulatory letter of Pope Paul VI to then Archbishop of Milan, Cardinal Giovanni Colombo. The second was written in 1610 by Giovanni Pietro Giussano who, after practicing medicine for a few years, was received into St. Charles' household and eventually became a priest of the Oblates of Saint Ambrose. Giussano's biography was translated into English as *The Life of St. Charles Borromeo*, volumes 1–2 (London: Burns & Oats, 1884).

A saint

The first and simplest reason that made Borromeo such an effective reformer was his personal virtue and holiness. He pursued a life of abiding intimacy with Jesus Christ in and through the Catholic Church. Cardinal Giovanni Colombo, Archbishop of Milan from 1963 to 1979, writes, "The secret of St. Charles is love: a pure, immense and total love. He spent long hours before the crucifix and the Eucharist, day and night, meditating, adoring, loving, weeping."[6] His deep union with the Lord Jesus meant that the Lord could work powerfully in him. This character emerges clearly in the very first oration he gave to his brother bishops gathered in their first provincial council when he exhorted them to pursue God's interests, not their own. He did not begin by setting out to reform the Church; he began with, and remained constant in, the conversion of his own life to Jesus Christ.

When seen in the light of the Counter (or Catholic) Reformation, this fundamental quality of Borromeo could be summarized as "reform from within," for it encapsulates his entire approach to reform. As with others who saw a need for reform, including Martin Luther (1483–1546), John Calvin (1509–64) and Ulrich Zwingli (1484–1531), St. Charles saw that many in the Church were not living, or not even trying to live, Christian lives. The practice of the Christian Faith was clearly deficient. The Protestants differed from Catholic Reformers like St. Charles as to the *reason* for this deficient practice. Protestant Reformers believed that the reason lay in deficient doctrine, while the Catholic Reformers insisted that the reason lay in misunderstanding or ignorance of doctrine, and most especially in ignoring doctrine and not bothering to implement it into daily living. If the people were not living according to right teaching, it was due to bishops (even the Pope sometimes), priests and the religious not living according to the Faith. For Borromeo, doctrine did not need to be changed; people needed to change by the proper understanding and application of sound doctrine to their daily lives. And the bishops, who represent Christ the Head of his Mystical Body, should be the first and foremost in this effort. Charles' preaching and writing reflect this approach. He did not seem overly concerned with theological controversies, although

---

[6]*La Più Grande Riforma: San Carlo e la sua passione per l'uomo*, edited by the Priestly Fraternity of the Missionaries of Saint Charles Borromeo (Milan: Fraternità di San Carlo, 2005), 47. [author's translation]

he strongly promoted the study of Christian doctrine among the faithful. While other Catholic Reformers, like Sts. Robert Bellarmine (1542–1621), Peter Canisius (1521–97) or Francis de Sales (1567–1622), were engaged on the theological and apologetical level, Borromeo spent his efforts on addressing doctrine-not-being-lived, warning his listeners that the bad example of Christian living among Catholics gave fuel to Protestant objections.

Furthermore, St. Charles was convinced that the Church had within herself the capacity and the means to be reformed because this capacity and means of conversion to Jesus Christ existed in each member of the Church. Borromeo's approach to reform emphasized one's own personal, interior conversion to Jesus Christ in and through the Church, and then the extension of this interior reform outward into larger spheres of influence, like ripples in a pond. Since St. Charles was nephew to the Pope, those larger spheres were large indeed. When the individuals comprising the head and members of Christ's Mystical Body were converted, then the Church would be reformed. In other words, reform does not begin with "the Church," "her teachings," "those bishops" or "you." Reform begins with "me." What in *my life* needs to change in order to follow Christ more closely?

What kind of a person was Charles Borromeo? Even from a young age, he was known for his cheerfulness, virtue, sobriety and exemplary moral life. Yet in his initial days as the "Cardinal Nephew" at Rome, one can detect a certain ease of life. He was a man of the late Renaissance and a true humanist. He collected art and hunted; he loved to sing and play the lute and the cello; he was attentive to his family's position. He gathered leading intellectuals in Rome into an informal academy called the *Noctes Vaticanae* (the Vatican Nights), which would meet at the Vatican Palace at the end of the day's work to discuss humanist topics and texts. In all these pursuits, of course, there is nothing really blameworthy, but in the science of the saints it is also nothing overly praiseworthy. This period of his life shows that "[he] was not born a saint, but he became one."[7]

In 1562, however, St. Charles' life began to change. Being shouldered with an enormous amount of power and responsibility at a very young age, he underwent what Marco Navoni calls a "maturation" or "deepened examination of conscience." This happened during the time Borromeo was directed by his uncle to reconvene the Council of Trent and to ensure its

[7]Navoni, *Carlo Borromeo*, 12. [author's translation]

completion. As a 22-year-old Cardinal, he once remarked, "The dangers are infinite. I am young and have no experience." But the heavy blow came later that year when his older brother, Frederick, died unexpectedly at the age of twenty-seven. Charles had remained at his brother's bedside in the final part of his illness, and Frederick's death hit hard. Charles describes his inner state as "being thrown to the ground" combined with a deep realization of the misery of the present life and the happiness of the life to come. The grief from his brother's death was compounded by family pressure, including that of the Pope, to give up his ecclesiastical path and marry so that he could take responsibility for the hereditary wealth and estates of the Borromeo family and carry on the Borromeo line. Charles decided to make the spiritual exercises of St. Ignatius and emerged from the retreat determined to become a priest.

He was ordained a priest in the Basilica of St. Mary Major in Rome on September 4, 1563. He offered his first Mass in St. Peter's Basilica and soon after was consecrated bishop. He shifted the focus of the Vatican Nights from humanist topics to discussion of the Church's needs in this time of crisis. His manifest increase in zeal for ecclesiastical matters led some of his fellow humanists to tease him with the name "Borromeo the Sacristan."[8] Following the plan of reform, which would begin with himself and ripple outward, he petitioned his uncle to release him from his duties in Rome so that he could take up residence in his diocese of Milan as the Council had demanded, since he was convinced that the residence of bishops in their dioceses was the essential key to reform. Pius IV took much convincing to release him and for a time St. Charles had to rely upon a Vicar General to run his affairs in Milan until he could go and reside there himself.

But even while still in Rome, St. Charles began the reform of his household. He reduced his annual income from about 100,000 to 20,000 crowns, and would have reduced it further if not for the necessity of maintaining a household.[9] At the time, a Cardinal was expected to maintain a household of servants, a kind of "mini-court," commensurate with the princes of European monarchies. He decided that it was unbecoming for a Cardinal to have a household comprised primarily of gentlemen and knights, whose presence was to increase one's social status, so he dismissed them with generous bonuses. The bishop was not a Renaissance prince but a shepherd of souls, a spiritual father following in the footsteps

---

[8]Navoni, *Carlo Borromeo*, 21.
[9]Giussano, *The Life of St. Charles Borromeo*, volume 1, 85.

of the apostles. He reduced the members of his household from 150 to 100 and recomposed the household to be primarily ecclesiastics and only those domestics who were absolutely necessary for the running of the household. The laypeople who remained were given a rule of life to follow. He paid his staff well and did not allow them to accept bribes and favors. He would dismiss from his household anyone who remained obstinate in giving a bad example. He himself began to live with increasing austerity and personal mortification to conform his life to the suffering Christ. He fasted and used the discipline often, wore a hair shirt most of his adult life and usually slept only about four hours each night. Because of these austerities he appeared older than his age. These penitential practices, which seem rather severe today, can also be interpreted as a positive response to the dissolute times.

It took two years of convincing, but eventually Pius IV allowed St. Charles to take up residence in Milan as Archbishop. On September 23, 1565, he entered Milan amid loud acclaim. He was nearly twenty-seven years old. The following day he wrote to the Bishop of Vercelli: "That was always the greatest of my desires, to find myself close to my church and my flock. Nothing for me is dearer or more joyful; yesterday by the grace of God I finally attained it."[10] He was determined that the diocese of Milan would become the living proof that the Tridentine reform could succeed. The following month he held the first provincial council of all the bishops of his province, whose task would be to implement the reforms of the Council as a group for that region.[11] Taking up residence in the Archbishop's palace, he and his household lived in radical simplicity, keeping only two small, sparsely furnished rooms for himself.

Borromeo pushed reform strongly, confidently and serenely. He radiated a calm, composed and cheerful countenance. He was no mere enforcer of ecclesiastical discipline. Lasting reform cannot take root only by rooting out and disciplining what is bad. Borromeo also imparted a positive vision of where he wanted to lead people. He was not afraid to mete out correction to those who were obstinate, but it was a means to an end: clearing the ground so that a more authentic living of the Christian life could flourish. This approach can be noticed in his preaching. Any denunciation of vice,

---

[10] Luigi Crivelli, *San Carlo: l'uomo, il pastore, il santo* (Milan: Ancora, 2010), 23. [author's translation]

[11] At the time, the ecclesiastical province of Milan was comprised of fifteen suffragan dioceses: Acqui, Alba, Alessandria, Asti, Bergamo, Brescia, Casale, Cremona, Lodi, Novara, Savona, Tortona, Ventimiglia, Vercelli and Vigevano.

in which he often includes himself, is followed by a positive note exhorting his listeners that divine grace can change the human heart. People soon recognized that he was out for their well-being, and not his own.

Though he could be a formidable opponent, Borromeo possessed a mild and gentle disposition and a tender heart. For example, he would go barefoot at night in the house so as not to awaken his servants, and he would not hesitate to enter the homes of the poor no matter how squalid. He was undaunted by opposition and showed no annoyance when things went awry. It seemed as if he expected such things. His gaze was fixed on Christ and, though problems and opposition abounded, they were relativized to that gaze. I am suggesting that he could move reform forward effectively not simply because he was talented or because he was the Pope's nephew, but because he had already inculcated those reforms in himself. The force of his personal integrity and example, which even his enemies often recognized, made people more willing to accept and follow his preaching, edicts and decrees. Though he readily admitted he was a sinner, he was not a phony.

He had a great love for people and an ardent zeal for their salvation. He burned with a passion to see his brother bishops, his priests and his people follow Jesus Christ and become holy. He wanted parish priests to be holy and joyful shepherds. He once rebuked a brother bishop who wrote to him lamenting that he did not have much to do. Borromeo wrote that such a phrase is dishonorable and reason for a bishop to be ashamed, since a bishop has as much work as he wants in proportion to either his zeal or his negligence.

Borromeo's spiritual life was immersed in the ordinary means of sanctification: Liturgy and Sacraments (especially Confession and the Holy Eucharist), personal prayer, virtuous living and the works of charity. He had a great love of the priesthood and the sacred liturgy, and cultivated devotion to the Lord's Passion and to the Blessed Virgin Mary. In his private chapel hung pictures of two bishops to whom he was especially devoted: St. Ambrose (c. 340–97), his predecessor, and St. John Fisher (c. 1469–1535), the sole English bishop not to capitulate to Henry VIII's takeover of the Church in England. Borromeo loved processions, relics, pilgrimages and the Sacred Shroud of Turin, before which he wept. He promoted a frequent reception of Holy Communion among the faithful. A true ascetic himself, he promoted the contemplative and monastic life in the diocese.

His union with Jesus Christ, manifested in his personal virtue and holiness, helped to inoculate him against the corrosive nature of power, rendered him less susceptible to peer pressure and making decisions based upon human respect, and made him courageous and dauntless in the face of those who opposed reform. Pope St. Pius X (1903–14) expressed this quality of Borromeo in the following way:

> Even though his outstanding virtue, his marvelous activity, his never failing charity commanded much respect, he was nonetheless subject to that law which reads, "All who want to live piously in Christ Jesus will suffer persecution." His austere life, his defense of righteousness and honesty, his protection of law and justice only led to his being hated by rulers and tricked by diplomats and, later, distrusted by the nobility, clergy and people until he was eventually so hated by wicked men that they sought his very life. In spite of his mild and gentle disposition he withstood all these attacks with unflinching courage … He yielded no ground on any matter that would endanger faith and morals. He admitted no claim (even if it was made by a powerful monarch who was always a Catholic) that was either contrary to discipline or burdensome to the faithful.[12]

This virtue was soon put to the test. Upon arriving in Milan, the new Archbishop immediately set about the implementation of the disciplinary decrees of the Council of Trent throughout the diocese. This created more than a few enemies, especially among priests and religious who had grown lax. Lazy, undisciplined or greedy priests and those who had grown old in concubinage did not want him as bishop. Priests who lacked piety and obedience, who insisted on priestly authority and remuneration without manifesting priestly service and zeal for God and for souls, did not want him as bishop. Religious who wanted to retain private property and to disregard their community's rule or to observe the cloister did not want him as bishop. Two dramatic events in 1569—with the canons of the church of La Scala and the friars of the *Humiliati* congregation—illustrate his courage and sanctity.

Matters came to a head with the canons in August 1569. Almost forty-six years earlier, Pope Clement VII (1523–34) had declared that the church of La Scala was exempt from the jurisdiction of the Archbishop of Milan provided that the Archbishop gave his consent. It seemed, however, that there was a discrepancy as to whether this consent had been obtained,

---

[12]Pope St. Pius X, Encyclical Letter *Editae saepe*, May 26, 1910, numbers 40–41.

and thus whether the exemption had taken effect. The canons claimed exemption from the Archbishop's jurisdiction and relied upon the secular authorities for support. The Governor of Milan had been incited by St. Charles' enemies to declare that anyone who violated the jurisdiction of the King of Spain, who at that time controlled Milan, would be severely punished. The Archbishop announced his intention to make a visitation of the church in accordance with the wishes of the Pope. He first sent a legate, who was met with strong opposition and open insult. Then, in early September, Borromeo himself went to make a visitation, and the canons did the same with him. He was prepared for such a response, and taking a cross into his own hands he stepped forward to pronounce their excommunication. Armed men supporting the canons raised their weapons against the Archbishop, while the canons closed the church doors against him. The men opened fire and one of the bullets struck the cross he held. His Vicar General posted the public notice that the canons had incurred censures. This act was followed by violence and outrage, the removal of the notices, with some declaring that the Archbishop himself was suspended from office.

During this controversy with the canons of La Scala, a conspiracy was hatched among some of the friars of the *Humiliati* (The Humiliated) congregation. The community had an auspicious beginning in the 1200s, but like many religious communities at the time had grown lax in their observance of their rule. In fact, when Borromeo began his reform the nearly 160 members of the community owned an incredible 94 houses, each of which could have housed 100 friars.[13] For two years they strongly resisted his reforms, until some of their members took drastic measures. On October 26, 1569, St. Charles was praying vespers in the chapel of the Archbishop's palace. It was his practice that vespers in the Archbishop's palace would be attended by any in the household who were able, as well as those from the general public who wished to attend. Two friars disguised themselves in lay clothes, gained admittance to vespers and positioned themselves about five yards from the Archbishop, who was kneeling at the altar. During the singing of Orlando Lassus's motet *Tempus est ut revertar* ("It is time that I return"), one of the would-be assassins opened fire. The ball struck Borromeo in the back. He fell forward thinking he had been mortally wounded and telling the people to keep praying. A commotion immediately broke out, allowing the two friars to escape. Miraculously the ball did not

---

[13]Giussano, *The Life of St. Charles Borromeo*, volume 1, 188.

pierce his body, although some shot had embedded itself in his skin. The ball left a welt on his back that remained for the rest of his life. Eventually the two friars were discovered along with two fellow conspirators. Although Borromeo pleaded with the civil authorities to spare their lives, his efforts were in vain, and the disgraced friars were executed. The following year the Pope suppressed the congregation. This terrible turn of events moved the canons of La Scala to reconcile with Borromeo.

As Archbishop of Milan, Charles also was in frequent conflict with representatives of the Spanish Crown over various jurisdictions within his diocese. He opposed any perceived encroachment upon the rights of the Church, which made him enemies. For example, in 1573 the Archbishop reluctantly excommunicated the Governor of Milan over one such controversy of jurisdiction. The Governor retaliated by confiscating the family castle in Arona, and Charles was attacked with calumny both in Milan and in Rome. Eventually the Governor yielded and recognized the Archbishop's jurisdiction in the matter.

Other examples of St. Charles' charity and humility are when he saw to it that 3,000 people were fed daily from his own table for three months during the famine of 1571, or the way he would personally wash the feet of the pilgrims during the Jubilee Year of 1576. But perhaps the most dramatic testimony of his sanctity took place during the plague of 1576, which killed over 25,000 people in Milan. At its initial outbreak, the civil government and the nobility fled the city, leaving people to fend for themselves. Borromeo assured the people that as their bishop he would not leave, and he asked his priests to remain with him in the city with the people. He said to his priests, "We have only one life and we should spend it for Jesus and souls—not as we wish, but at the time and in the way God wishes." His passionate appeal to the religious clergy of the city can be found in Chapter 3. Most of the clergy remained and more than a hundred of them died. The sacrificial service and death of these heroic priests shows how deeply St. Charles' reforms had already taken root among his clergy.

The Archbishop himself was in the front lines of assistance during the plague. He organized hospitals and work projects, and provided for orphans. Borromeo personally took Holy Communion to thousands of the sick and dying quarantined in their homes. He organized Masses to be offered in the squares and at crossroads so that people could worship from their windows and doorways. He sold off his furniture to gain funds for the poor. He had the tapestries of the Archbishop's palace made into makeshift cloths for the poor to protect them during the winter. By the time the plague ended, almost nothing remained in the Archbishop's palace. When the dead could not be buried quickly enough, and their bodies had to be stacked in the street outside the infirmaries and hospitals, the Archbishop was seen climbing up a pile of corpses to give Viaticum to a man who was still conscious.

In true reform, there is no substitute for personal virtue and holiness. Such an example gives force to a remark he made to one of his priests: "Do not be so forgetful of your priesthood as to prefer a late death to a holy one." In summing up Borromeo's personal holiness, Cardinal Dionigi Tettamanzi, Archbishop of Milan from 2002 to 2011, writes: "The example of St. Charles is revealed as convincing and attractive. The exemplarity of his life, the incisiveness of his works as pastor and reformer are the fruit of the intensity of his love for Christ crucified."[14] Borromeo took as his episcopal motto one word: *Humilitas* ("humility"), the springboard of all virtue and holiness. Pope Benedict XVI highlights St. Charles' possession of this singular virtue: "It was humility that motivated him, like the Lord Jesus, to renounce himself in order to make himself the servant of all."[15]

A friend

A second quality that made Borromeo such an effective reformer was his ability to make friends and inspire others with his vision. It would be unfair to reduce his effectiveness to mere political influence as the Pope's nephew or for bearing the name of a well-respected family. His many and powerful connections inside and outside the Church certainly did not hurt, and he would use them to further the cause of reform. However, Charles was a man of friendship. He may have been the tip of the spear, but a tip is no good without the shaft; he was by no means alone or isolated in his efforts. He made friends with others who shared his desire to see the Church reformed and to live a more radical life for Christ.

His primary friendship, of course, was with Jesus Christ. He radiated a deep, intimate and vibrant inner life with Jesus. The lack of this friendship was the fundamental problem in a Church needing reform. An early key friend was Bartholomew of the Martyrs, O.P. (1514–90), Archbishop of Braga in Portugal. For Borromeo, this Dominican prelate, who played a

[14]Navoni, *Carlo Borromeo*, 5. [author's translation]
[15]Pope Benedict XVI, Angelus Address, November 4, 2007.

prominent role in the final sessions of the Council of Trent, was a living icon of what a bishop should be. He wrote to Archbishop Bartholomew in 1565: "Your figure is continually before my eyes. I have taken you as an example, your life under every virtuous and laudable aspect."[16] Archbishop Bartholomew wrote a treatise in 1564 called *Stimulus Pastorum* (*The Motivation of Pastors*), in which he wrote, "Who is the Bishop if not the sun of his diocese, a man on fire, completely dedicated to conquering souls for Christ, who preaches so very often with the Word and always by example?"[17] Moreover, at the time Borromeo was deciding about the priesthood, this prelate had convinced the young Cardinal not to abandon a public life in favor of entering a monastery. Charles had been apprehensive embracing the life of a bishop and Cardinal, as he saw it fraught with danger for his soul, and perceived the monastic life as a safer path to his own salvation. Archbishop Bartholomew responded:

> I cannot do otherwise than applaud so pious a desire, and I know also by experience the advantages and the security of life in the cloister. But the question is not which is the safest way, but what is that way which the will of God designs you to follow... In leaving the world and entering religion, I forsook no duty; but with you it would be otherwise.[18]

A great leader knows how to form a team and is not threatened by the talent of others. On the contrary, he cultivates it. Whereas we may expect a 22-year-old Cardinal to feel insecure in his power and threatened by the talent of others, we actually find quite the opposite in Borromeo. St. Charles consulted many while working through the complicated and delicate negotiations of the final sessions of the Council. He wanted to consult people he considered holier and more talented than he. He once said: "Every other error is more able to be remedied, except that of not wishing counsel."[19] Not a few of his associates became great reformers themselves. Borromeo assiduously studied the issues being discussed and sought the counsel of the members of the Vatican Nights and other learned and holy

---

[16]Navoni, *Carlo Borromeo*, 20. [author's translation]
[17]Cited by Danilo Zardin in *San Carlo Borromeo: La casa costruita sulla roccia*, edited by the Archdiocese of Milan and the Veneranda Biblioteca Ambrosiana (Bari: Pagina soc. Coop., 2011), 46. [author's translation]
[18]Giussano, *The Life of St. Charles Borromeo*, volume 1, 44.
[19]*La Più Grande Riforma: San Carlo e la sua passione per l'uomo*, 48. [author's translation]

experts in Rome, such as Hugo Boncompagni from Bologna, the future Pope Gregory XIII (1572–85). He did the same after the Council, when presiding over the writing of the Roman Catechism and the revision of the Roman Missal and Breviary. After his uncle died, Borromeo worked hard to not put himself forward, but to advocate the election of Anthony Michael Ghislieri, O.P., and when he succeeded in this, suggested that the reforming Dominican take the name Pius V (1566–72).

After the Cardinal reformed his household, his house became a place of formation for priests and a *de facto* training ground for future leaders. Twenty of these household members eventually became bishops. He also established the Oblates of Saint Ambrose, which would be an association of secular priests not tied to a parish but rather at the immediate disposition of the Archbishop of Milan. After drawing up the rule for this community, he submitted it to his friend in Rome, St. Philip Neri (1515–95), asking his advice. St. Philip urged the Archbishop to remove the vow of poverty for this kind of community, which he did.

Borromeo was also an acute judge of character and worked hard to find and recruit the best. This eventually led to a sort of falling out with his friend St. Philip when St. Charles convinced some prospective members of St. Philip's Oratory to come to Milan. Neri therefore called him "the great thief of men." But whenever the Archbishop was in Rome, he would always visit St. Philip, kneel before him, kiss his hands and ask for his blessing. He knew other saints as well. While staying at the home of Marquis Gonzaga in 1580, St. Charles met Marquis' son, the future St. Aloysius Gonzaga (1568–91), and during that visit the Cardinal gave the boy his first Holy Communion. Also that same year Borromeo met with the Jesuit priest, St. Edmund Campion, S.J. (1540–81), who was making his way back to England and eventually to martyrdom.

St. Charles surrounded himself with talented and loyal lieutenants who believed in his vision and would labor tirelessly to see it realized. One such lieutenant was Monsignor Niccolò Ormaneto (1515–77), a priest of the diocese of Verona and member of Cardinal Reginald Pole's household. Borromeo recruited this priest to be his Vicar General and to administer the diocese of Milan until the Pope would give him leave to take possession himself. Monsignor Ormaneto became St. Charles' right-hand man in Milan and even conducted the first diocesan synod. As Archbishop, St. Charles relied on and helped to expand the influence of those religious communities in Milan dedicated to ecclesial reform, such as the Jesuits, the Theatines, the Barnabites and the Capuchin

Franciscans. One of his suffragan bishops was Niccolò Sfrondrato, who became Pope Gregory XIV (1590–1).

Borromeo wanted to be close to his clergy and promoted a strong priestly identity and fraternal life among them. For example, he revived the ancient tradition, practiced by Saints Ambrose and Augustine, of the bishop living in community with his clergy. When one of his priests lay dying from illness, St. Charles personally went to his bedside and prayed for his cure. The priest recovered and, responding to the surprise of people, Borromeo simply said, "You do not know the value of the life of a good priest."[20]

A practical genius

"A practical genius" was the phrase that Pope Paul VI (1963–78) used to describe Borromeo.[21] It is true he was exceptionally gifted with a practical sense. His father had been a good ruler, and Charles was also well trained in the law. He possessed the ability and the zeal to translate lofty ideals into a lived reality and to persevere in making changes so that they did not simply remain at the level of theory and proposal. He also knew how to strategize toward the most effective means to attain his goals. He was prudent, knowing when to press forward with changes and when to wait for a more opportune moment.

At the time of the final sessions of the Council of Trent, although the previous sessions treated primarily doctrinal matters, St. Charles insisted that something more was needed. Assuredly, the Catholics needed to respond to the objections of the Protestants by clearly pronouncing on matters of doctrine. Nevertheless, a major problem for lasting reform was enfleshing these unchanging truths in daily life. If teaching clearly on faith and morals helped to dissipate the problem of the misunderstood doctrine, a further step was needed to overcome the problem of the ignored doctrine. The faith has to be lived, and for this to happen one needs not only clear teaching but also disciplinary decrees to give the necessary teeth for the reform of discipline and morals. This is precisely what emerges in the final sessions of Trent under the influence of Borromeo. In a letter to Tolomeo Gallio (1527–1607), then secretary to Pius IV, at the conclusion

---

[20]Giussano, *The Life of St. Charles Borromeo*, volume 2, 28.
[21]Quoted in Angelo Majo, *San Carlo Borromeo: vita e azione pastorale* (Milan: Edizioni San Paolo, 2004), 27.

of the Council, the young Cardinal wrote that it was no longer the time for disputation but rather the time to act.

In Milan, he pursued reform first of all by force of his personal example, by his constant presence and visitation in the diocese and by his preaching. Another bad habit that had crept in over the centuries, in addition to their nonresidence in their diocese, was the fact that bishops of the late Renaissance rarely preached. As Archbishop of Milan, however, Borromeo preached constantly. He was convinced from the example of his friend Bartholomew of the Martyrs that the bishop's primary duty was preaching the Word of God. Enforcing decrees may change external observance, but effective preaching changes hearts. Preaching helped people not only to understand the truth of the Gospel but also to translate it into daily living.

Another aspect of his practical genius was his choice of focusing on the building block of the local Church: the parish. In the parish the ordinary means of sanctification are cultivated. One finds Borromeo continually repeating the importance of living the faith at that local level: frequent reception of Holy Communion and Confession; daily prayer; the works of mercy; and the sanctification of the workplace, the home and civic life. He resisted anything that would interfere with the flourishing of parochial life, which was why he vehemently opposed the annual celebration of the Carnivale, which had all the revelry of a bacchanalian festival and none of the sobriety and prayerfulness required for a spiritual preparation for Lent.

St. Charles' efforts at the internal reform of the Church could be summarized in the practical phrase: Be who you promised you would be. Every member of the Mystical Body of Christ must be intentional about pursing a life of holiness, according to one's particular state of life. If you are a bishop, then live according to the promises you made at your consecration. Live not like a Renaissance prince but like the apostles and the great bishops of the past, in imitation of the Good Shepherd. If you are a priest, live according to the promises you made at ordination, and serve your people, not yourself. Be zealous, poor, chaste and joyful. If you are a religious, then live according to the evangelical counsels of poverty, chastity and obedience according to the particular rule of your community, and do not seek a comfortable life while retaining your private property. If you are married, then live to your vows faithfully and live like a Christian, not only on Sundays in church but in your homes and places of work. Live with integrity, live radically for Christ.

Perhaps the most well known aspect of Borromeo's practical genius is his constant state of visitation in the diocese. Not content with simply residing in his diocese, he wanted to be close to his priests and people. He went everywhere. We can easily forget how difficult and even dangerous traveling could be at that time. Even if the roads were safe from brigands, they were often treacherous or nonexistent. There was little protection from the elements, and just getting caught in a rain could mean pneumonia, which could prove fatal. Sometimes he was on horseback, but more often, especially in his later years, he went on foot. He never traveled in a carriage. He crisscrossed the city and the region, even going deep into the remote mountain areas of the diocese where no Archbishop of Milan had ever gone. He went up into the Catholic cantons of Switzerland. His practice of visitation meant that the Archbishop had first-hand knowledge of people and of situations. He had a remarkable ability for remembering people's names and abilities. So when a position needed to be filled, he often had a good candidate already in mind. After a visitation he would keep a written record of what was discussed, what needed to be done and who would be involved for the inevitable follow-up.

Besides reviving the ancient tradition of episcopal visitation, Borromeo implemented two institutions mandated by the Council of Trent: provincial councils and diocesan synods. These structures fostered collegiality and consultation in a bishop's governance.[22] A provincial council was a meeting of all the bishops of the ecclesiastical province, and it was in these meetings that the decrees of Trent were read and promulgated. The task of the bishops united in a provincial council was to discuss and to decide in a collegial manner how best to implement the reforms in their particular region. Chapter 1 of this book contains a selection of the opening addresses, which as Archbishop he gave to his brother bishops at these councils, exhorting them to the task. Borromeo also convened diocesan synods, which were a meeting of the bishop and clergy about implementing the reforms on the diocesan level. The final text in Chapter 3 is a sermon he gave to his clergy gathered in diocesan synod. These texts show Borromeo's practical genius in utilizing these structures to give a platform to disseminate more effectively his reforming vision.

St. Charles was attentive to the fact that lasting reform not only needed good laws, it needed structures and institutions. Those essential administrative realities allow reforms to extend beyond the present

---

[22]It seems that initially Borromeo had mandates already prepared for the bishops to adopt at the provincial councils. Later, he would hear from Rome that the provincial councils should be scheduled for more days precisely to foster more collegial action. I am grateful to Jared Wicks, SJ, for clarifying this point.

generation. Borromeo built seminaries, established colleges and founded institutions for the care of orphans, the destitute and girls and women at risk of prostitution. He was not the one who allowed problems to fester or for needs to go unaddressed. He fought for the protection of the poor against tyrannical masters, usurers and the enslavement of children. He founded the Oblates of Saint Ambrose, convoked provincial councils, held diocesan synods and promoted lay confraternities devoted to the Blessed Sacrament and Our Lady, who involved themselves in various spiritual and corporal works of mercy. All these initiatives would bear fruit for many decades.

Another example of his practical genius is seen in the economic dimension of his reforms. Some of the abuses that had crept into the Church were driven by deficiencies in the benefice system. These abuses were sometimes due to greed but sometimes they happened because, with the passage of time or a change of circumstance, a particular benefice was no longer able to support adequately the priest or religious community that relied upon it. The individual or group then would be tempted to "supplement" their income in the wrong way. When such situations came to his attention, St. Charles reorganized or combined benefices so that they would provide an adequate income for their holders, who then would be less tempted to seek ill-gotten gains.

St. Charles' practical bent is reflected in his works. He was not interested in speculative ideas in theology or philosophy, or in composing complex orations to be appreciated for their erudition and rhetoric. Nor did he write apologetical or polemical works on the theological controversies with the Protestants. His interests were elsewhere. He wanted to ensure that the wisdom of the Council of Trent would be implemented and lived, so he wrote decrees, orations, homilies and letters. These writings do not so much dazzle with their rhetoric as much as edify with the direct, plain-talking practically of a wise pastor. On the other hand, his writings do reveal a command of Scripture and the Church Fathers. Although naturally intelligent and the recipient of an excellent humanistic and theological education, he was more a man of action than of speculation. He was a legislator, a tactician and a builder.

Saint Charles' life, according to one biographer, was "brief but intense."[23] Indeed, his tireless labor and constant visitation, in addition to his austerity and penitential practices, took their toll. In January of 1584, he came down with a bacterial infection in his leg (erysipelas), which confined him to bed

---

[23]Majo, *San Carlo Borromeo*, 26.

for a time. In October of that year he was struck with a fever and his health began to fail rapidly. He died in his bed on November 3, 1584, as the Passion of the Lord was being read to him. He was only forty-six. True to his own advice, he pursued a holy life rather than a long one. He was canonized a saint a mere twenty-five years after his death. His cousin, Frederick Borromeo, succeeded him as Archbishop of Milan and was known for his holiness of life and good governance.

Many today do not realize the debt of gratitude the Catholic Church of today owes to St. Charles Borromeo. It is inconceivable now that a bishop would not live among his flock or would not preach regularly, or that prospective priests would not undergo seminary training. Borromeo was a major reason that turned these ideals of the Council of Trent into reality. The Tridentine reforms created an environment more conducive to living the Christian life, gave impetus to one of the most fruitful periods of evangelization in the history of the Church and produced such remarkable and diverse saints as Vincent de Paul, Alphonsus Ligouri, Benedict Joseph Labre, Thèrése of Lisieux, John Vianney, Katherine Drexel, Joseph Vaz, Mary MacKillop, Damien de Vuester, Josephine Bakhita and thousands of martyrs.

Although the Council of Trent and the Second Vatican Council differ in style, tone and intended audience, Borromeo's preaching and writing highlight the often underappreciated continuity between these two ecumenical Councils, especially in light of the strong influence Borromeo's life and work had on Angelo Giuseppe Roncalli, who became Pope St. John XXIII (1958–63) and convoked the Second Vatican Council.[24] A largely forgotten fact is that when Pope Paul VI took the reins of this Council in 1963, he directed that twelve of St. Charles Borromeo's orations to his brother bishops and sermons to priests were to be published and sent to all the bishops of the world, with the desire that those participating at the Council would be inspired and guided by this great reformer.[25]

Cardinal Henry Edward Manning, Archbishop of Westminster from 1865 to 1892, in his introduction to the English translation of Giussano's biography aptly summarizes the importance of this figure:

---

[24]Cf. Jared Wicks, "Tridentine Motivations of Pope John XXIII Before and During Vatican II," *Theological Studies* 75.4 (2014): 847–62. In his footnotes, Wicks provides additional useful sources on Borromeo's influence on Pope St. John XXIII.

[25]*Sancti Caroli Borromaei. Orationes XII, ad usum episcoporum in concilium oeacu. Vaticanum II convenientium Pauli VI Pont. Max. iussu denuo editae* (Rome: [no publisher given], 1963).

He broke through the traditions of worldly ambition, avarice, inertness, which crushed and stifled the spiritual life of men, and revived in the midst of a sunken age the image and the reality of the Good Shepherd, surrounded by His apostles … St. Charles comes as a voice calling us to the greatest of our duties, the end for which all things are ordained, the care of souls for whom Christ died, and the forming and multiplying of pastors, not hirelings or worldlings, but shepherds, willing to give their lives for the sheep.[26]

Charles Borromeo should have been part of the problem. Instead he was a driving force in the solution, becoming one of the foremost reformers in the history of the Catholic Church. It is remarkable that from out of the epicenter of what looked to be the most problematic and irreformable elements in the Church came the very man who would make reform happen. Borromeo's life and work give shining testimony to the possibility of reform from within.

---

[26]Giussano, *The Life of St. Charles Borromeo*, volume 1, xxvii.

EDITOR AND TRANSLATOR'S NOTE

The translation that follows has its origins in a conversation on November 4, 2005, the liturgical feast day of St. Charles Borromeo. The Office of Readings of the Liturgy of the Hours for that day presents a selection from one of his addresses to priests, and a discussion of this text with a fellow priest inspired a search for further material. It was discovered that in the 430 years since his death Latin and Italian editions of his works had been published (especially in the eighteenth century) but precious little of his work had made its way into English. This present volume, which is the first collection of the saint's preaching and writing ever to appear in English, is the fruit of an often-interrupted attempt to address this unfortunate situation.

The collected works of Borromeo are substantial.[1] There are five volumes of his homilies alone. In addition, volumes two and three of the *Acta Ecclesiae Mediolanensis*, the collections of the acts of the Church of Milan, are dedicated to other works of his, and there are also volumes of his correspondence. Editorial choices had to be made about what to include in a book of this size. Much of his work still awaits translation.

Texts were chosen that highlight the timeless wisdom of this great saint and that would inspire the reader of today. As a bishop, Borromeo's primary vehicle for reform was the spoken word—his preaching—and this reality guided the choice of texts. A renewed emphasis on the preaching of bishops was a major disciplinary reform of the Council of Trent. The works selected, furthermore, are arranged under four different categories, according to four indispensable aspects of reform for Borromeo: Bishops, the Eucharist, Priests and Laity. The texts within each chapter appear chronologically.

Chapter 1 is a selection of three orations that St. Charles gave as Archbishop of Milan to the other bishops of his ecclesiastical province gathered in provincial council. These texts were among those that Pope Paul VI sent out to the Bishops of the world in 1963 during Vatican II. They reveal the saint's foundational ideas of reform, which for Borromeo is

---

[1] Cf. Carlo Marcona, "The Resources of the Ambrosiana for the Study of Borromeo," in *San Carlo Borromeo: Catholic Reform and Ecclesiastical Politics in the Second Half of the Sixteenth Century*, eds. John M. Headley and John B. Tomaro (Washington, DC: Folger Shakespeare Library, 1988), 300–12.

more a matter of living the Church's teaching with integrity than theological controversy about doctrine. His particular focus in these orations is on the role of the local bishop in the reform of his priests, religious and laity. If reform were to begin, it would have to begin with the bishops themselves, because their poor example and neglect of duty were most at fault for the sad state of affairs in the Church and were being cited by the Protestant reformers to justify their positions. Using familiar biblical and agrarian imagery, Borromeo exhorts his brother bishops to seek the interests of God rather than their own, to be vigilant, wise and persistent in going about the reform, and to do so together.

Chapter 2 is a selection of homilies on the Eucharist, which for St. Charles was crucial for authentic reform. Contrary to the common practice of his time, Borromeo vigorously promoted frequent reception of Holy Communion, like so many reformers in Church history who have led people to both sacramental confession and the altar of the Lord in eras of infrequent communion. St. Charles' attention to propriety in the sacred liturgy, and especially his meditations on the meaning of the sacred orders conferred on clerics show that he would have welcomed the well-known teaching of the Second Vatican Council that the Eucharistic sacrifice is the source and summit of the Christian life.[2] In these Eucharistic texts themselves, Borromeo highlights the importance of receiving Communion and the effect this Sacrament should have on one's daily life, as well as showing the essential link between the Eucharist and the loving service of one's neighbor.

Chapter 3 treats the reform of the clergy, the reform for which St. Charles is most known and on which he spent most of his efforts. For this reason, Chapter 3 contains more texts. Priests are the indispensable collaborators with the Bishop in the work of preaching, sanctifying and shepherding the faithful. St. Charles was convinced that any lasting reform could occur only if the clergy were reformed. Recurrent Borromean themes to his priests are the greatness of the priestly vocation and the consequent necessity to live that call with integrity through humility, prayer, poverty and self-sacrifice. Included is his moving letter to the clergy of Milan, asking them to remain in the city with him and heroically care for the people during the time of the plague. He even provides practical tips, such as advice on how to preach more effectively.

---

[2]Cf. Second Vatican Council. Dogmatic Constitution on the Church *Lumen gentium*, number 11.

Chapter 4 presents Charles' efforts at mobilizing the laity in their own reform. In this chapter we have included his "Booklet of Reminders," which in plain language instructs lay people on how to cultivate holiness within the household and the workplace, such as setting up a place to pray in the home and how a shop owner should run his business and treat his employees. As with bishops and priests, he reminds fathers and mothers that raising their children in holiness and imbuing the secular world with holiness begins first and foremost with their own personal example.

The translation is based on two original sources. The homilies and most of the orations were translated from the Latin edition of his homilies and orations compiled by the Milanese priest Joseph Anthony Sax, then Prefect of the Ambrosian Library, in the eighteenth century.[3] The version used for this translation is in the holdings of Mount Angel Abbey Library: Joseph Anthony Sax, ed. *Sancti Caroli Borromei Homiliae*, volumes 1–5, printed by Joseph Marellum at Milan in 1747–48. The other texts were translated from the *Acta Ecclesiae Mediolanensis*. The edition of the *Acta* used in this translation is the one available for consultation in the printed book section of the Apostolic Library at the Vatican.

The translation is intended to be faithful to these Latin or Italian texts, while rendered into contemporary English. Therefore, long Latin sentences, especially in the orations, have been broken up into smaller segments, and long sections of text have been broken into smaller paragraphs. Capitalizations and italics reflect as much as possible the Sax edition. Titles have also been added to each individual selection to orient the reader to the main point expressed in that particular text. In some texts the reader occasionally will find elisions indicating that a sentence or paragraph was not translated. These portions have been omitted because they repeat what the saint had already stated in that text or because they are tangential digressions from the point at hand. Footnotes have been provided by the translator and sometimes by the editor in those instances that require historical, theological or liturgical explanation. Since Borromeo's scriptural citations are taken from the Latin Vulgate, the English translation of these quotations is taken from the Douay-Rheims Bible (Challenor version) with slight modifications for the sake of avoiding arcane English expressions.

---

[3]Carlo Marcona observes that St. Charles preached to the people in Italian, but his sermons were recorded in Latin by a secretary as he heard them (cf. Marcona, "The Resources of the Ambrosiana," 305).

A word of gratitude is owed to those who helped bring this project to fruition. First and foremost to Monsignor Gerard O'Connor for his initiative in the genesis of this project and for his collaboration on researching and selecting texts. Gratitude is also owed to the Right Reverends Gregory Duerr, O.S.B. and Jeremy Driscoll, O.S.B. the Abbot Emeritus and 12th Abbot, respectively, of Mt. Angel Abbey, for their agreement as monastic superiors of the translator; to Fr. Jared Wicks, S.J., for his invaluable expertise, suggestions and encouragement; to Fr. Derek Lappe, Msgr. Edward Lohse, Fr. Andrew Menke, Dr. Michael Cihak and Dr. Alexis Crow for their helpful suggestions on the Introduction; and to the Most Reverend Alexander Sample, Archbishop of Portland in Oregon, Prof. Tracey Rowland and Fr. Thomas Weinandy, O.F.M. Cap. for their encouragement in this project. Finally this work is dedicated to Father Jerome Young, O.S.B., who first began the work of translation but who was called home to the Lord after a long battle with leukemia. Brother Ansgar would like to dedicate his share in the work to his monastic community, and to the faculty and students of Our Lady of Guadalupe Seminary in Denton, Nebraska.

CHAPTER 1
DEFINING REFORM FROM ITS CENTER

Pursuing God's interests, not ours

Oration at the first provincial council[1]
October 15, 1565

By a very great blessing from God, Most Reverend Fathers, the Ecumenical Council of Trent, begun twenty years ago, interrupted more than once, but then reconvened by the singular piety and prudence of the Supreme Pontiff Pius IV, was wonderfully concluded last year by the outstanding virtue and doctrine of the Fathers who were so constant in attendance. In this Council, everything for explaining the truth of the Faith and restoring the integrity of ecclesiastical discipline was established with the greatest clarity. It was entirely by divine inspiration, Fathers, that you decreed that the practice of holding provincial councils, which had not been held for a long period of time, was to be renewed at last. It is most certain that Christendom will receive the richest fruits of salvation from it.

Indeed we are led by nature and reason itself to seek out the counsel of others in our deliberations about the most important things, because deliberation is more careful when the considered opinion of many is joined to our own judgment, and because our directives will have greater authority and weight in the mind of those whom we desire to guide from the agreement of many others with us. The author of this institution in the Church is Christ the Lord and the teachers, the Apostles. For indeed

---

[1] A provincial council is an assembly of the bishops of an ecclesiastical province, that is, an Archdiocese with its suffragan dioceses to discuss church matters and to enact disciplinary reforms in the province. Ecclesiastical provinces were formed organically from the earliest centuries. The assembly is convoked and presided by the Archbishop of a Metropolitan or first See ("See" is from *sedes*, the teaching chair of a diocesan bishop) to which a cluster of neighboring dioceses is attached with a very limited degree of subordination. The Council of Nicaea ordered that provincial councils take place twice a year, but history shows that such frequency was rarely followed. The Council of Trent ordered that these gatherings be held once every three years. The province of Milan under St. Charles was exemplary in adhering to this norm.

his promise is most certain when he promises his own strength, his own help and, in the end, his very self to these gatherings of Fathers rightly celebrated. *For where*, he says, *there are two or three gathered together in my name, there am I in the midst of them* (Mt. 18:20). And likewise: *If two of you shall consent upon earth, concerning any thing whatsoever they shall ask, it shall be done to them by my Father* (Mt. 18:19).

Although each of the Apostles had received a rich knowledge of all things from the Holy Spirit as teacher; nevertheless, especially if it was a question of something important and public, they were accustomed to take counsel in this way, and by law they laid down the practice for others to keep, namely that twice a year bishops should meet in council. From that time on innumerable sanctions and decrees have been established and promulgated both by Supreme Pontiffs and by provincial and ecumenical councils to continue or indeed to restore this practice of synods as demanded by the needs of the times. So we conclude that with piety we ourselves should continue up to our day and ever after that practice of provincial councils, which has been cultivated by those most holy men and handed on for the salvation of the Church, and that we should employ as much piety and diligence in defending this excellent institution as they did with counsel and zeal to hand on to posterity!

It is difficult to say how many calamities the breaking of this custom has brought upon Christendom, because with the fear of negative judgment taken away, there was no one apart from the Supreme Roman Pontiff to evaluate the guarding of the Deposit, the distribution of grain, the cultivation of the vineyard and the exercise of the stewardship by the shepherds of the Lord's flock. There was no one to demand the principal with interest, or an account from each one of his serious and multifaceted tasks, according to the custom of the ancients. Then the institution of ecclesiastical discipline slid and fell miserably, and those who were supposed to keep others to their duty, themselves turned away the most from the path of duty. Fathers, the wounds of the Church of God are known to you here, and I willingly pass over them in silence, because I judge that I cannot recall them, and that you cannot hear them without the bitterest pain. Therefore it was with a singular great virtue and prudence of yours that the remedy was found for most of the grave evils in the restoration of provincial councils. Now there remained only to administer wisely this rediscovered medicine to the sick provinces.

[W]e have all come together here, as if each and every part of our province were in view from this watchtower, admonished as we are by the divine voice of the prophet Ezekiel: *We will seek that which was lost: and that which was driven away, we will bring again: and we will bind up that which was broken, and we will strengthen that which was weak, and that which was fat and strong we will preserve* (Ezek. 34:16).[2]

In order to provide all of that, we must first beseech God by resounding prayers and the highest integrity and innocence of life, as well as by charity to our neighbors, that he surround us with his light and follow our counsels and actions with his grace. None of us, according to the condition of each, was prevented by age, work, strength or length of journey from arriving here together before the appointed day, because we placed private comforts after our common duty. In the same way we must take care that, for the express purpose of consulting and discerning, we bring an upright and perfect mind and will, preferring the weight of public service to private comforts, serving the interests of those over whom we preside, not our own purposes. This is indeed the task: to seek the things which are of God, not our own (cf. Phil. 2:21). This is the ministry of the pastor. This is the office of the leader. These are the responsibilities of the pilot, namely, that he look out for what is best for the flock, the soldiers, the ship. For the safety of the superior is found in the salvation of his subjects. And since there are three things that the Tridentine Council especially ordered to be carried out and put into practice: namely, that delicts should be corrected, customs recalled to the highest standards of discipline and controversies settled, the first of those will have to be laid as a most firm foundation for the whole edifice. So that when all the things defined and established by the sacred Council of Trent without exception have been publically received, then we, detesting all heresies condemned by the sacred canons and ecumenical councils, especially the Tridentine, may vow true obedience to the Supreme Roman Pontiff. And from the order of that same Council, and according to the manner and formula of our Most Holy Lord [the Pope], profess the faith *without which it is impossible to please God* (Heb. 11:6), and make use of what the divine benevolence has granted us up to this day: opportune defenses and the greatest diligence and vigilance, in proportion to the danger of places and times.

The method to be used in correcting delicts, following the nature of illnesses, is the one that adapts the medicine to the strength and quality of the sicknesses—now punishing faults with the light remedies of admonitions

---

[2]St. Charles rephrases the subject of the scriptural verse in the plural "we" rather than "I" seemingly for rhetorical effect with his audience.

and blame, now employing a sharper cure, and finally applying iron and fire to the irritated parts, as the nature of the evil and the danger of contagion will demand, always remembering that we are fathers, not lords. We will restore discipline of morals easily if, in restoring, we use that same method, and whatever deeds first established and preserved it, following in the footsteps of those who, with God as First Author, by their virtue first brought forth to us this abundance of good things.

Let us propose for ourselves, I ask you Fathers, their holiness of life and their wisdom in discharging their duty. With integrity they were chaste, sincere, modest, humble, upright in morals, assiduous in prayer and reading, not high in their self-estimation, keeping in view the salvation of their neighbor, beneficial in their counsels and works, hospitable, sparing with adornment and meals at home, but beneficent and liberal with others: *they were watching over their flocks* (Lk. 2:8), cultivating and guarding the vineyard of the Lord with the greatest diligence and labor. Assiduously they pastured the sheep entrusted to them on the three fold food of salvation: word, example and the Sacraments, remembering and imitating the chief Shepherd, Christ, who for the salvation of his flock poured forth his blood and life. They themselves did not hesitate to take up any labor, undergo any hazard, or bear any violence and injury, in sum, to lay down their lives for their sheep like that Good Shepherd of the Gospel (cf. Jn 10:11), not expecting any return from that in this life, that they might obtain the greatest fruits in the heavenly reward.

If we, Fathers, keep these things before our eyes as we must, we will easily understand what should be done by us in this age for the restoration of ecclesiastical discipline. For this, it will first be necessary to bear in mind that just as in designing and establishing the order of the Church, Christ the Lord began with the Apostles themselves, whom he willed to be teachers of the Christian life, so we too, in the reform and restoration of discipline, should begin with ourselves, the pastors who must hand on to others the right examples and precepts of living.

If we fulfill these functions of ours with the necessary zeal, it will be a very light business for us to settle conflicts, as the Tridentine Synod intends us to do. For if covetousness, which is the root of all evils and the seed of dissension (cf. 1 Tim. 6:10), is removed, we will easily pacify the discords of the present time, and we will leave to no one in our province any ground for dissensions in the future.

Therefore, Fathers, let us apply ourselves wholeheartedly and with paternal piety to these necessary cares of our office. *Now is the acceptable time; behold, now is the day of salvation* (2 Cor. 6:2) *which the Lord has made* (Ps. 67:24), so that, with the Holy Spirit leading and guiding, we may bring as much as we possibly can by our counsel, work and actions to the work of establishing the wholeness and health of our common province. This great and most noble city of Milan begs these things from your charity and wisdom. Each and every one of your respective flocks most urgently requests this of you. The whole province demands it more in reality than it can with its words. This is desired by the most excellent and great King Philip,[3] in whose royal dignity, if I may sum it up in a word, we may recognize a priestly soul. It is also desired by the other princes of the province, solicitous as they are for the salvation of their peoples. I have no fear that these men's efforts and services will ever be lacking to us and to the Holy Synod's decrees, or fail to most willingly join the power they received from God to his will and service. The most Holy Synod of Trent requests it of you that so many and so great labors, undertaken by the most holy Fathers, not come to naught in a short time. This is expected vehemently of you by the Supreme Pontiff Pius, especially since that day on which he released us to you from the administration of his own counsels and services to the Church. Bring it about for him, I beg you, that I may bear back rich fruits from my departure and your labors, that is to say, glorious and salutary actions from this Council. This is demanded by your virtue which, observed and known to the world in this gathering, you must now express in the life of your peoples, and in their safety that you must defend. Finally, this is entreated of us by Christ Jesus, that he may note how we carry out our office on behalf of his sheep which, redeemed by the price of his blood, he commended to our faith and prudence. May it never come about that he should require their blood from our hand. God forbid that we allow them to be destroyed or scattered on account of our faults or negligence.

---

[3] King Philip II of Spain (1527–98).

Charles Borromeo

Cultivating the field persistently

Oration at the second provincial council
April 24, 1569

You have already come to know in what state of disturbance Christendom finds itself, what deadly torches of heresies have long been aflame in neighboring provinces, what turbulent riots have arisen from them in France, how many massacres, how many battles have broken out. Specifically, you ask? How many churches, even the most majestic, have been torn down, stripped of the most sacred images and signs and despoiled of their ornamentation. How many sacred vessels have been carried away, sacred relics scattered, priests and religious killed, holy virgins dishonored, divine things polluted, in sum everything has been laid prostrate.[4] How long, O Lord, will you be angry? How long will we see *the vine which your right hand planted* (Ps. 79:15–16), and the people whom the blood of Christ Jesus your Son atoned for so cruelly, so horribly torn down, devastated, scattered? *How long will you feed us with the bread of tears: and give us for our drink tears in measure* (Ps. 79:6)?

Even if they seem to be somewhat distant from us, these deadly and pernicious evils nevertheless surround us on all sides and are here even at the gangway of the ship. It is to be feared that at any hour or moment this force of waters will burst into our province and carry it away entirely in its waves unless we meet the danger with the help of God and the greatest vigilance of the pastors. But there are other, certainly not light

---

[4]Borromeo is speaking during the Wars of Religion, but the Protestant revolution in Switzerland and France was distinguished from the beginning by its "purifying" the country and the churches of "superstitions" and "idolatries," that is to say images, relics, vestments, the Mass, consecrated Hosts and the tabernacles, all held to be contrary to Scripture. Real abuses regarding relics or images, together with clerical corruption, sometimes provided a popular justification for their destruction in those regions. Iconoclasm in France, whether by individuals or mobs, resulted from the preaching and pamphlets of reformers who incurred swift convictions and executions when caught by civil authorities who had largely replaced the Inquisition in the kingdom. Massive iconoclasm was largely rejected or avoided by Luther and other German reformers whose theology and methods were less radical. See Jean Dumont, *L'Église au risqué de l'histoire*, with Preface by Pierre Chaunu (Paris: Éditions de Paris, 2002); Carlos M.N. Eire, *War Against the Idols: The Reformation of Worship from Erasmus to Calvin* (Cambridge: Cambridge University Press, 1986); Ole Peter Grell and Bob Scribner, eds, *Tolerance and Intolerance in the European Reformation* (Cambridge: Cambridge University Press, 2002).

misfortunes as well, which must also move us greatly because they are found at the very doors of our province.[5]

Even if at our last gathering we decreed many things with divine approval, and afterward accomplished many things by our pastoral attention, giving some sign of a province heading in the right direction, nevertheless many inveterate errors of life and discipline remain, and other things as well, which our care and solicitude must now keep under our vigilant gaze, since they plainly call for emendation and correction by us. Such is the condition of these times. Some men, lovers more of the world than of God, unite their souls to the things which pertain first to care and solicitude for riches and the flesh. Others are entangled in other shameful, false pleasures as if by chains, held fast as they are by the perpetual enemy of the human race, who *as a roaring lion goes about seeking* mortal men, *whom he may devour* (1 Pet. 5:8). In short, if we cast our glance over the whole province, we see everything leading, despite the Apostle's lament, to *an occasion to the flesh* (Gal. 5:13) in such a way that the condition of true and solid Christian piety appears rather nonexistent.

These evils, since they are indeed internal, though they be less than the kinds afflicting neighboring provinces, are nevertheless of such a sort that they provide the heretics a specious argument for defending their errors to common minds. It could easily happen (which God forbid), that channels will be opened and entrances pointed out to the reprehensible stain of heresies to our own people as well, if we allow our people to sully themselves with a depraved state of conscience.

Although this danger can be known by many other, almost innumerable examples, we know it most especially from this one: namely, that the Israelite people, when it immersed itself in feasts, banquets and licentious living and was stained with an impure conscience, fell all the more readily into the deadly sickness of idols. When the Apostle Paul became aware of this very thing, he admonished his disciple Timothy with these words:

---

[5]To prevent the diffusion of heretical ideas in his own diocese and other regions of northern Italy, St. Charles urged the observance of the laws concerning libraries and bookshops. In regard to heretics themselves, he employed prayer and preaching, and went to great lengths to ensure fair judicial procedures for accused heretics and to spare them being handed over to secular authorities for punishment; he was also capable of allowing the penal process to run its course on the incorrigible and recalcitrant (cf. Bascapé, *Vita e opera di Carlo*, 145–7; Jean-Pierre Giussano, *Vie de Saint Charles Borromée*, trans. Edme Cloysault [Avignon: Seguin Aîmé, 1824], 120–3).

Having a good conscience, which some rejecting have made shipwreck concerning the faith (1 Tim. 1:19). From where, Fathers, do so many old heresies once extinguished resurface again in our times if not from the depraved and contaminated morals of people? For as an old illness returns if the body is affected by some recent, even minor problem, so we see pestilential heresies, which already have troubled the Church in various ages and which were once restrained by the virtues of the ancient Fathers, return again like some old illness because of the corruption of our times.

In this crisis, therefore, see how great is the obligation laid upon us, who are the chosen standard-bearers of the Christian army and the doctors of souls, to enter into council, so that coming together as many into one, with the Holy Spirit leading, we may more easily implore aid from *the Father of mercies and the God of all comfort* (2 Cor. 1:3). Also, if matters are established more carefully by the judgment and consent of many, we will find those for whose salvation we must above all have regard that much more prompt of soul and willingly disposed to accept.

This, Fathers, is our task. This is our office. If indeed we have been placed in the exalted Chair of episcopal dignity, then we must as if from a watchtower be on the lookout for and repel whatever dangers hang over those who come under our faithfulness and our care. If we are fathers, then likewise we must show paternal solicitude for the danger the children are in. If we are shepherds, we must never cast our eyes away from the sheep, which Jesus Christ rescued from the jaws and gullet of hell by his most holy death. And if any of them are wasting away in the impure stain of vices, we must heal them with the salt of keen correction. In short, if any are wandering in the darkness of bad habits and ways, we must shed light upon them.

When the greatest workman, the One who made all things, in the beginning gazed upon heaven when he made it, he adorned it with a multitude of stars which, sharing the light and splendor of the sun, would shine upon earth in the night. Likewise in the spiritual renovation of this world, he placed in the Church, as in a new firmament of heaven, prophets and apostles, pastors and teachers, who, reflecting the light of that eternal Sun—Christ the Lord— would be placed over the darkness of this gloomy age, and dispel darkness from human minds with the splendor of a bright and holy discipline.

Therefore, consider those men whom heavenly wisdom willed to be pastors and to succeed to the Apostles, as if taking the place of the parents, for the prophet says, *Instead of your fathers, sons are born to you* (Ps. 44:17). Why should we not imitate them, parents, leaders and teachers that they were? They who in founding Christendom at its birth amidst the greatest difficulties, made use of this method of councils when they enlightened with the light of evangelical discipline that confused face of the world, enfolded as it was in the darkness of errors. They also provided us an example for restoring it, so that we who are in their place and are the mouth of the Lord, from whose lips, as from the angels of the hosts of the Lord, the people seek the law (cf. Mal. 2:7), may teach the people of our province *to walk as children of the light* and to carry *the fruit of the light in all goodness, and justice, and truth; proving what is well pleasing to God: And have no fellowship with the unfruitful works of darkness* (Eph. 5:8), in the midst of such great disturbances and black darkness of sins, and draw salutary laws of life from the font of the light of the Holy Spirit, in whose name we are gathered today.

Let us not think, Fathers, that we completely did our part by the many things we established three years ago in this very place. For if we examine the whole matter in the way we really should, we will find that we indeed only began the work of our ministry. We certainly have not finished it. Rather we have reason to see it through to its completion, as demanded by the state of things. As the Apostle often warns each of us in many places: *Take heed to the ministry which you have received in the Lord, that you fulfill it* (Col. 4:17); *and he gave pastors and doctors for the perfecting of the saints, for the work of the ministry, for the edifying of the body of Christ* (Eph. 4:11–12). Therefore if the whole reason for our ministry looks to consummation and a certain perfect discipline of sanctity, our efforts would be truly vain, and in vain the labors undertaken, unless, once those foundations have first been laid, we strive with the greatest zeal to finish what remains necessary for the edification and completion of the building. For at the time when we first came together in council, if indeed we gave to our people not only milk but also food, nevertheless at that time we were hardly able to give them the more solid foods (cf. 1 Cor. 3:2). That was taught by Christ the Lord, who although he had many things he could still say to the Apostles, nevertheless did not teach everything at one time, since they were certainly not then capable of bearing them (cf. Jn 16:12). Although he could have provided the same in a mere moment, he willed to illumine his Church more and more with the splendor of doctrine over a long period of time both by rousing the minds of the holy Fathers and through the most holy councils that were held. In the same way, we who care for and watch over Mother Church should hope that in his goodness he will both now and in the future, as the times demand, open up and make plain to us whatever things were not opportune, nor suggested to us by the Spirit of God himself at the time of our last council, that we may then hand them on to our faithful.

Besides, it frequently happens that once farmers have cultivated a field well, purged it of useless weeds, pruned the vines and the trees, unless they repeatedly apply the same cultivation, the good field that came up by their efforts, will turn up wild and rough. So too it will be with the faithful, who *are God's field* (1 Cor. 3:9), when they have been brought to a splendid state by our vigils and efforts, which we applied in the last council. Unless we frequently go back and pull out what grows up afterward, that first cultivation with the passage of time will easily become wild, especially if any depraved habit strengthened by long duration has, like far-spreading ivy cast, its roots so deep as to be nearly or actually impossible to pull up.

Therefore, since almost our entire ministry must consist in a certain perpetual method of cultivating the field of the Lord, God has set before us in Jeremiah an example in words of the diligent farmer we must imitate: *Lo, I have set you this day over the nations, and over the kingdoms, to root up, and pull down, and to waste, and to destroy, and to build, and to plant* (Jer. 1:10). But if perhaps we will see only a few things to be added to our other Constitutions, nevertheless there will be no meager fruit or slight usefulness if, having our previous decrees in mind as a mirror, we will set our gaze on whether any fault has been incurred in carrying them out, either by us or by those to whom they were commanded, or if there are some things which it has not yet been possible to provide, either through ourselves or others, on account of certain reasons. With this agreed upon, if some fault is to be admitted because we have been deficient in our duty, we will correct it persistently, and if it was for some reason of difficulty, which we will bring up and diligently explain right here, let us apply the suitable remedies.

Therefore let us direct our counsels, thoughts, efforts and actions to the certain norm of the will of God … so we may take care to restore by our decrees, not a mere sketch, but the express image of Christian discipline, which with the breath of the Holy Spirit at the Church's birth, was instituted by *the word of God*, which *is living and effectual, and more piercing than any two edged sword; and reaching unto the division of the soul and the spirit, of the joints also and the marrow, and is a discerner of the thoughts and intents of the heart* (Heb. 4:12).

For if we do not strive to tear up the seeds of vices by the roots, but instead consider it sufficient to use a light touch to correct only certain external matters that cause offense to the popular mind, then it will turn out for us as it does for farmers. They neglect to tear out weeds by the roots, but only cut off those that spring up and do not purge the field of noxious stems. In doing so they bring about what they plainly do not want, namely, that after a few days the weeds spring up more abundantly. Nor is there any reason to be frightened off from carrying out our essential task, either because in our pastoral efforts and actions we see the aroused irritation of mind of those who are sons of perdition, or because we hear those voices of the people, the voices with which, like bad figs with leaves, depraved morals are also accustomed to cover themselves. It is the severity of the ancient canons that these times cannot bear. They say: "This is how we have been living for a long time, thus did the previous generation live and behave. There is no need to change anything in our way of life."

But let us despise this type of thing and everything like it, and let us set before our eyes that freedom of spirit and virtue that armed our fathers the Apostles, fortified the martyrs and equipped the holiest men of our order: Athanasius, Chrysostom and Ambrose, bishop of this Church, and imbued other religious men who burned with a firm apostolic ardor for souls. They were not broken or weakened by anything, be they threats, the shouts of men or fury from judges. Rather with that freedom of spirit and virtue they exercised something like that resolute virtue that most sharply avenges sin for God's glory, for the salvation of the flock committed to them, and with strong and constant soul. Let us also act and bring to completion what the Gospel teaches, what Christ commands, what reason prescribes, what the salvation of the flock requires, what the authority and dignity of the Church demand, without fear, but with constancy and sureness, and with that apostolic constancy and evangelical virtue of which alone there is nothing more brilliant, nothing more necessary in the Church's pastors.

For if we act otherwise, then in that fearful judgment of God to whom we will render an account for the souls that were entrusted to our faithfulness and care, we are going to hear the outcry of others accusing us and the irate judge likewise bitterly reproaching us with the following: "If you were the watchmen, why were you blind? If you were the pastors, why did you allow the flock entrusted to you to wander? If you were the salt of the earth, how did you lose your flavor? If you were the light, why did you not shine on those *that sit in darkness, and in the shadow of death* (Lk. 1:79)? If you were apostles, why did you forgo apostolic strength and instead do everything for the eyes of men? If you were the mouth of the Lord, why were you mute? If you felt yourself to be unequal to this burden, why were you so ambitious for the office? If you were in fact equal to it, why were you so lazy, so neglectful? The voices of the Prophets, the laws of the Gospel, the examples of the Apostles, piety, religion, the tottering state of the Church, the fearful day of judgment, rewards, punishments and eternal torments: did those things move you not at all?" ... Amen.

Charles Borromeo

Reforming together

Oration at the fifth provincial council
May 7, 1579

Now from the Gospel you have just heard,[6] Most Reverend Fathers, you fully understand that the Apostles were called together by Christ the Lord and sent to preach the kingdom of heaven with power for healing illnesses and expelling demons. From that evangelical reminder you have also observed the laws of that apostolic commission and duty, prescribed by the mouth of divine wisdom, and have again called to mind the great zeal the apostles applied in carrying them out to the great admiration of all.

In this very moment, this clergy and people of the province of Milan see you, successors of the Apostles, having been convoked from the laws issued in the spirit of Christ the Lord by the Sacred Tridentine Council, you come together with me to celebrate this fifth provincial council. Accordingly, they will now observe set before their eyes an image, as it were, of that apostolic convocation and legation recalled in the words of the Gospel. For Christ the Lord, when he saw in that time the crowds wandering here and there like sheep without a shepherd, scattered in various directions and infected with multiple kinds of illness, had mercy on their condition from the depths of his sacred kindness. He did not think it sufficient to have traversed villages, towns and all the neighboring places preaching and healing. Rather in the midst of such a great multitude of people streaming together from all sides, he also willed to make use of other men as his associates in the preaching of the Gospel and the curing of illnesses. He therefore ordered his disciples to pray, convoked the twelve apostles, and sent them to carry out those tasks.

Now in like manner, when the One who never turns his gaze from the care and protection of his Church: *my eyes*, he said, *shall be there always* (1 Kgs 9:3), perceived our Milanese province from highest Heaven, as from the highest watchtower, he saw it greatly troubled on all sides, especially by the plague of these last years, and he cast his eyes of mercy on a province lost and miserably afflicted not so much because of the loss of lives, as by the detriment and harm in the spiritual realm, which flowed from all those afflictions. And he roused us, the ministers of his Gospel, not only to the celebration of holy prayers and supplications, but also to providing remedies by synods and episcopal labors.

---

[6] Cf. Lk. 9:1–2.

You were present, most holy Fathers, at the exercises of prayer that we held in this sacred place without interruption before the most holy Nail[7] of our Lord Jesus Christ; that we might implore the light of the Holy Spirit, with whose help we were able to enter into our consideration of how best to govern our province and repair the spiritual damage. For that very reason, there is no hamlet, no town, no city in the province that has not been powerfully motivated to prayers, the Sacraments of Penance and the Holy Eucharist, and the other exercises of Christian piety.

But now today, Fathers, convoked by the same guiding Spirit of the Lord, we are present in this place, so that with official prayer and the other synodal actions, we might offer him our work and our ministry.

And it is to be hoped not only that Christ the Lord will hear our prayers (for he said, *if two of you shall consent upon earth, concerning any thing whatsoever they shall ask, it shall be done to them* [Mt. 28:19]), but also that he will be present to us who are engaged in carrying out a discussion so important for salvation. *For where*, he says, *there are two or three gathered together in my name, there am I in the midst of them* (Mt. 18:20).

And so this whole action of the provincial council shows forth that, as we said, the image of the apostolic mission and mandate. When we treat our affairs and those of our Churches together with mutual charity, when we inquire concerning the right and proper ways of celebrating the divine Offices, when we investigate the state of discipline of clergy and people, when we contemplate first of all the execution of our own and the Apostolic Visitation's decrees,[8] when we place before our gaze the entirely ruined state of so many things, when we consult each other on how to restore them, when with the authority of the Holy Spirit we labor to establish new constitutions and decrees suitably adapted for remedying those ills, this

---

[7]Borromeo is referring to the relic purported to be one of the nails used in the crucifixion of Jesus. One of the earliest sources regarding this relic in Milan is St. Ambrose himself in his funeral oration for Emperor Theodosius in 395. The tradition holds that this nail is one of the two nails brought back by St. Helena from her sojourn in the Holy Land in 326–28. One nail was incorporated into a bridle for her son Constantine's horse and eventually kept in the Cathedral of Milan. The Holy Nail's shape and features are completely different from the medieval understanding of a crucifixion nail, but consonant with the relevant details of the Shroud of Turin. See "Il Santo Chiodo della Croce, Intervista con il professore Ernesto Brunati di Giovanni Ricciardi," *30 Giorni* 6–7 (2010), accessed March 17, 2016, http://www.30giorni.it/articoli_id_22806_11.htm#.

[8]An Apostolic Visitator to a province or diocese is a special papal legate sent to inquire into chronic local abuses, possibly with the authority to himself decree the necessary measures for reform.

entire method and way of proceeding is such that with these helps from God, our mind may be enlightened, our charity enkindled, our zeal for the salvation of souls set afire, our episcopal power and ardor more and more set aflame, so that a certain new spirit may be aroused in us who are strengthened by the power and authority of provincial decrees. May it be vehemently aroused for expelling all foul spirits, for driving out the plague of vices, for healing spiritual illnesses—in sum, for bringing every possible cure to the peoples entrusted to our care.

O how salutary are the labors of the councils of bishops! Christ is present with you. The guide of your actions is the Holy Spirit. You are the teachers of right living and customs, the governors of the peoples, the authors of holy laws. By your wisdom all manner of Christian discipline is restored; controversies are settled by your prudence, discords removed by your charity, *feeble hands* are raised up again by your efforts, *weak knees are strengthened* by your power (Isa. 35:3), new strength is brought to men's minds. Why go on? The holding and celebration of a council teaches, instructs, restores, recreates and motivates us as well, who hold the office of teacher and are the physicians of the Church.

Therefore, how miserable were these recent times when for so long and in many places provincial councils and diocesan synods were no longer held, but neglected and became entirely a thing of the past. As a result, a veritable forest of multiple evils came to be: basilicas left uncared for, the adornment of church furnishings reduced to nothing, the ritual and use of the ceremonies barely known, the correct celebration of the Divine Offices entirely disturbed, the discipline of choir rescinded, the duties of ecclesiastical functions disregarded and despised, sacerdotal and clerical residences deserted, all the duties of discipline at length thrown off and entirely laid aside, and furthermore the instruction and forming of the people was distorted. Corruption of morals appeared on all sides. The honor of feast days was violated by many sins. The upkeep of sacred places in many places suffered injury. The dignity of the sacerdotal order was treated as if it were nothing. In sum everything was reduced to such a state as to be worthy of tears, mourning and commiseration. We ourselves saw the face of our province deformed and manifestly resembling in its appearance the lamented temple of Jerusalem when, with everything devastated and uprooted by Antiochus, the most valiant Judas Macchabeus looked upon the temple swept clean of everything, with its altar violated, its gates burned away, everything struck down and prostrate: with vestments rent, his head covered in ashes, and with sighs, groaning and the most mournful cries, he powerfully poured forth his tears before such a ruined condition of an august temple (cf. 1 Macc. 4:38–40).

But let us return to the Gospel event we have just recalled, for the whole passage shows and describes not only the reason for this our episcopal gathering and council, but also the tasks and duties which we must now provide or at least plan for. Therefore, Fathers, let us first understand why Christ the Lord convoked all the apostles at the same time for their apostolic commission, since he could have sent each apostle with his own personal instructions. With that we will clearly see why almost from the beginning of the infant Church it was established that bishops of a province should come together in metropolitan synod, and there to decree provincial laws sanctioned by all, to be received and observed by everyone living in that same province.

One reason which stands out among the rest is so that those who were sent into the various different parts of the world to propagate the Gospel might have one teaching, one apostolic office and one apostolic way of life common to all of them. Certainly that teaches us that bishops of the same province, although presiding over distinct and diverse dioceses, should nevertheless be bound as by a single chain in one province, and that the faithful entrusted to them should be directed in the way of salvation by one and the same form of ecclesiastical discipline, the same prescribed laws and the same rules of life. That is what the decrees of the most holy Fathers and the canons of councils show and even order, for by the canons on these matters and others besides, the other dioceses of a province are forewarned to conform themselves to the ecclesiastical rules of the metropolitan Church.[9]

So from this united pastoral solicitude and concord and from concerted zeal, the greatest advantages and the greatest helps spring forth, not only for the smooth governing of the Churches committed to the bishops, but also for the entire progress of the peoples in the way of the Lord. For from this sprang forth the greatest protection for each one of the salutary rules

---

[9]As in footnote 1 above, Borromeo is referring to the structure of an ecclesiastical province. A bishop is given ordinary jurisdiction over a geographical area called a "diocese." Dioceses in turn are organized around the first See, called a metropolitan See or "archdiocese." An archdiocese united with its suffragan dioceses comprise a "province." Although each individual bishop is directly answerable to the Pope, certain laws of the Metropolitan See, like St. Charles mentions here, can be binding for the suffragan dioceses of the province. For the sake of their own greater flourishing, dioceses of more recent foundation were traditionally expected to follow the examples of the founding and earliest diocese of their regions, in other words, of the Metropolitan Sees.

adopted. From this came the perennial conservation of ecclesiastical rites and holy customs, from this a most holy strength for all salutary things, from this the most prompt and ready willingness to obey. From here came that glorious rivalry and religious emulation in carrying everything out correctly and well. But in regions where such councils did not meet, it can hardly be said what disadvantages and how many difficulties emerged.

Fathers, you are aware of the truth of what we have been saying, but let us look at it from another angle. If anyone among you is frequently at prayer and in contemplation of heavenly things, regularly present in the episcopal residence, and likewise totally dedicated and given over to episcopal duties, zeal and tasks, abstinence and fasting; if anyone among you is hospitable, a true father and pastor of the poor, widows and orphans, a patron of the holy places and assiduous in promoting holy observances; and if on the other hand another bishop of the same province is remiss or negligent in all these things, or what is worse, does the opposite, or speaks disparagingly about his fellow bishop who acts rightly and diligently; well it is certain that all possible disadvantage will come from that, and the greatest harm.

But this is the place, Fathers, where we should ignite our own ardor if we examine the matter more attentively. Consider a bishop who holds himself to the rules of the best kind of pastor and unceasingly puts into practice the Tridentine Council's precept of the duty of preaching. But then consider another bishop, who sets his soul on the grandeur of the episcopal dignity, not its labors; on its recompense, not its burdens; on a leisurely life, not the solicitude perpetually entwined with many cares, or who rarely, if ever, administers the nourishment of God's words to the people. One bishop will normally celebrate an annual diocesan synod, but you will indeed find another who never holds the appointed meetings of clerics and priests, to say nothing of convoking a synod. The first bishop strives with perennial zeal to perform the diocesan visitation, but the other knows not the face of his flock, nor does he make any effort in paternal charity so that he might be known by them. There is nothing the first bishop will not do or undertake in order to sweep out all corruption of morals, to correct and amend vices and sins, and to recall to the way of salvation all those who are wandering away. But this other one, since he measures all things with the standard of popular opinion, wants to please people, to cover over their sins, and often he himself proves to be the reason why many deviate from the right way.

But the concern of the vigilant bishop is directed also to the splendor and upkeep of the churches, so that basilicas may be well protected and in good repair, furnished and brilliant with every appointment and adornment, shining on all sides; so that devotion to the Divine Office is in a flourishing state, the ritual of the ceremonies cultivated, the order of the choir not only entirely retained, but also improved, the clergy educated in sacred doctrine and held to the duties of their state, bound by laws, edicts and rules most holy, kept not only innocent of all crime, but upright, pure and free from every suspicion.

How different from that is the character and manner of a remiss, negligent and self-indulgent pastor—you yourselves can see this—almost no discipline in his clergy, no instruction of the people, no restoration and upkeep of the churches. In sum, everything which should shine brightly on account of the bishop's care and concern instead lies in decay and squalor right in front of him. May it never be the case, Fathers, that on account of these contrasts between bishops, the effort and solicitude of a bishop whose ardent zeal was tending to the heights should end up practically extinguished. May it never be the case that there is no longer any of that holy emulation between bishops, which is so much to be desired and so potent for the propagation of all discipline. When, however, that unfortunately is the case, then there is another disadvantage, and the greatest of all, namely that on account of observing the differences in pastoral care, people in the vigilant bishop's diocese become more obstinate and difficult in their obedience. They pull back from their pastor and father, wickedly censure his many good deeds, ignore his warnings; and since the human race is inclined to make excuses in sins (cf. Ps. 140:4), they find protection for their stubbornness and for every vice, since they are able to use the neglect and excessive indulgence of another bishop as justification for themselves.

And so we see tremendous detriment and harm to the Christian republic, brought in by bishops having such a dissimilar spirit, even though Christ the Lord wished the spirit of the pastors to be one, joined in one bond of charity and spurred on by one concern and solicitude. To this end he instructed us, when in today's Gospel he entrusted the office of preaching and the curing of diseases to his apostles convoked together, and prescribed to all of them certain rules for that apostolic office.

For which reason, Most Reverend Fathers, let us be persuaded that, with God's help in the first place, we will bring no small benefit to our province by our deliberations at this fifth provincial council, provided that at length we plainly set out on the examined way, with a certain and right method. Let us carry out the laws, enactments and all discipline prescribed for us, the clergy and the people of our province. Let us all apply ourselves to that perpetual concern, with minds most united, with a most united will and with the same devotion and equal zeal, as with one pastoral and episcopal spirit.

But you, Lord God Almighty, who ordered seventy elders of the people to be convoked by Moses at the entrance to the tent of the covenant, and ordered them to be present, remaining together in the same place, and who deigned to grant one and the same spirit (cf. Num. 11:16–17); you who sent your Holy Spirit to your apostles gathered together in one place (cf. Acts 2:1–4), illumined their minds, and inflamed their hearts to the point that, burning with incredible ardor, when they knew and accepted that they were legates of the divine preaching, they carried out that mission most admirably, with one most burning zeal and with the same enactments of apostolic discipline over the whole world: we beg you today, be present to us who are called together into one in your name. Enlighten our minds with the splendor of your divine light, tend them with goodness. Rule and direct them by wisdom, and cause us so to carry out the duties and tasks of our commission with one counsel, the same vigilance, the same admonitions and the same example. May we do so in such a salutary way that we and the faithful of our province, made one in you, may entirely enjoy that eternal glory which is in you, the one God. Amen.

CHAPTER 2
BEING TRANSFORMED BY CHRIST
IN THE EUCHARIST

Washing feet as Christ did

Homily for the washing of the feet of the Cathedral Chapter[1]
on Holy Thursday
March 27, 1567

Nowadays the lamentable condition of Christians is such, as well as the same miserable state to which the Christian religion has been reduced, that people often wonder more about a man who does his duty than about a man who neglects it. Many (what sorrow this causes!) can be found who judge it hypocrisy if a man professing a holy life actually follows in the footsteps of the saints, or if a Christian actually follows the example of Christ. We see this happening in so many other areas as well, but we hear it the most in regard to the washing of the feet, that washing of the feet which both the saints and the Lord of the saints used in order to teach a very deep mystery in a most admirable way and with a certain singular humility.

If I may begin from the most ancient times, the great patriarch Abraham, ready to give hospitality to angels of God in human form, could not better express his good will and love toward them than by washing their feet. His nephew Lot did likewise to these angels (cf. Gen. 18:4; 19:2). In the Gospel, the Lord was able to answer Simon with a reproach because Simon had not washed his feet when he received him into his house (cf. Lk. 7:44). Also, the apostle Paul was unwilling to admit into the number of the widows supported by the Church any woman who had not been accustomed to wash the feet of the saints (cf. 1 Tim. 5:10). For this practice of foot-washing not only shows forth humility, but is also the greatest indication of devoted love, and has an admirable power to

---

[1]The modalities and times for this rite have varied across the centuries. In the tradition followed by St. Charles in his time in Milan, a strong focus was the superior humbling himself before the inferior ranks of the clerical order, reflecting the relationship between Christ and his apostles, the first priests; hence the archbishop St. Charles washed the feet of the canons of his cathedral.

join souls together in mutual love. For this reason, our Savior seeing his passion imminent, and wishing, as he was about to depart, to leave them some splendid teaching and example to imitate, first washed all their feet himself. Then he commanded them to do the same to others, saying: *For I have given you an example, that as I have done to you, so you do also* (Jn 13:15).

In this matter, most beloved brethren, and if I may omit the rest, the admirable humility of our Savior is to be not only diligently considered but also imitated with the greatest zeal. For three degrees of humility are found to exist: the first is the minimum, the second is an abundance, and the third is the fulfillment of all justice. In the first degree are found those who willingly obey and honor every superior; in the second, those who also submit themselves to their equals; in the third degree are to be numbered those who do not disdain to serve their inferiors. In each of these degrees, Christ our Lord clearly showed himself to be both the most humble and the most obedient. To the Father who was Christ's superior, if you consider His humanity, and equal to Christ according to divinity, he was so obedient and submissive that he said he never did anything other than the Father's will. And both his own testimony and the gospel story are in agreement on how much humility and obedience he showed toward men, who were so far inferior to him: *I am not come*, he says, *to be ministered unto, but to minister* (Mt. 20:28). But if you will together with me consider that gospel passage which narrates the things he did and said in the washing of the feet, then you will most clearly perceive all the things I have only introduced and suggested; I mean the gospel passage beginning, *Before the festival day of the pasch* (Jn 13:1).

Everything we find in the mystery of the Incarnation of Christ teaches the greatest humility and shows an immense love. For on account of love he descended from heaven, for love of us he was baptized, for love of us he fasted and suffered trials, afflictions, opprobrium, and finally death. He showed this admirable love as well in the Last Supper, instituting the Most Holy Sacrament of his Body, and the other devout mysteries and duties of religion. Moreover, this washing of the feet, concerning which we have determined to say a few words, wondrously commends that same love of his to his own, and teaches his ministers moderation and mildness of soul. Wherefore the holy evangelist says, *Jesus knowing that his hour was come, that he should pass out of this world to the Father: having loved his own who were in the world, he loved them unto the end* (Jn 13:1), as if meaning to say: since he had always given signs and performed deeds of his singular love toward his own, so he persevered unto the end, continuing to show forth the same kind of deeds with the greatest and most perfect love, until his death.

For when the devil had put it in the heart of Judas to betray him, our Lord, who knew he had received all things from his Father, had gone forth from his Father and was to return to God in glory, nevertheless did not disdain to wash the feet of poor fishermen like a humble slave, and to do everything in this service in such a way as to bring out his supreme diligence, modesty and submission. For the Lord arose from the supper with his disciples still reclining. He laid aside his outer clothing so as to better execute the whole service. He girded himself with linen to show himself fully prepared to minister, to help and to do good. Finally, he himself put water into the basin, humbly ministered, bowed himself before the feet of his servants, and did what is usually left to the lowest class of men: he washed their feet. He did all these things alone: he alone poured the water, he alone washed, he alone dried their feet. To all he showed an equal proof of goodness, and gave a sign of his love.

He humbly washed the feet of all, he fed all with the Sacrament of his Body, but not all received an equal fruit from it. For Judas, who was going to betray him, who willingly carried the money-box for the Lord, ate the same food with the other apostles, offered his feet to be washed, and wanted to have and enjoy all advantages with the other disciples. Moreover, he could not be restrained from betraying innocent blood by any kindness or benefits he had received. In this affair, we can only stand in wonderment at the detestable perversity of the traitor who could not be moved by fear of the Lord, nor by reverence for his majesty, nor by his innocence of life, nor by the magnitude of the benefits he had received. But all the more worthy of wonder is the goodness of the Lord, who seeing and knowing the obstinacy of the traitor, did not cease to treat him with goodness and instead tried to soften his obdurate heart with every kind of benefit, leaving us an example so that we too might seek rather the conversion of our enemies than their ruin, and try to gain their souls rather than lose them. But the gifts of the Lord, which bore the most abundant fruit in St. Peter and the others, brought the bitterest damnation in Judas.[2]

He came therefore to Simon Peter (Jn 13:6–10). Three times Peter spoke, but in three different ways. Three times the Lord responded, and he adapted

---

[2]Borromeo's mentioning of Judas' damnation may have been inspired by the Holy Thursday liturgy; like the Roman Rite in its ancient use, the Ambrosian Rite of Milan mentions Judas as having "received the punishment of his guilt," and the crucified thieves' "diverse" deserts. See the Ambrosian prayers of *Feria V in Cena Domini* in *Das ambrosianische Sakramentar von Biasca. Die Handschrift Mailand Ambrosiana A 24 bis inf., 1 Teil: Text*, ed. Odilo Heiming (Münster: Aschendorffsche Verlagsbuchhandlung, 1969), 63–4.

each response to Peter's word. For it was out of ignorance that Peter first asked, *Do you wash my feet?* as though he considered it absurd for the Son of God to cast himself before the knees of a most lowly man. The second time he spoke obstinately: *You shall never wash my feet.* The third time, seeing that his Lord entirely willed him to obey, he offered more than the Savior had earlier asked, saying: *not only my feet, but also my hands and my head.* So the Savior instructed him in his ignorance, saying, *What I do you know not now; but you shall know hereafter,* as if to say, you are as of yet still ignorant of this mystery; if you understood it, you would not have questioned me. Then he pounded Peter's obstinacy with threats: *If I wash you not, you shall have no part with me.* Afterward, he commended the faith and obedience with which Peter submitted himself to the will of his Lord, saying: *He that is washed, needs not but to wash his feet, but is clean wholly. And you are clean.*

From this passage, we will be able to understand that subjects must not despise the precepts of magistrates with great obstinacy, nor out of embarrassment refuse what they offer to us, even though what is held forth seems unworthy to us. Moreover, superiors are taught to persuade their subjects even if at first they resist, and to compel them with threats, so they will accept sound teaching. Peter was obstinate enough in refusing, but when he saw that the judgment of his Lord was firm and definitive, he easily acceded to it. For all that, both of his actions were from charity and reverence. It was in character for him when, seeing his indignity and the majesty of the Savior, he asked that such a lowly service not be done for him, just as in another place he had said: *Depart from me, for I am a sinful man* (Lk. 5:8); which we also read was done by the Precursor of the Lord, when he said: *I ought to be baptized by you, and you come to me?* (Mt. 3:14). Truly, a wise man would rather change his judgment for a good reason, than stick to it obstinately. Therefore the obedience of Peter is praised, since once he knew the will of his Lord, he entirely renounced his own, and entirely subjected his whole self and all he had to the Lord.

Here we see two washings suggested by the Lord, one by which the whole body is washed, and another by which the feet are washed. This latter should be done often, if the first is done once, since the feet cannot be washed often enough. For right away they are dirtied again and again, and since they are soiled by daily dirt and mud, daily must they be washed. We are also taught by this twofold ablution of the body and of some members of the body that there is a twofold spiritual cleansing of the soul and its affections. The one cleansing, which washes the whole soul, takes place in Baptism by which man is purified from the innate impurity, that is, from Original Sin. This washing is never to be repeated. But the feet, that is, the affections of the soul, must be washed often since we sin daily: *If we say that we have no sin, we deceive ourselves, and the truth is not in us* (1 Jn 1:8). These feet of our souls, which need to be washed, we ought to place before Christ the Savior, who washes them, as in heaven he intercedes for us without ceasing, and infuses grace for the remission of sins through the Sacrament of Penance.

Nor is a mystery lacking in this, that once the Jewish supper was completed, that supper in which the paschal lamb was consumed, he then first washed the feet of the disciples before he instituted the Holy Sacrament of the Eucharist, thereby showing that we must make a greater preparation as often as we approach communion than the Jews did when they ate the paschal lamb. It was with unwashed feet that they ate the lamb, for it was only a type and a figure. Moreover, at the Last Supper, only after washing the feet was it fitting to approach the tremendous mystery of the Eucharist. It is not enough to show an external devotion to the world unless interiorly the soul is purged sincerely and without deception by penitence. Therefore when our Redeemer said, *Not all are clean*, his words did not strike the traitor Judas only, but all those others who live badly under the title of the Christian name, who with the tongue profess themselves disciples of Christ, but crucify him with their ways of acting. For not just anything that glows with the appearance of gold is gold. Externally, Judas also had his feet washed, and lived like the disciples of Christ, among them, but within he bore a malicious spirit, and he offered himself as a guide to the captors of the Son of God.

Then after he had washed their feet, etc. (Jn 13:12). It was the custom of our Savior to first do and then teach, so that he might at the same time show something by example and institute it in words. Therefore here, where he showed an example of humility and charity by washing the feet of the disciples, he taught that this was not done by him to no purpose, but in order to entice them to imitate him: *If then I being your Lord and Master, have washed your feet; you also ought to wash one another's feet; For I have given you an example, that as I have done to you, so you do also* (Jn 13:14–15). In this event, which the Redeemer has proposed for our consideration, three things should be noted by us. In the Savior himself we are taught what the prelates of the Church and the ministers of Christ must do. In Judas the traitor we learn that there are some who partake of sweet foods with Christ, eat his bread and openly proclaim themselves to be disciples of Christ, but interiorly are conspirators against Christ. Such are those who want to be seen as Christians, and who on account of ecclesiastical benefices and dignities take up the ministry of Christ, not from love of piety, but desire for gain and honor. In the other apostles besides Judas are meant those who interiorly present all their affections to Christ to be washed, so that they may have a portion with him in heaven. Let us, most beloved brethren, flee the deception and obstinacy of Judas, and with Peter let us show Christ our head, our hands and our feet, that is, our intention, our works and our affections, to be washed, so that when these will have been purified and washed by his grace, they may also be crowned by him in heaven.

Moreover, if we desire to consider entirely the things that are mystically contained in Christ's example, we will find the whole duty of an apostle expressed by him. He rose up from the Jewish supper. In like manner his ministers too must leave behind the lifestyle of the old man and Judaism, and put on the new, rising from just knowing to putting it into practice, from the meal to labor, from the letter to the spirit. Then they must lay down their garments, that is cast away all impediments to the virtues, that they may be able to labor strenuously and gird themselves with white linen, that is, integrity of life. Then they draw the water of saving doctrine and wash the character and conduct of their subjects with doctrine, the Sacraments and example. This, our leader and standard-bearer Christ did, so that we might do the same. *The disciple is not above the master* (Mt. 10:24), nor is it fitting for servants of the humble Lord to be proud. Again and again, most beloved brethren, I am embarrassed, as often as I compare our pride, the pride of dust and ashes, with the humility of our Lord. For he, though he was God and Lord of the angels, did not disdain to minister to the poor, but we refuse to serve our fellow servants. The Son of God rose from the table to wait on his servants still seated. We consider it contrary to our dignity if a poor fellow servant, I will not say sits with us at table, but gets too close to us while we are eating. The Creator of heaven and earth washed the feet of poor disciples; but among us, how many there are who would more readily wash their own feet with wine than extend a cup of cold water to a poor man! He showed the services of kindness to his betrayer; we deny to friends the services we owe them. What could be called or thought more unworthy than that? Disciples, servants, creatures and mere dust and ashes refuse to be like the teacher, the Lord, the Creator, the Man from heaven. Let us be affected in spirit, brethren, by the indignity of such a thing. Let us be moved by such humble submission in such majesty, and let us humble ourselves with the Lord, if we desire to be exalted with him. With him let us serve the poor, if we wish to reign with him. Let us wash one another's feet, if we wish to be considered disciples of Christ. Let us conform ourselves in life to our head, and he will deign to conform us to himself in glory. Amen.

God's overwhelming love in the Eucharist

Homily during the Mass of Corpus Christi
June 9, 1583

Dearly beloved souls, among all the other mysteries of Christ our Savior, which we and Holy Mother Church worship, all of which are most exalted and sublime, today's mystery of the institution of the Most Holy Sacrament of the Eucharist, by which the Lord left himself as food, is so elevated that it surpasses all understanding by the human mind. In this mystery there shines forth such condescension and such charity of the Most High God, that all understanding falls short, so that no one can either explain it in words or conceive it in the mind. But since by the duty of our pastoral office we must speak to you, we will say something even about this. And this sermon will comprise in particular two main points. In brief, we will make clear the causes of the institution of this mystery, and of its being celebrated at this time of the year.

In the Old Testament we read that most noble account of the paschal lamb, which was ordered to be eaten in every family, in every house. If anything was left over, it could not be eaten, but had to be consumed by fire. That lamb was the figure of the immaculate Lamb, Christ our Lord, who was going to be offered on the altar of the cross to the eternal Father on our behalf, Christ whom the precursor John exclaimed over, saying, *Behold the Lamb of God, behold him who takes away the sin of the world* (Jn 1:29). That most beautiful symbol and figure taught us that whatever could not be eaten from the paschal lamb with the teeth of contemplation had to be entirely consumed with the fire of love (cf. Exod. 12:10). But when I meditate within myself on the fact that the Son of God has bestowed himself entirely on us as food, there no longer appears to be any place for that distinction, but it is the whole mystery which is to be consumed by the fire of love. I ask you, my children, what impelled God, all good and most great, to communicate himself as food to this most miserable creature man, a rebel from the beginning, who for having tasted the forbidden fruit at the beginning of his creation had been expelled from the earthly paradise into this most miserable valley; who had daily provoked God himself by the most varied crimes. What, I ask again, so impelled God if not love alone? This creature man had been created for the sake of being like God, and established in a place of delights, presiding over all creatures, and in fact all others had been created for his use. He transgressed the precept of God by tasting the forbidden fruit, *and when he was in honor did not understand*, wherefore *he is compared to senseless beasts, and is become like to them* (Ps. 48:13), so that he was now constrained to eat of the food destined for them.[3]

But God had always loved man to such a point that he was immediately thinking of man's restoration as soon as he had fallen. And in order to turn him away from the food of beasts (see his infinite charity in this), he gave his very self to men as food. You, Christ Jesus, who are the bread of angels, did not disdain to become the food of rebellious men, the food of most ungrateful sinners. O dignity of human excellence, and how much greater is the restoration than the fall! How much the sublimity of this dignity surpasses previous calamities! O most singular favor bestowed on us by God! O inexplicable love of God toward us! Only love impelled God to do so much. O how ungrateful the man who does not think on these things in his heart, who does not meditate on them often! God the creator of all things had foreseen and foreknown our infirmity, and how much this spiritual life of ours would need spiritual food just as our temporal life needs temporal food. For this reason did he prepare such abundant food for both: bodily food for this life, but for our spiritual life he gave us himself whose presence the angels now enjoy in heaven, so that on earth we might feed on him hidden under the species of bread and wine. Elizabeth, a most holy servant of God, sensing that it was the Mother of God who was coming to her, could not help exclaiming: *And whence is this to me, that the mother of my Lord should come to me* (Lk. 1:43)? But how much more should a man exclaim, as he receives God in himself: "How is it that for me, a most unhappy sinner, a most ungrateful and unworthy worm and not a man, the shame of men and the abject one among the people; how is it that my Lord, Creator, Redeemer and God, upon whom angels desire to gaze, is coming to me, entering my house, inhabiting my soul which I have so often made into a den of thieves?"

Let us now approach our second main theme, dearly beloved: it is on this day that the Church, not without reason, celebrates the solemnity of this most holy mystery. It would seem that the proper day for this celebration would be the Thursday of the Lord's Supper, the day on which we know this Most Holy Sacrament was instituted by our Savior Christ. Nevertheless, just as a son, if he is upright and brought up well, cannot think about his

---

[3]Borromeo seems to be following the theological tradition that sees the eating of meat by man as something that is a consequence of original sin. Before the Fall, man was given plants for food, but after the Fall is more like the other animals who feed on each other.

inheritance while his father, who has left him an ample and rich patrimony, is still in his final days rendering his soul to God, so also Holy Mother Church, the spouse and daughter of Christ, is so spiritually involved at that time with the lamentable torments of his most bitter passion and death, that she cannot celebrate, as she would like, the Sacraments most holy that were instituted at that time, most especially this tremendous inheritance which has been left to her. Therefore the Church instituted this day on which we are to express in a particular way the enormous thanks to Christ our King, even though on account of our weakness we are incapable of doing that, since the Son of God, who knew all things from eternity, himself gave thanks to the Father, as he blessed and broke the bread (cf. Mt. 26:26) coming to the aid of our infirmity. By the very institution of this Sacrament he most clearly taught us that we must always and to the utmost of our ability give him thanks for such a great gift.

But why did Holy Mother Church institute this particular time for keeping this memory, the time following the celebration of *all* the other mysteries of Christ: after the days of the Nativity, of the Resurrection, of the Ascension into heaven, the sending of the Holy Spirit? Not thoughtlessly and not without reason, my beloved children, for this most holy mystery corresponds to the others so much, and is so efficacious as a remedy in comparison with *all* the other Sacraments, that rightly is it added on. For by this vivifying consumption of the Eucharist, the faithful are so efficaciously joined to Christ—adhering, so to speak, by the mouth of the body to the opened side of Christ—that they draw in the most abundant treasures of all the Sacraments.[4] But pay attention to another reason as well: among the mysteries of the Son of God that we have observed up to now, the last of all was his Ascension into heaven, which we have said was done so that he could take possession of his kingdom in his and our name, so as to manifest that power about which he had said a little before: *All power is given to me in heaven and in earth* (Mt. 28:18). Just as any king about to take possession of some kingdom goes first to the city that is the metropolitan capital of the whole kingdom (and as a new magistrate or prince similarly makes his approach to begin his administration of that kingdom), so Christ, having obtained the greatest power and the fullest authority over heaven and earth, first took possession of heaven, and poured forth gifts of the Holy Spirit upon men, thus manifesting that fact.

---

[4]The thought seems to be that since the Eucharist potentially gives more sanctifying grace than all the other Sacraments, its feast day crowns all the other feasts.

But since it has been decreed that he is to reign also on earth, he also left himself present here in the most holy sacrifice of the altar, in this Most Holy Sacrament whose institution we venerate this day. For this reason, in a kind of extraordinary way, the Church orders this Sacrament to be carried with honor in procession through cities and towns on this day. When that most powerful Pharaoh, king of Egypt, wished to honor Joseph, he ordered him to be led with honors through the city, so his greatness would be known to all, for when Joseph had explained Pharaoh's dreams, the king told him: *You shall be over my house, and at the commandment of your mouth all the people shall obey: only in the kingly throne will I be above you ... Behold, I have appointed you over the whole land of Egypt. And he took his ring from his own hand, and gave it into his hand: and he put upon him a robe of silk, and put a chain of gold about his neck. And he made him go up into his second chariot, the crier proclaiming that all should bow their knee before him, and that they should know he was made governor over the whole land of Egypt* (Gen. 41:40–43). Similarly Ahasuerus, when he wished to bring the same honors to Mordecai, for that same reason ordered him to be led by Haman in procession while clothed in royal vestments and seated on the king's horse, and to be acclaimed: *This honor is he worthy of, whom the king has a mind to honor* (Est. 6:11).

God wishes to possess the hearts of men; he wishes to be worshiped with due honor by all men. Therefore on this day he passes through cities and towns with the greatest honor and magnificence, led in procession by clergy and people, prelates and magistrates. And in this way the Church publically professes that he is our King and God, from whom we have received all things and to whom we owe everything. Most beloved children in the Lord, while we were traversing the city just now, I was thinking about such a great multitude and variety of people who even until the present time and up to this very day have been oppressed by such miserable servitude, and for so long a time have served the most vile and cruel lords. My mind was turned to so many young people caught up in evil pleasures and lusts, who have made the belly their God, as the Apostle says (cf. Phil. 3:19), for those who aim at something as their favorite and ultimate goal in life, want that to be their God, for God is the end of all things.[5] Let them renounce the flesh, their dissipations, dives and taverns, bad company and sins, and let them come to know the true God whom the Church proclaims to us here today. I was weeping over the

---

[5][Q]ui enim finem sibi ponunt, hi nunc Deum suum esse volunt; omnium enim finis est Deus.

intolerable pride and pomp of certain vain women who make themselves into idols unto themselves, who expend so many morning hours, which ought to be dedicated to prayers, in order to embellish their faces and to twist and turn their hair; who daily demand new dresses, and so make their husbands unhappy, leave their children impoverished and use up their patrimony. Consequently, we find illicit contracts, failure to repay debts and pass on legacies to their intended recipients, and complete forgetfulness of God most good and great and of their own souls. I was contemplating so many avaricious men, purchasers of hell, since they gain eternal fire for themselves at such a high price. About these the Apostle rightly said avarice is a serving of idols (cf. Eph. 5:5, Col. 3:5). Besides gold, they have no other God, and they direct all their actions and words to this one end, with all their actions and thoughts aimed at acquiring money, buying fields and comparing their riches to others'. I could only marvel at the unhappiness of certain men who say they are dedicated to the art of governing States, and who have nothing else ever before their eyes. If the divine law commands something contrary to what they call the law of good governance (how miserable and unhappy they are!), they do not hesitate to trample on the divine law, and they compel God to yield to these diabolical designs of their own. What lamentable people! And we are supposed to call these people Christian? Men who place themselves and the world higher than Christ and publically profess it? All these different kinds of idols the Lord comes to destroy with this holy institution of the Eucharist, so that we shall be able to exclaim with Isaiah the prophet, *Only in you is God, and there is no God besides you. Verily you are a hidden God, the God of Israel the savior* (Isa. 45:14–15). O good God, up to now we have served the senses, the flesh and the world. Until now our God was our belly, our flesh, our gold, our State. We now renounce all these idols, and venerate and worship you, the only true God, who has bestowed on us so many benefits, and this one above all: you have left yourself for us as food. I beg you, make this heart of ours yours from now on. May nothing ever more uproot us from your charity. We prefer to die a thousand times rather than to offend you in the slightest way. For thus advancing here in your grace, we shall likewise enjoy your glory perpetually. Amen.

Charles Borromeo

Taste the sweetness of the Lord

Homily in the Cathedral of Milan after Compline
Corpus Christi
June 9, 1583

How delightful is your spirit, Lord, for in order to demonstrate the sweetness of your goodness to your sons, having granted them bread from heaven you filled the hungry with good things, sending the rich away empty.[6] Thus sings Holy Mother Church in today's solemnity while she recalls the celebrated memory of such a gift. Therefore how much, dear children, should we taste of this most sweet memorial of God, than which nothing is more delightful, nothing more joyful, and by which the highest love of God toward us is shown. It is indeed a most eminent effect of that divine love, which by its own power makes itself tasted. Let us all consider, I ask you, those words of the apostle Paul, by which he describes the institution of this Most Holy Sacrament, and we will see how everything about it breathes forth a great love: *the Lord Jesus, the same night in which he was betrayed, took bread. And giving thanks, broke, and said: Take you, and eat: this is my body, which shall be delivered for you: this do for the commemoration of me* (1 Cor. 11:24).

O Christians, how much force those first words have: *the same night in which he was betrayed*; at the time when so many traps were being laid for him by his disciple, to whom he himself had done so much good; the time of so many injuries, such opprobrium, so many torments, and finally death itself, a most vile and cruel one, at the hands of the people; at that time, I say, when such things were being planned against him, and he who scrutinizes the *hearts and reins* of men (cf. Ps. 7:10) saw them all most clearly. In a word, at that time and hour Christ was preparing a most singular benefit for sinful men still hostile to him, he was mixing such a powerful medicine for us who were sick; he was providing delightful food to us who were famished. See, O man, what kind of injuries he was repaying, and what benefits he answered vicious deeds done to him! How much even the consideration of this hour should inflame you with love of God, and love of him who has pursued you with such love, traitor though you be! O wondrous sign of love that has been given! They prepare death for you, O Christ, and you see it and think of life for them. They arrange ambushes for you, and you determine to free them from the traps of the devil. What should I wonder at more, the traitor's ingratitude or your

---

[6]A Magnificat antiphon that had been sung for the feast.

goodness? The latter is indeed the more wonderful of the two, for it is your very own characteristic to spare and to have mercy, since you have always loved men so much that you could say in another place, with the fullest justification: *I am come to cast fire on the earth; and what will I, but that it be kindled* (Lk. 12:49)!

How much you desire this, in how many ways did you dedicate your efforts to this, how many means and instruments you used to this end! Listen, dear children, to those many ways. In the beginning God created man from nothing and fashioned him after his own image and likeness; he placed him in a paradise of delights; he placed him over all creatures; he created all those things for his use. But not at all content with all that, he also wanted angels, such noble rational creatures, to be at the service of men and to guard them and to be present to them the entire span of their lives. These things seemed like nothing to God. When he himself personally descended from heaven to earth, made man, he did not disdain to be subject to human infirmities, but went even further. He gave himself to us while living as a companion and dying as our price. Departing from us, he left himself as food in the Most Holy Sacrament, and he will afterward give himself as our reward in heavenly glory. O how rightly can we all exclaim with the royal prophet David: *What is man that you are mindful of him? or the son of man that you visit him* (Ps. 8:5)? Man, within whose memory and awareness you so strongly desire to have the first place, that on this account you left yourself to him in this most excellent Sacrament! You who need no one's goods, since heaven and earth belong to you, what advantage or increase of glory and honor can you expect from man, that you so seek to be honored by him? But it is for our good, O dear children, to acknowledge this immensity of divine love, on this depends our greatest benefit. Therefore, the Lord willed to show it to us with so many works and signs.

And because this reality is of such great importance, we who as your bishop strive above all to help and promote you in the Lord, and always give great attention to this, will see to it that Reverend Father Francesco Panigarola, very well known to you, will speak to you every afternoon about its dignity, excellence and spiritual benefit, even as Holy Church by her divine offices and sacrifices attends this most holy mystery through this whole octave.[7] And we, for whom the task is most fitting, will give a

---

[7]Francesco Panigarola, O.F.M. (1548–94) was from a noble Milanese family, studied at the University of Pavia and became a Franciscan priest. The Sax edition indicates that Panigarola was a preacher highly esteemed and relied upon by St. Charles. Panigarola was eventually named bishop of Asti, and was chosen as the preacher for Borromeo's funeral in 1584.

sermon about the same thing this Saturday, which will be the day sacred to the Apostle Barnabas, to whom all you Milanese owe so much since he was as a father to your ancestors, the first to bring the Christian faith into this province and sow in it the seeds of religion. Likewise on Sunday we will give a sermon on the same thing.

What, I ask, does your Holy Mother the Church mean to hold before your attention in all of this? Nothing else, dear children, except that you acknowledge such a great benefit, that you be grateful, that you taste this most immense sweetness, that these things penetrate your heart. Why should a Christian not derive the greatest devotion from this when he knows himself to be standing before God Most Holy, before the Most Holy Altar? What is this condescension of God, that as often as we wish, he permits us to be present? When Christ, before he ascended to heaven, was living among men, he worked so many miracles by his bodily presence and restored life to so many dead, sight to so many blind, and health to so many sick. So now, why would he be unable to break apart and soften our iron hearts by his most holy presence, and thus dispose that once their companionship with the devil is broken up, they may give place within themselves to the Holy Spirit?

In the time of that most holy servant of God, Bernard [of Clairvaux], there was in the region of Aquitaine a certain most stubborn count, William,[8] who living in schism had perverted all divine and human laws, had expelled a great many bishops from their sees, had usurped ecclesiastical goods, and did not cease to persecute all the faithful of Christ, showing himself to be a man of obstinate and obdurate heart, like another Pharaoh. This despite the fact that many other religious men as well as Bernard, first of all, had approached him multiple times to move him away from his wicked purpose and lead the stubborn son back into the embrace of the kindest Mother. One day, with Mass almost finished, after the kiss of peace and having taken the Most Holy Sacrament in his hands, Bernard, while approaching this count standing outside the church as her bitterest enemy, is related to have said in complete freedom the following words:

Up till now, O Count, you have always resisted the servants of God, neglected their words, and instead of listening have brought injuries

---

[8]Borromeo seems to be referring to William X, Duke of Aquitaine (1099–1137), who had sided with the Antipope Anacletus against Pope Innocent V in the papal schism of 1130. Apparently, he was one of the most difficult for St. Bernard to convince of quitting his schism.

upon them. We have appealed to you, and you have spurned us. In another meeting which we had with you, a multitude of servants of God gathered together beseeched you, and you had contempt for them. Will you be contumacious even to the point of not giving due obedience to the Lord of those servants, who is approaching you in person? Will you not fear him who can destroy your body and send your soul into Gehenna, him who shall come to judge the living and the dead? Will you not revere this very God himself, the Son of God born for you, who suffered so many things and died? Behold, to you comes forth the Son of the Virgin, who is the Head and Lord of the Church which you persecute. Here present is your judge, into whose hands your soul will arrive. Will you despise even him? Will you despise even him, like you despise his servants?

Such power did the sight of the Most Holy Sacrament have, so much was its presence capable of doing, that he who earlier had been a most fierce lion, suddenly turned into the mildest lamb; and he who had wanted to give commands both good and wicked to everyone, submitted in everything to Bernard commanding him. He restored the expelled bishops to their sees, returned the goods taken away by trickery, became respectful of all religious men, and having been made an entirely new man, he went pale and stiff, and with his legs trembling with fear and giving way, he was cast to the ground as if out of his mind. Lifted up by his soldiers, he again fell on his face, and of course without saying anything to anyone or looking at anyone, he appeared epileptic, with saliva flowing down his beard, and emitted deep groans.

This, my children, was the change wrought by the right hand of the Most High. This is the efficacy of the presence of this vital Sacrament. When you publically adore this Sacrament, and when you see it carried to the sick or through the city, may this same efficacy move you and soften you, so that each of you say, "This is my God, this my Lord, this my shepherd, this my judge, this my remunerator, whose delight is to be with the children of men, who is so pleased to be with us. For his sake I will extricate my heart from earthly affairs and will try to fill that space, once emptied, with the love of God. Now may everything in me yield to God: *Shall not my soul be subject to God? for from him is my salvation*" (Ps. 61:1). Sinners, let your hearts be broken down. The Lord has asked you so often through his servants, and you have spurned them. In a thousand ways he has called you to repentance, and you have despised him. With preaching, inspirations, scourges and pestilences has he tried to correct you, but all was in vain. Behold, the Son of the Virgin goes forth before you, God and man, himself in person, whom you persecute with your wicked deeds, whom you exasperate with dishonor and injuries, whom you blaspheme, whom you never cease to provoke. Your judge is present, will you spurn even him? Will you not hear even him? But now give the usual alms for the poor, while I touch on the other things briefly.[9]

Second part

Concerning the spiritual use of this Most Holy Sacrament, as I have said, we will speak to you on the two approaching feast days. Now let us say a few words about the honor which must be shown to it by all, both when it is carried in public and when you approach frequently to consume it, which is by far the way in which God is most honored, and the end for which especially these mysteries were instituted. This morning you have heard from us that Holy Church by these processions makes profession of the Christian religion she has received, and that this is our God, and there is no other God beside him. Now just as he always has since Christ's ascension into heaven, the devil is arming his accomplices, but now more energetically and diligently. Daily he incites heresies in order to remove this great remedy from our midst, to delete all memory of this Sacrament from the minds of men. What does he not do, in order to attain this, what does he not contrive, what does he not attempt? See for yourselves what he has done in so many provinces of the Christian world: I mean in Germany, in England, in Flanders, and in neighboring France. Why therefore should you not arm yourselves to struggle more energetically for the honor of God, the confounding of the devil, and the glorification of this Most Holy Sacrament by which our spiritual life is strengthened with every help?

For this reason so many societies and so many confraternities have been instituted in every parish of this city, but how many of those enrolled in them fail in their duty! When it is carried to the sick, how few there are to follow behind! And among these few, how many without lighted candles! The very King of heaven and earth deigns to dwell in our midst, and we disdain to honor him! Looking out as much as we can for you and for

---

[9]Felice Carnaghi informs us that St. Charles would have added an exhortation to charity here, as the alms were being taken up, before proceeding to the second part of the sermon (Felice Carnaghi, trans. *San Carlo Borromeo, Omelie sull'Eucaristia e sul Sacerdozio* [Rome: Edizioni Pauline, 1984], 147, footnote 9).

your salvation on that account, as in everything else, we gave order for the erection in this cathedral of the kind of society, of the Most Holy Body of Christ, to which we concede and connect all the indulgences conceded by the Supreme Roman Pontiffs to societies of this kind everywhere, especially the one in the church of Santa Maria Sopra Minerva in Rome, with the authority communicated to us by our most holy lord Gregory XIII, by divine providence Pope, the present Vicar of Christ the Lord on earth. In the greatest detail we will study everything that will be helpful for its confreres to do. In the meantime, we beg you all in the Lord, that with concern for your salvation you enroll yourselves in it; that you take part in the processions which take place every month according to custom; that when the saving Viaticum is carried to the sick, you accompany it in a fitting religious spirit; and finally that you come frequently to this school of Christ. Nor let there be anyone among you who says, "I have to be at the store; I am tied up with much business." Or is this the principal business of your souls? Will the store dismantle the school of Christ, and will earthly affairs prevent us from worshipping God? Seek first rather the kingdom of God, and all these things shall be added to you and everything will proceed successfully.

And there are not a few who when they pass before the most holy altar, God's resting place, scarcely know how to genuflect; they bend only one knee. Miserable and unhappy people! God so often lowers himself to earth for you, and you refuse to adore in every possible way him for whom every knee bends in heaven, on earth and below the earth! You do not wish to expend yourselves and all your things for his honor! You vain women have abundant silk and gold clothing, rings, jewels, pearls, necklaces, earrings and a thousand such gold chains by which devils hold you bound; and you men daily dream up new types of boots and clothing, while in your parishes the poor and naked Christ rests on bare altars with no pyx in some places, no fly net in others—and this leaves you unmoved? Are you not steeped in shame? The most holy David speaking to Nathan was ashamed that the ark of God was in animal skin tents, while he himself was in a royal palace; he said, *Do you see that I dwell in a house of cedar, and the ark of God is lodged within skins?* (2 Kgs 7:2). Are you not terrified at the thought that you cover yourselves in gold and silk, but the flesh and blood of Christ are covered in linen rags? You dissipate yourselves in so many pleasures, and so many members of Christ in monasteries, both of religious men and nuns, perish from hunger. Love, love is what you need, O hearts of steel, at least a little. If you were not entirely lacking in that, if there were even a spark of it in you, believe me, you would clearly recognize that you can never provide as much as you ought for God's honor and your own lowliness.

I wish two things to come to mind for you, as often as you see Christ in this Most Holy Sacrament, and they are contained in those words of the prophet: *if then I be a father, where is my honor? and if I be a master, where is my fear?* (Mal. 1:6). The Lord speaks from that altar to you, the people of Milan, saying: "O you merchants, I made you for myself, that I might be your end and goal, and you think about everything else except me. I gave you all things in my possession, and you do not wish to return even the smallest portion of them to the poor man, who bears my person and is asking, or rather to me who can demand it. You drink the blood of the poor against my rights, you engage in illicit business contracts, you violate feasts and days sacred to me, you trample down the honor due me. And if I am Lord, where is the fear of me? If I am Father, where is my honor? Disgraceful children, I commanded you to honor your parents so gifts of grace would follow you, and to keep your bodies, which are the temples of the Holy Spirit, pure and clean. But you dissipate yourselves in pleasures, living to get drunk and gorging yourselves at the table. If I am Lord, where is the fear of me, and if I am Father, where is my honor? Most vain women whom I created as a help for the men, why are you the perdition of men? With your pompous displays and make-up, with your accessories and hairstyles, by which you tie up men's souls in the strongest cords, are you going to take the time which should go to prayer and worship of me, and use it instead for decorating your fetid flesh?[10] If I am Lord, where is the fear of me? If I am Father, where is my honor?"

O how much you will have learned today, my children, if on your hearts you would engrave as your firmest maxims these two things: the fear of God and the honor owed him! You would say, "I want this to have first place before all worldly things. I decide to direct all my actions to this end. I prefer to meet death itself rather than come up short in any matter concerning the honor owed to God." The greatest help for you in persevering in this path before all else is frequent reception of the Most Holy Eucharist. Whatever things the world finds hard and bitter, Christ himself will render most

---

[10]We have translated the adjective *foetidis* literally, "fetid," although Carnaghi's Italian rendering, *destinato a perire* ("destined to perish," *San Carlo Borromeo: Omelie*, 150) brings out an appropriate meaning beyond the rhetorical and ascetical exaggeration of St. Charles. But then again, perhaps people living before the age of convenient daily showers and quickly applied chemical deodorants were more keenly aware than we that the natural condition of the human animal is not that pleasant to smell.

easy for you. The prophet Elijah, as you heard in the first reading at Mass this morning (cf. 1 Kgs 19:2ff.), was quite frightened by the persecutions and threats of that most impious woman, Jezebel, so that he was brought almost to the point of despair. The Lord sent his angel, who aroused him a second and third time from sleep, and brought a barley loaf for him to eat. In the strength of that bread, Elijah walked forty days, until he arrived at the mountain of God, Horeb. Jezebel the demon, Jezebel the world, Jezebel the flesh, O how miserably do they bring terror and fright to men, how difficult they make Christ's precepts to men, how difficult they make it for men to humble themselves, to leave bad company, to forgive injuries! But eat this barley bread, the body and blood of Christ, frequently, and believe me, you will overcome all difficulties of the journey and finally arrive at the mountain of God, Horeb, at the heavenly Jerusalem, where face to face, together with the holy angels, you will truly understand him whom you now see under the appearances of bread and wine. May that be granted you by him who died for us on the wood of the cross that we might obtain it, Christ Jesus, blessed unto ages and ages. Amen.

Charles Borromeo

Receive this Sacrament frequently, worthily and zealously

**Homily for the second Sunday after Pentecost, in the octave
of Corpus Christi
given in the Cathedral of Milan
June 12, 1583**

*And it came to pass as he was sitting at meat in the house, behold many
publicans and sinners came, and sat down with Jesus and his disciples*
(Mt. 11:10). This morning the holy Gospel recounts, O most beloved souls,
the story of the banquet prepared for our Lord Jesus Christ in the house of
Matthew, to which many publicans and sinners came flocking to be seated
at table, attracted by the example of Matthew himself, whose sudden and
deliberate change of life they marveled at. Matthew followed Christ at
the mere sound of his calling, "Follow me." They were also drawn by the
utterances of Christ himself, who had the words of eternal life. Seeing these
things, the Pharisees began to murmur, saying to his disciples, *Why does
your master eat with publicans and sinners? But Jesus hearing it, said: They
that are in health need not a physician, but they that are ill. Go then and learn
what this means, I will have mercy and not sacrifice. For I am not come to call
the just, but sinners* (Mt. 9:11–13). Therefore we can say that he spent time
in the company of sinners in order to lead them to repentance. It is indeed
opportune and fitting that this gospel narrative falls within this octave, for
this banquet, to which so many flocked, signified the riches of that heavenly
banquet which Christ puts on for the world, and to which he invites all,
saying: *Come to me, all you that labor, and are burdened, and I will refresh
you* (Mt. 11:28). Our Lord admitted all publicans and sinners to that table;
now that does not mean sinners should approach this table of the Eucharist,
does it? Should those stained by mortal faults receive communion? Of
course not. In what way you should approach here, I will now undertake
to tell you, although concerning this very thing you have sufficiently and
elegantly heard the religious man Father Francesco Panigarola speaking
to you, yesterday and the day before yesterday. Nevertheless, so as not to
fail in our duty, we will deal briefly with what preparation the Most Holy
Sacrament is to be received and with what zeal we should frequent it.

Yesterday you heard at length that some Sacraments have been instituted
as life-giving, that is, instituted to free the soul from the death of sin, and
restore it to the life of grace. These are two, namely Baptism first, and after it,
Penance. But the Most Holy Eucharist is properly a Sacrament of the living,
it requires that those who receive it be spiritually living, for it was instituted

for the sake of sustaining and increasing life. Therefore he who remains in death, who is in mortal sin, should stay far from this table. Let him first hasten to life, to penance, the second plank after the shipwreck. Let him confess his sins to the priest with sorrow and with the resolution to avoid them in future. For the Sacrament of Confession is the first and necessary disposition for the Eucharist. He who, though actually dead, would approach to receive the life-giving bread, ought to hear what the apostle Paul, speaking about the solemn institution of it, would say to him: *But let a man prove himself: and so let him eat of that bread, and drink of the chalice. For he that eats and drinks unworthily, eats and drinks judgment to himself, not discerning the body of the Lord* (1 Cor. 11:28–29). He sins against the Body and Blood of Christ, therefore he is said to be guilty of them, because he does not judge, does not discern, does not consider what he consumes, namely that it is the Body and Blood of God, that is of Christ, who will judge the living and the dead, who suffered for us and reigns in heaven, the dazzling white font of all purity. But a Christian is not going to be content with such a preparation as that, merely avoiding the stain of deadly crimes, is he? Not at all, in fact. Rather he will make use of another preparation as well, to make the reception of the Most Holy Eucharist more fruitful. He will also try to wipe out venial sins by confession, or at least by sorrow. Although they surely do not take away grace, they nevertheless make charity grow cool, and he who treats them as nothing, little by little slips into bigger sins. Just as a long illness brings on death, so venial sins prepare the way to mortal sins. And just as a great quantity of water completely extinguishes fire, while a little water only weakens it, so mortal sins take away all grace, but venial sins render a man weaker and sick. The greatest zeal must be applied to the curing of that sickness, and that before the Most Holy Synaxis, so we may be able to perceive more abundant fruits in us.

And any Christian, my dear children, when he stands before the sacred altar, should excite in himself the strongest particular sentiments of actual devotion, sentiments which will be enkindled the most by meditations like this: "Just whom am I approaching, I who am but a worm? Whom have I come to receive? What am I about to do? I have determined to eat of him who created heaven and earth with a word, by whose providence all things are governed, who by a mere nod could reduce everything back to nothingness; to whom all power in heaven and on earth has been given, to whom the Father has given all judgment, on whom the angels desire to look, before whom demons tremble. In his name every knee bends in heaven, on earth, and the regions below the earth; in his presence iniquity is found in angels and the columns of heaven shake; before him all our just deeds are a filthy rag. He is to judge the living and the dead, he who is the font of all brightness and purity. He abhors all impurity and stain. I who am utterly impure, the lowest of creatures, having fallen a thousand times into sin, approach to eat of him to whom I owe so much, who loved so much that he gave his life for me, accepted death and left himself as food. I, who am the most ungrateful traitor, approach to eat of this Bread."

Thus a meditation on his majesty and holy fear, but also on his goodness and charity, will awaken in us the sentiment of love, and by these two things most of all a man will render himself fit to receive an abundance of heavenly fruit. For just as causes here below bring about greater effects in those things which are found to be more disposed to them, so God acts in the same way. And just as the waters of the sea would fill a glass up to its capacity, so in the same way our heart will be filled with the water of divine grace, which is an immense and deep sea, if indeed our heart is found empty of all cares and business of this world and all impurity. This sentiment of devotion will be most helpful, as I have said, dear children, and a notable absence of it, joined to a disdain for the Sacrament, can be such even as to inundate men with mortal sin. So we must be on guard against such a state of soul.

I would like, most dearly beloved, to lament the misery and calamity of some who are probably now absent, I mean those who spend the entire year in offending God a thousand times, expend themselves to commit innumerable crimes, fall into all kinds of impurities and sins, but when Easter is approaching, toward the end of Holy Week, and in order to avoid ecclesiastical censures and the taint of infamy in the eyes of everyone, come flocking on Holy Thursday, wanting to confess immediately, on the spot, and immediately receive Communion.[11] These most unhappy people have become hardened in sin, have contracted bad habits, grown old in evil days (cf. Dan. 13:52); and in the twinkling of an eye they want to be purified and united to God. Do you know where such great zeal could come from? I mean, like dogs they return more quickly to their vomit, resume their old way of life, and lose no sweat in preparing themselves for the Sacraments. O what a judgment these people eat and drink upon themselves! It is not with this intention, not to this end, my children,

---

[11]This was because at that time those who did not do their Easter duty, that is, confessing and receiving Holy Communion at Eastertime, were reported to the ecclesiastical authorities and their names were made public in their parish.

that we are to receive Communion. But like all other actions, so this reception of the Most Holy Eucharist is to be ordered to God's glory and honor; and then, so that the soul's salvation may be provided for, its weakness healed, grace increased, and life conserved and sustained. The Lord wanted the sons of Israel to be prepared and disposed in so many different ways; therefore what preparation could there be, for one who is to receive the author of the law and of grace that will not be far short of what is required? There is much I ought to say concerning the right way of receiving Communion, and many topics could also be given you for meditation, but since you will hear at greater length concerning all this from the Religious Father, I therefore pass them by, and will set before your consideration the manner and frequency with which we should avail ourselves of God's mercy.

Second part

As this part, dearly beloved, is so useful and necessary, it cannot be treated in a single sermon, but should rather be talked about daily. For it concerns our life, since the Lord promises eternal life to those who eat of him, saying: *If any man eats of this bread, he shall live forever* (Jn 6:52). The Eucharist was instituted precisely for this purpose (as we have often said, and will show again): to be food for us. For whatever food brings for the body, the Eucharist brings to the soul. There are two things in man by which he is kept alive, natural heat and a basic liquid.[12] Now fire is fed by what it burns, so natural heat is always consuming this liquid, that is always burning this liquid away, rather than body tissue. So man has daily need of food by which the liquid is replenished, for just as in a lamp or torch the wick remains lit on account of oil and would quickly go out if oil were not added, even though as oil is added over sufficient time, the wick is also consumed. So it is in the lamp of the soul. The wick is concupiscence, that is the tinder for sin (*fomes peccati*), and the oil is divine grace that must be added. Natural heat is the ardor or smoldering of concupiscence, and the basic liquid is grace already present; thus if new food is not added daily, if there is no increase of grace, then the burning heat of that tinder will take over everything, and our soul will quickly waste away like a wick is burned away when oil is

---

[12]St. Charles here employs the physiological understanding of the human body of that time to construct his analogy, which illustrates the Catholic doctrinal distinction between sin and concupiscence (the tendency toward sin).

not constantly added.[13] This food and increase of grace is conferred by the Most Holy Eucharist. It is the Eucharist that repairs the harm proceeding from the burning of concupiscence. If the harm is continual, why should a continual remedy not be applied? Why do you think such great mysteries were hidden under these visible species of bread and wine, dearly beloved? For no other reason than for us to consume the Most Holy Eucharist daily, just as we use bread and wine daily as nourishment of the body.

But let us scrutinize even more deeply the reason for this, relying on this axiom most true, namely that all things are conserved and increased by those means and ways by which they were first generated. I beg you, let us look and see what the first beginnings of the nascent and flourishing Church were, how it grew and spread so widely. You will surely find no other cause than this: the Christians of that time were persevering in the breaking of the bread (cf. Acts 2:42). O Milan, every day the whole people received Communion; not only priests and religious, but also laity and people living in the world did this, and what great increases resulted for the Church! What a propagation of the faith! How much liberty for preaching the Gospel followed in the wake of that, how much constancy in bearing martyrdom! How much alacrity in undergoing death, how much contempt for all human things and life itself by comparison! From this and after suffering many things was brought to Diocletian, Sebastian all the more freely accused the emperor of impiety. From this, Vincent, God's athlete most strong, could not be conquered by any torments. From this, Polycarp, finding himself in front of Marcion and asked whether he knew him, most freely said, "I recognize the first born of the devil." From this, Ignatius wrote to the Romans:

> Would that I could have beasts prepared for me, and which, I pray, will be quick to punish and destroy me, enticed with desire to eat me. May they not be afraid to attack me, as has happened with other martyrs. But if they do not want to come near, I will force the issue. I will press on so as to be devoured. Now I am beginning to be a disciple of Christ, desiring no visible thing, but rather to find Jesus

---

[13]The translation attempts to adjust and interpret the analogies presented by St. Charles, somewhat incoherently, from true *principles* of nature, but partly misunderstood physiological details. The basic point is that divine grace must be constantly present in the soul to counterbalance the tendencies to sin inherited from Adam; if not, then one or more of those evil tendencies will grow into the basic character of the person.

Christ. Let fire, the cross, beasts, breaking of bones, tearing apart of limbs, crushing of the whole body, and all the torments of the devil come upon me, as long as I attain and keep Christ.

From this, the Levite of Christ Lawrence triumphed over the men serving him burning coals, and called out, "I worship my God, and him alone do I serve; therefore I do not fear, O tyrant, your torments." But also in the virgins and the whole feminine sex, what a virile and unbreakable spirit was caused by this alone, the frequent reception of the Eucharist! Listen to Lucy when she was before the prefect Paschasius: when he said, "Your words will cease, when it finally comes to blows on you." She manfully responded with, "Words cannot fail the servants of God, to whom Christ the Lord has said: And you shall be brought before governors, and before kings for my sake, for a testimony to them and to the Gentiles: But when they shall deliver you up, take no thought how or what to speak: for it shall be given you in that hour what to speak" (Mt. 10:18–19), and many other words to the same effect. Listen to Agnes resisting and reproving Symphronius with unbroken spirit: "Nor do I wish to give divine honor to Vesta, who is nothing other than a wooden or stone statue, and if you should bring my virginity to the test, I have with me a guard of my body, the angel of the Lord, who will preserve me inviolate." How audaciously the young girl Catherine reproached Maxentius! But why should I spend time in calling to mind these things, which fill a thousand books? It is no wonder there was so much fortitude in those first Christians of both sexes, who, according to Cyprian's testimony, were armed for martyrdom with this most sacred food, and rightly so, for strength was given them by this bread of the strong, as the Sacred Scriptures called it. From this, chains, fetters, handcuffs, jail, fasts, hunger, many days without eating, vigils, the rack, the pillory, clubs, swords, crosses, the wheel, blades, the gridiron, hot coals, fires, beasts, hot lead and pitch poured down their throats, thorns, and in sum all the other innumerable torments like that were sweeter to them than honey on the comb, and they rushed to their death with more alacrity than we to life.

But when people stopped consuming this food, when communion ceased to be frequent, O what weakness followed! What sickness! What infirmity! How easily people are conquered today! How easily they are overcome! They barely catch sight of the demon and immediately they surrender, they succumb, they turn their backs on Christ their leader. Or irritated with the slightest injury, provoked by the slightest word, they attack and dishonor God and the saints with their blasphemies, shed the blood of their brethren, break concord, sever charity, sunder peace, lose love. Led on by the consideration of their own benefit and profit, no matter how small, they neglect God, think nothing of heaven, look down on the eternal goods, attach no value to their souls, and rush headlong into hell.

When Christ the Lord had raised the dead daughter of the leader of the synagogue, he ordered that food be given her, so that we might know that without spiritual food, our souls once brought to life cannot long remain in life. Isaiah lamented over that fact, saying, *Therefore is my people led away captive, because they had not knowledge, and their nobles have perished with famine, and their multitude were dried up with thirst. Therefore has hell enlarged her soul, and opened her mouth without any bounds, and their strong ones, and their people, and their high and glorious ones shall go down into it* (Isa. 5:13–14). This, my children, is the ruin of cities and towns, this, the origin of all calamities: that the nobles are perishing from hunger, that the magistrates wish not to eat, that those persons, after whose example the whole world forms itself, dishonor the frequent reception of the Most Holy Eucharist, ridicule those who do so often, call them hypocrites, give them the name "simulators of sanctity"; and the whole people follow them. For this reason hell extends itself, opens its mouth wide, swallows and devours so many every day. I would indeed openly acknowledge, my children, that many good things have been established in this, your city, over the past few years, that many have succeeded in improving. I acknowledge that a great many are leading moral and praiseworthy lives, that many pious works are flourishing, that worship more fervent than before is being shown to God, that ecclesiastical ceremonies are more diligently observed, and prayers better attended. I acknowledge that crowds come more frequently to hear the word of God, to hear sacred discourses and readings. But whatever good comes from that, or will come from it in the future, whatever fruit we shall notice resulting from our labors and vigils, we will attribute it to this sole cause: the frequency of the most holy Sacraments of Penance and the Eucharist. O people of Milan, *look unto the rock whence you are hewn, and to the hole of the pit from which you are dug out* (Isa. 51:1). Consider the Church's beginning; think over the roots of the fruits which you see among yourselves; cultivate and grasp them.

But there will not be lacking someone who will say: "I receive Communion often, but I remain always cold and tepid; I barely recognize any fruit in me." This is itself a fruit: to know that you are cold. This is merely your infirmity, than which, I ask, is there anything more powerful for taking it away, than grace and Christ who bestows it? You sin every day, says Ambrose; receive every day. O how miserable we are! What a terrible thing, that for those actions we are held to do, we are so tardy and find so many kinds of excuses! You the storekeeper, what do you say? "I have to work at my business, be at the store daily, take care of lots of affairs, therefore I cannot receive Communion every day." See how light and frivolous this type of excuse is. Storekeeper, either you are a Christian or you are not. If you wish to be a Christian and conduct your business according to the precept of the rule of Christ, what prevents you from receiving Communion every day? Or is it not true that if you seek first the kingdom of God and his justice, all these other things will be added to you? But if you do not wish to run your business like a Christian, but rather a Gentile or pagan, my words are not directed to you, for you have already condemned yourself out of your own mouth. All the Fathers and holy Doctors of the Church, the Gregorys, Augustine, Chrysostom, and Ambrose with one voice profess and preach what I myself instruct you to do: this food is to be received most often. But I know there are also many who, led by reverence for such a great Sacrament, say they do not consider frequent reception to be recommendable. But these people are entirely wrong, for the ways of God are far different from the ways of men. For too much familiarity among men breeds contempt on account of the fact that long association with them brings out their faults more easily. But frequenting God makes reverence toward him greater, for those who approach more closely to God, by knowing his power, wisdom and goodness better, and by enjoying his gifts, are compelled to love and revere him more.

But now I seem to hear many of you, who are burning with desire for this saving reception, asking me to fix a certain time in advance, and give you a certain rule for receiving the Most Holy Eucharist. But I cannot give them a rule. This is the duty of the spiritual fathers of their souls, who more easily know what is most helpful for any of them. But I will prescribe that universal rule of our blessed father Ambrose: Let them live in such a way that they can receive Communion every day, for he who has not made himself worthy to receive this food, will be even less worthy after a year, according to the proverb, "He who is not ready today, will be less ready tomorrow." What, after all, is the preparation for the person who is receiving Communion at Easter? To be daily entangled in a thousand crimes, to grow old in sins, to contract bad habits, to permit the demon to sink the deepest roots in our soul and, with no opposition from anyone, to make himself its lord? On the contrary, those who receive Communion more often confess more often, have fewer and smaller sins, and dispose themselves more quickly to receive. Augustine advised that, as they were doing in his lifetime, laypeople should receive every week. My children, when you recite the Lord's Prayer, you ask that daily bread be given you. Ask this bread from the Lord, the bread by which he nourishes your souls. I know you will not feel the tremendous fruits which will come out of that just as soon as you begin, but you have to persevere, for neither does he who plants and daily waters a tree and tills the earth around it immediately see visible growth and the production of fruit. Patience is needed, my children, and perseverance.

Through the mercies of our Lord Jesus Christ I ask this of you, dearly beloved, as I conclude. I beg of you, try it, make the experience of it, begin to receive at least every month, then twice every month, afterward on every feast day, and you will see how much change there will be in you. How different your souls will become from what they were before. Taste, taste, place your mouth forward, so you may see how sweet and rich is the bread of Christ. It is the same Christ as in the primitive Church, the same Eucharist, the same strength as before. You will receive the same fruits as they did. But it is not enough to consume Christ, unless you also lead a life in conformity with him. It is not enough to be filled up with the gifts of the Holy Spirit, unless they are put to use. Therefore, *If we live in the Spirit, let us also walk in the Spirit* (Gal. 5:26). Flee *the works of the flesh, which are fornication, uncleanness, immodesty, luxury, idolatry, witchcrafts, enmities, contentions, emulations, wraths, quarrels, dissensions, sects, envies, murders, drunkenness, revellings, and such like* (Gal. 5:19–21). May the Lord grant you, my children, to abound in the Spirit, to receive the fruits of the Spirit, which are charity, joy, peace, patience, kindness, goodness, patience, meekness, faith, modesty, self-control, chastity; so that living by the Spirit, you may also walk by the Spirit, and by the bounty of that same Spirit, may you be filled here below with grace, and likewise in heaven with glory. Amen.

Uniting heaven and earth at the altar

Homily on the occasion of the consecration of altars
Parish Church of Galbiati, Diocese of Milan
June 30, 1583

Most beloved children, by a kind of special prerogative of love, the Hebrew people had been dear to God above all others, for they were the people whom he had provided with so many benefits, to whom he had prescribed the Law, to whom he had granted the manna, to whom he had declared and promised a land flowing with milk and honey, the people he had instructed in all rites and ceremonies, whose God he wanted to be, and by whom he wanted to be called their God, and specially worshiped and adored. But all these things were but shadows, night and figure; the night has given way to the day, darkness has given way to the light, the figure to the one prefigured, the law to the Gospel, the Hebrews to the Christians. And indeed, when I weigh in my own mind these gifts and the great dignity with which we have been sealed, I most clearly understand that as far as the east is from the west, God has left that people far from us. In us I see a great abyss of excellence above them, which it is not the right place here to treat of, and neither would the lateness of the hour permit it. But I absolutely cannot remain silent about this fact, namely that God willed to be adored by them in only one place, the temple of Solomon in Jerusalem. There alone did he wish to receive their sacrifices and hear their prayers with loving condescension. But the Son of God really existing with us and among us, has deigned to remain not in one single city, but in the world, and in many churches in whatever part of the world, in any church you please, on many altars. The magnitude of this benefit was known beforehand by Malachi, when long ago he predicted: *For from the rising of the sun even to the going down, my name is great among the Gentiles, and in every place there is sacrifice, and there is offered to my name a clean oblation: for my name is great among the Gentiles* (Mal. 1:11), so that truly all nations and people must say about us today, that *no other nation is so great and has gods as close to it as God is to Christians everywhere* (Deut. 4:7). And he is especially close in their holy churches and on their altars, two of which we just consecrated in this church, as you saw. Since they are so full of mysteries which should not be rushed over quickly, the quality of our office requires us to say a few words about their dignity, as well as the spiritual fruit of such a consecration, and above all, the duties assigned to you, so you the Christian Faithful do not appear ungrateful to God.

Dear children, the instituting and dedicating of altars is most ancient, for since human beings are naturally constituted in such a way that religion is seen to have been born with them, we also see that at all times men gave worship to God with sacrifices and services, and built altars for that purpose. Now we are not going to speak of those who sacrificed to God according to the guidance of a false religion, but only of altars erected to the true God. And so in the first place, Noah, that man most just and acceptable to God, when he had come out of the ark together with whatever animals were with him, *And Noah built an altar unto the Lord: and taking of all cattle and fowls that were clean, offered holocausts upon the altar. And the Lord smelled a sweet fragrance,*[14] and said: *I will no more curse the earth for the sake of man* (Gen. 8:20–21). But how *fragrant*, brethren, will the sacrifice of your own altar be to the Lord God, since it is not lambs and sheep, but his Son's Body and Blood, foreshadowed on those earlier altars! How much this oblation will please him and dispose him to withdraw the curse laid upon men! And Abraham the father of many nations, when he had heard that God was going to give the land of Canaan to his seed, built an altar to the Lord; altars were built in memory of the benefits received from God (cf. Gen. 13). But also Moses, and all those first patriarchs, are recorded, in Sacred Scripture, to have built many altars to God. Among those, the most famous was holy Jacob's altar, which he erected in stone, and which he saw touching the summit of heaven, *the angels also of God ascending and descending by it. And the Lord leaning upon the ladder;* and when he awoke, he said: *Indeed the Lord is in this place, and I knew it not. And trembling, he said: How terrible is this place? This is no other but the house of God, and the gate of heaven* (Gen. 28:12, 16–17). O what if Jacob had seen our altars, this celestial ladder fixed on our altars, over which the prayers and words of priests ascend to God and divine mercies and the very body and blood of God descend to men; how much more truly and vehemently would Jacob have exclaimed: *Indeed the Lord is in this place,* not, as in that other case, only promising the propagation of seed, but showing himself forth as food to be eaten by mortals, and bestowing together with himself all possible treasures! *How terrible is this place* to the demons, for here all their powers are broken, but lovely to men, for here they obtain all good things. *This is no other but the house of God, and the gate of heaven:* truly, here the Most

---

[14]The Douay-Rheims version translates the word as "savour," whereas in modern English "savour" is more linked to the sense of taste than of smell, which is the physical sense to which Borromeo is referring.

High prepared his tent; truly, here he dwells as he reigns in heaven; and he is the gate of heaven, he who about himself while still living among us had said: *I am the door* (Jn 10:9); nor is entrance to heaven granted to anyone, except through him.

And certainly it is our church which is most especially lovely, but also *terrible,* first of all on account of God's living presence therein, for God who scrutinizes men's hearts and reins[15] from heaven, does so in the same way from here. Therefore we can most especially and truly say about the altar: *The Lord is in his holy temple, the Lord's throne is in heaven. His eyes look on the poor man: his eyelids examine the sons of men. The Lord tries the just and the wicked: but he that loves iniquity hates his own soul* (Ps. 10:5–6). For here *the eyes of the Lord* are upon the *just, and his ears unto their prayers. But the countenance of the Lord is against them that do evil things: to cut off the remembrance of them from the earth* (Ps. 33:16–17). From this most holy altar God looks upon the repentant with a gaze of mercy, that he may forgive them their sins; upon the just with a gaze of friendship that he may bestow rewards upon them; on the impious with a gaze of justice, so that he *binds his hands and feet, and casts him into the exterior darkness* (Mt. 22:13).

In order that he not be compelled to confront us with that gaze of justice, our most benevolent and loving Lord warns us in today's Gospel: if in approaching the altar someone remembers that he has something against his brother, let him leave his gift there, and first go and be reconciled to his brother (cf. Mt. 5:23–24). On account of that, the church of God most certainly ought to inspire trembling in the hearts of sinners who enter, if they remember that they are approaching God, who sees their thoughts and hearts, and shall one day judge the living and the dead. As we have said, it also inspires terror and trembling in the devil, because here his tricks are laid bare to confessors by penitents, and by the confessor's advice and counsel, his traps are here sprung. The church is terrible to the devil because here he is often forced to give back the souls he had stolen from God, and because here there abundant images and relics of saints and crosses of Christ, and innumerable thousands of angels surround the most holy Body of Christ resting on the altar. But alas, sinners visiting the church do not take fright at any of these things, and at times some even dare to sin in the church and offend God who is present. In this respect, they are much worse than demons

---

[15]The Douay-Rheims translates *corda et renes* as "hearts and reins (kidneys)," respecting the concreteness of the Vulgate and Hebrew original.

who believe and tremble, and since these sinners have no fear, who knows whether they believe? About them the Lord makes complaint through the prophet: *What is the meaning that my beloved has wrought much wickedness in my house?* (Jer.11:15). He means to say, "This man whom I loved so much, for whom I laid down my life, whom I redeemed with my blood, *commits much wickedness* even *in this house of mine* which I chose for myself, I who did not disdain to dwell with him." In it he plans dishonorable loves, engages in empty talk, and makes business deals, even illicit ones, in sum he makes *my house of prayer into a den of thieves* (Mt. 21:13). But the church should inspire fear also because those who despise it are to be frightfully punished, since the most wondrous sanctity is what a church demands of us. Christ our Lord showed us this by a sign, since he, the kindest and humblest of men, dealt out the most severe punishment he ever imposed, on those who were buying and selling in the Temple, selling even those things that were to be offered to God, for zeal for the house of God consumed him (cf. Jn 2:17). If we are to procure the honor of God everywhere, then we must do so most especially here, where he deigns to dwell in a special way.

From all that, how great is the dignity rising up from this church, but first of all from the altar, which is the reason why the church itself excels in such great dignity! Indeed if that worthy Temple of Solomon, built and erected at such great expense and over so many years, was enriched with such gifts as the house of God, and so many things were granted in it to the Hebrew people according to the long prayer of Solomon to the Lord (cf. 1 Kgs 8:15–53), wherefore the same Lord God *appeared to him by night, and said: I have heard your prayer, and I have chosen this place to myself for a house of sacrifice. If I shut up heaven, and there fall no rain, or if I give ordered, and command the locust to devour the land, or if I send pestilence among my people. And my people, upon whom my name is called, being converted, shall make supplication to me, and seek out my face, and do penance for their most wicked ways: then will I hear from heaven, and will forgive their sins and will heal their land. My eyes also shall be open, and my ears attentive to the prayer of him that shall pray in this place* (2 Chron. 7:12–15). Then we can certainly ask, how much more will all these things be obtained by the Christian Faithful approaching this church and prostrate before this most holy altar, where we find not merely the ark of the covenant with the stone tablets of the Law, but the Body and Blood of Christ; where it is not Solomon who asks, but holy Mother Church, the Spouse of Christ utterly beloved to him, which earnestly entreats him with her common prayer, since she says: *Favorably hear us, O Lord, and grant that whoever shall enter this temple seeking your benefits, may rejoice in obtaining all that he asks.*[16] Here is where you will have as special advocates, the most glorious saints under whose patronage we have consecrated these altars, and the most holy pastor, our patron and father Ambrose, as well as the unconquered martyr of Christ, Maximus, whose venerable relics we have placed here. Our Lord promised all these things which Solomon sought, but in much greater abundance, when he said: *if you ask the Father anything in my name, he will give it you* (Jn 16:23). The poor man will enter here, and the Lord will lift him up from his poverty. The afflicted one will approach, and will receive consolation from the Lord. Here the weeping mother will obtain health for her children. Here we will beseech the Lord for abundance of the fruits of the earth. Here all will be able to lay down the most heavy burden of their sins. This is the most well equipped workshop for all the virtues. Here in your thirst *you shall draw waters with joy out of the savior's fountain* (Isa. 12:3). I shall be the guarantor of the divine mercy for you, since here *the eyes of the Lord are upon the just: and his ears* attentive to their prayers (Ps. 33:16), the prayers of those who shall pray in this place. Here the spirit of pride will be beaten down. Here the heat of anger will be cooled and the flames of lust tempered. Here all sluggishness will be taken away, and the ice of cold hearts melted. Whenever you like, you shall be able to draw near to this place. How much and how great is the benefit of being able to speak to God present at all times! Here you will cease to be poor any more, having the King of glory and all wealth among you, from whom you know with certitude that whatever you ask, you shall receive; and if you do not receive it, it will be on account of having asked badly that things turned out badly, or because the things you asked for what have been pernicious and harmful if you had obtained them. Therefore let the Christian be inspired by confidence in the consideration of so great a mystery, to bring due honor to such worthy churches, to such a noble altar; to receive such great fruits which will come forth from there, so that *you receive not the grace of God in vain* (2 Cor. 6:1).

But let us now turn our attention to what your parts shall be, and to what you must do in order to receive the benefits flowing from the altar.

Certainly in the first place you must love the worship of God exceedingly, and always have at heart the things pertaining to it, so that you treat all divine and spiritual things with splendor and your own things more

---

[16]This line can be found in slightly different form in the Collect of the Mass for the Dedication of a Church in the Roman Missal of 1962 or earlier.

meagerly and modestly. Thus you will want the altars to be covered only with gold and silver, and with the precious silk cloths which are fitting for the ministry which takes place at the altar. He who loves his wife provides her daily with new and precious clothes, gold rings, necklaces, earrings and a thousand other such things. If asked why he does that, he of course will reply on the spot that it is because he loves her. Why, therefore, if you love Christ, do you have no zeal to adorn and polish his house and his altar? Consider Solomon and see the wonderful and golden vessels, which he ordered to be heaped up for the worship of that earlier Temple, which nevertheless contained nothing but the stone tablets of the law, as you have heard. But here, where the Body and Blood of Christ are, do you think you should be sparing with money and expenses? "But we are poor," you will say, "we could hardly live if we did that." But whatever you have, did you not receive it from the Lord? Are not all things really his? Therefore, what prevents you from taking a little away even from things you need, in order to see to the adornment of the altar? Therefore this is the first thing your guest Christ requires of you, namely that in loving him, you also love his altar, tabernacle and dwelling place.

Secondly, you must approach these altars with the greatest veneration. For just as one guilty of a capital crime comes before the prince, from whom he can hope for clemency, with only the greatest humility and respect, so we too, who are worthy of death as often as we have sinned gravely, must enter and take up our station here with the utmost reverence, under the gaze of the One who, after he has punished our body with death, can do likewise in our soul. For this reason you will when in church avoid outbursts of laughter, ridicule, story-telling, empty conversations, and even more will you avoid obscene words, detraction, murmuring and the like. For the same reason, women will approach with heads veiled, and guard themselves from spiteful glances, but rather, intent only on their prayers, they will keep themselves attentive to the One before whom stands an innumerable multitude of angels.

And finally the third thing: since God has enriched us with so many gifts, and pursued us with so many services, he requires of us that we promptly embrace, accept and love them, and make use of them. For what would it profit a sick man, if medicine were given him, if he refused to take it? Or which of you, giving some gift to a friend, would not take it hard if the friend disdained to accept it, or barely looked at it? If there were only one church in a given diocese where an altar could be found, we would all have to set out and crowd around it in order to obtain heavenly treasures, to see our King, our God. But now that God draws so near to us, what will excuse us if we do not frequently approach the church, since it is especially from here that we can receive so many benefits? Therefore I beg you, most beloved brethren (since the lateness of the hour presses upon us, on account of the length of the consecration ceremony) let your souls in the future be altars consecrated to the Lord God, and just as these altars are perpetually given over to divine worship, so that they can never be converted to any other use, so dedicate your hearts and your souls to the living God. And I ask you earnestly, to whom could you be dedicated with more benefit to yourself? To the world, which is hypocritical, and whose joy is *the joy of the hypocrite but for a moment* (Job 20:5)? To the world, which promises so many things, but actually gives nothing? The whole world which *is seated in wickedness* (1 Jn 5:19)? The world which has been inimical to God? Shall you be consecrated to the flesh, which is always striving against the spirit and trying to drag you headlong into the abyss? Or to the devil, the ancient enemy of the human race? Will you not rather be dedicated to Christ the Son of God, who pursues you with such love, who has prepared such a great inheritance for those who follow him? *For as* up to now *you have yielded your members to serve uncleanness and iniquity, unto iniquity; so now yield your members to serve justice, unto sanctification* of the Holy Spirit (Rom. 6:19).

Maintain your temple in purity, or rather strive daily to adorn it with virtues and good works, so that possessed by the love of your souls, the dwelling places you are may never by deserted by him who does not *dwell in a body subject to sins* (Wis. 1:4). Of course I know that you have not the strength to prepare the adornment which is due such a great host. But he himself will furnish a house for himself, and adorn it. He comes to you this day to give the fullness of his grace by the holy chrism. He only requires a house that, if not ornate, is at least purified from all worldly cares, and above all, free from sins. Offer him an empty house. Promise him whatever you can do, and show him all that is within you. And do not be afraid because he will himself prepare, adorn and here dispose your souls for himself with his grace, and afterward fill them with heavenly glory.

Since great kings and princes planning a stay in someone's house are accustomed to send ahead servants who furnish it with tapestries and draperies, in a similar way, my children, humbly beseech the Son of God today, that he may send his Holy Spirit into you. That he who is ready to do this, may do it all the more willingly, dedicate yourselves to him this day as altars, offer yourselves as tabernacles when he is placed in your mouth. No palace delights him as much as your hearts. Christ the Lord will come to you, surrounded by thousands of cohorts of angels, to feed you and nourish you with his flesh. But hasten to meet him, and as soon as he enters, humbly pray to him in this way: Up until now, O good God, our souls were dens of serpents and demons, utterly disgusting sewers of sins. Behold, now we abhor the indignity of sin and desire to dedicate our souls to you as altars. Grant that they may always be reserved for your worship and service. May nothing unworthy of your majesty sneak into them. Anoint these altars with the oil of your grace and wash them with the waters of your mercy. May you be worshiped with incense sacrifices of prayers in them. We have resolved that they shall always be yours, that in them there shall no longer be any place for the devil, the world or the flesh. But help us in our infirmity. May there be only offerings and prayers to you in them. May the sacrifice of our heart ever be shown forth; may we prove this pious intention by deeds. Hedge in our hearts with the iron railings of the fear of you, O Lord, so that everything unworthy is prohibited from drawing near. Just as you reside in material tabernacles upon stone altars, may you also inhabit our hearts always, as long as we live, until you unite us to yourself perfectly in that heavenly Jerusalem, where with the Father and the Holy Spirit you live and reign as God through endless ages. Amen.

CHAPTER 3
IMITATING THE GOOD SHEPHERD

Preaching the Word of God

Oration to all those having the charge of preaching sermons in the diocese and province of Milan, according to the decree of the third provincial council (1573)

...

Those upon whom the charge of preaching falls

I charge you, before God and Jesus Christ, who shall judge the living and the dead, by his coming, and his kingdom: Preach the word (2 Tim. 4:1), says the most holy apostle Paul in the epistle he writes to Timothy, bishop and his disciple.

From those words, let that be perfectly clear what the Ecumenical Tridentine Synod recently decided, coming to us perpetually from the monuments of Sacred Scripture and demonstrated by the example of the other apostles and the ancient Fathers, namely, that the preaching of the word of God is the principal duty of the bishop, as well as the most necessary.

Therefore, devoting himself wholeheartedly to this concern, the bishop will feed the flock committed to him with the word of God, both by himself and through others, according to what that Tridentine Synod and the provincial councils have prescribed.

Furthermore, as a faithful worker sent into the harvest to aid the works of the bishop, the parish pastor too, and any priest with care of souls, should be mindful of pastoral solicitude, called as he most certainly is to a portion of this solicitude. The priest with care of souls, therefore, must also take and carry out the ministry of preaching the word of God, which has likewise been laid upon him, according to the prescriptions and decrees of the same Tridentine Synod and the provincial councils.

If at times a priest cannot provide this service, then let him by all means make use of that aid and assistance which has been pointed out to him by those synods, in order that on the prescribed days the nourishment of the word be in no way lacking to the flock entrusted to his care.

And although the bishop, entirely occupied with the assiduous labors of his pastoral office, is often unable to preach to the whole people committed to his care, still, he will take care to employ that most ancient means which goes back to the times of the apostles: sometimes preaching by pastoral letters to the peoples far away from him in his diocese.

For this way of preaching was upheld not only by the apostle St. Paul, but also by the other apostles, who preached by epistles to those who were absent.

…

And since it often happens that the bishop must often delegate the ministry of the divine word not only in his cathedral church, but also in his whole diocese, how diligently he should examine anyone to whom he gives that faculty, so that no injury or outrage is done to such a great ministry and most holy reality. We are especially warned by [St. Gregory] Nazianzen, *Not just anyone should discuss or preach about God and the things of God.*

Therefore a bishop will not lightly grant the faculty to anyone who is not a priest, as was established in the canon of Pope St. Leo.

But if for some just and necessary reason he does permit a deacon to preach, the deacon selected should have the right character, both in doctrine and discipline of morals (which are both required in a preacher), and also the right age, since in the judgment of the most wise and holy Pontiff Gregory the Great, a preacher should manifest firmness and strength. And in no way should the bishop give power or permission to preach to anyone who is not a deacon.

…

The discipline, virtue and innocence of the life of a preacher

He who receives the task of preaching should be persuaded above all, that unless he lives rightly and in harmony with the laws of the Gospel which he preaches, he will not have much effect on the souls of his listeners. For just as in the ark of the covenant those two cherubim were placed in such a way that they always regarded one another, so the preacher's life must correspond with his teaching, in such a way that his teaching gives him light by which to live, and his life likewise strengthens his teaching, giving it ever greater vigor.

Since he preaches about abstinence, fasting, tears, prayer, almsgiving, patience and any other Christian virtue, his words will carry the greatest weight and importance for his hearers, if they can see in his whole life the virtue whose precepts he hands on by preaching.

…

For he must be purified before he purifies, as the most blessed Pontiff Gregory the Great says.

Therefore, the preacher will be prepared by a singular innocence of life, the purest morals, and Godlike virtues.

Thus he will be endowed with the fear of God, contempt for worldly things, zeal for the salvation of souls, humility, meekness, patience, charity and the other elements of religious discipline.

On this whole subject, he will listen to that holy man John Chrysostom warning us as follows:

> *The teacher or preacher must be perfected with all virtues.*
>
> *For he must be poor in spirit, that he might freely rebuke all avarice and desire for gain.*
>
> *He must perpetually mourn over his own and others' sins, that he might disturb those who have no fear of sin before they sin, and after sinning conceive no sorrow for the crimes they have committed.*
>
> *He must hunger and thirst for justice, so that those who are growing tired in their efforts and good works may be inspired by the word of God and rekindled with zeal by his example.*
>
> *He must be meek in order to be loved more than he is feared.*
>
> *He must be merciful toward others and strict with himself.*
>
> *He must be pure of heart, so that he neither takes on the empty and useless thoughts of this world, nor involves himself in worldly pursuits.*
>
> *He must be peaceful, so that the people whom he teaches will be solicitous to preserve the unity of the spirit in the bond of peace.*
>
> *He must be prepared to bear all things, even the most difficult, for the glory of God and the Church, not by a certain vain impulsiveness of soul, but by a true constancy worthy of the martyrs.*

Not only will he conform himself to these admonitions of Chrysostom but he will also imitate the discipline of two other Greek Fathers who are celebrated with praise for their holiness and teaching, namely Basil and Gregory Nazianzen.

In the first book *On Theology*, which he wrote with great diligence, and then Basil in his letter about the solitary life, which he wrote to Gregory himself, both of them taught what kind of man was necessary to carry out the office and the person of the preacher.

He will follow that greatest kind of perfect life, which any of the best preachers lays down according to the prescription of the Pontiff Gregory the Great, who so often fashions the model of the preacher indeed both in the *Book of Pastoral Care* and in the *On Morals* especially in Book XXX, Chap. 21 and in Book VI, Chap. 25[1] and in other places, in which it becomes quite clear that whoever takes up the ministry of the divine word has to be the kind of person which St. Paul describes himself to have been with these words: the world is crucified to me, and I to the world (Gal. 4:14).

The knowledge a preacher should have

Before the man designated to preach sets himself to that task, he must be as well versed as possible in all studies of sacred and ecclesiastical doctrine, especially if he has never held any teaching position.

> He will have learned and examined all the branches of theology.
>
> He will strive for knowledge of apostolic and ecclesiastical traditions.
>
> He will be very well versed in the writings and the sermons of the holy Fathers.
>
> He will be learned and well versed in the use of the most holy and spiritual interpretations.

And he shall likewise know the sacred rites of the Church, which have been instituted for the Sacraments, for the celebration of the Divine Office, in sum for all ecclesiastical activities. By knowing the mysteries and their significance of these, his explanations will enkindle the minds of the faithful to zeal for devotion.

Likewise he will be familiar with all which has been done in the Church and preserved in the memory of ecclesiastical antiquity, but mindful above all of the history of the holy Fathers and the lives of the Supreme Pontiffs and bishops who most especially shone with holiness.

---

[1] English translations of these two works of St. Gregory the Great include: *Moral Reflections on the Book of Job,* trans. Brian Kerns (Athens: Cistercian Publications, 2014); *The Book of Pastoral Rule,* trans. George Demacopoulos (Yonkers: St. Vladimir's Seminary Press, 2007).

Besides that, he will have some knowledge of the ancient canons, the recorded laws and enactments of the Supreme Pontiffs and the decrees of the councils.

He will be well versed in that part of theology which is entirely taken up with the practices of the spiritual life, with interior reformation, and which is therefore called *Mystical* or *Therapeutic* theology.[2] He will thoroughly understand the basic spiritual precepts and exercises.

Through his own experience he will be familiar with holy meditation and mental prayer, so that his preaching may instruct others in the acquisition of heavenly contemplation.

He will be instructed in the theology of giving solutions in cases of conscience. He will have right knowledge, and not only an orderly list, of the maxims of Christian morals and virtues.

…

He must be well supplied with teachings, to make use of as the need arises, for refuting the audacity of impious men who, thinking falsely about the Catholic faith, attack the truth of the Church; also for rightly and devoutly showing forth the dogmas of the Church and for various other needs of that kind.

…

And in this vast area, the preacher will certainly see to it that, as St. Gregory wisely teaches, he does not disclose and pour out whatever he has read, or expertly understood, but he will prefer to expound some of his teachings, passing over others with silence, as the place, position and condition of his listeners may require.

…

The preparation a preacher will always make for a salutary ministry

In order that a preacher may be more zealous and religious in carrying out his share of this most excellent ministry, which he must accept and bear in a holy manner, he will first of all reflect upon its dignity and authority. And he will perceive these four truths:

First, that the whole nature and power of preaching is concerned with the glory of almighty God and the salvation of souls.

---

[2] "Therapeutic Theology" is likely an archaic term for what was later called "Ascetical Theology."

Second, that he who undertakes the office of preaching is the minister through whom the word of God is brought from the very font of the divine Spirit to flow into the souls of the faithful in a divine way.

Next, that the preacher is to treat of holy things that have been divinely handed on.

Then, he will reflect that the office of preaching which he undertakes has not only been committed to the holy men of God, the prophets and apostles, but also bestowed by the Son of God, Christ the Lord himself.

But the more he exercises his zeal, the more attentively will he see how supremely difficult is the task given to the man who strives to recall the souls of the faithful to the way of the Lord in the midst of the great and perpetual assault made against them by Satan and the world. And indeed since he senses himself unequal to resisting these perpetual adversaries, he will not only fortify himself with the weapons of the virtues, as we have shown, but will also implore the help of God by assiduous prayer and frequent fasting, in order to repel the attacks of such troublesome enemies.

…

And neither will he trust in his own powers, but rightly acknowledging his own weakness, he will cast himself before God, from whose heavenly kindness he will receive help, no matter how cast down and unworthy of the preaching office he may be.

And in order that he might be the more powerfully inflamed to employ all holy means which will help him, he will often reflect on how great is the reward for those who lead a sinner away from the error of his ways.

He who causes a sinner, says Saint James, *to be converted from the error of his way, shall save his soul from death, and shall cover a multitude of sins* (Jas 5:20).

…

The preacher will take great care to fulfill the obligation of Matins and the other prayers of the canonical hours and Divine Office, every day, correctly, intelligibly and devoutly, according to the prescriptions of the rule he professes if he is a religious, or if he is a cleric bound to choir, then according to his own discipline, in church when possible, and in choir, with the others.

When the Office has been recited, he will spend some time in contemplation of divine things and in devout mental prayer. In this way, the preacher who is inflamed and glowing with the ardor of divine love, thanks especially to prayer and meditation, will more effectively enkindle in his listeners zeal for charity, the seedbed of all the virtues.

He will not omit to offer the sacrifice of the Mass every day, unless impeded by a legitimate reason. By the custom of frequent offering of the Most Holy Sacrifice, he will obtain great benefit for living a holy life in every way, as well as motivate the faithful to more diligent and religious participation in the Most Holy Sacrifice.

The preparation needed before each sermon

First of all, since the sacred orator understands that the preaching ministry depends not on human knowledge or eloquence but on divine power and the grace of the Holy Spirit, he will judge that he must avoid above all else saddening the Holy Spirit by mortal sin, which adversely affects this work, which was not only the ministry of the apostles, but of Our Lord Jesus Christ himself. And so before he undertakes to handle the word of God, he will first purge his conscience of all impurity of sin by the Sacrament of Penance. He will certainly have the greatest fear of that most grave rebuke of the prophet: *But to the sinner God has said: Why do you declare my justices, and take my covenant in your mouth* (Ps. 49:16)?

Then when he gives himself to the study required for the sermon which he is soon to give, he will take for his model St. Thomas Aquinas and other men illustrious by the praise they merited by sanctity, for they were accustomed to make devout prayer before giving themselves to study.

And finally, having made a short prayer to God, he will make sure that he has a good knowledge of what he is going to say in his sermon before he gives it. If more preparation has been needed, in order to learn and acquire what he is going to say from study and books, then he will devoutly and repeatedly turn over in his mind the different parts he has composed for his sermon. He will try in this meditation to become so devoutly affected that, in as much as it is in him, he will move the souls and minds of his listeners to that same devout spirit and ardor for holy living.

In order to inflame himself with ardent piety, even while he is studying and working out his sermon, he will place before his eyes the image of Christ the Lord nailed to the cross, or the apostle Paul preaching (as Chrysostom is said to have done), and consider it in silent meditation.

His greatest preparation will be the night before the sermon. Let him ardently pray to the God of all wisdom and author of all holy virtues, beseeching him to bestow the help needed for his divine service and the salvation of souls. In our own age, there have not been lacking those who are accustomed not only to shedding copious tears for those graces, but also to taking the discipline to petition for them.

Before ascending the pulpit, he will also resolve that his intention will be to preach a sermon suitable for a multitude of people hungering and expecting nourishment from his preaching, or suitable for a crowd of the lame, the paralyzed, people afflicted with dropsy, the mute, the blind, the deaf, those agitated by the Evil One, lepers and others seeking benefit and strength.

Since he must keep this in his mind's eye, he will therefore prepare himself in every part of his sermon to look only to the people's condition and to their salvation, by counseling, consoling, and by every service and excellent remedy.

Besides this, he will consider himself to be a fisher of men. Therefore he must strain every nerve to keep fishing until he fills that Gospel net, by gaining the souls of men who are perishing for Christ the Lord. Therefore let him see to it that he does not grow faint in his office of preaching.

But in order to call forth holy movements of soul in others, he will first conceive and arouse them in himself, in his own soul, in such a way that, to others he will show forth the same emotions which he has rightly conceived in his own mind, and which he desires to transfuse into the minds of others.

He will strive to attain that, first by ardent prayer and then by deepened knowledge of the thing he is going to speak about; likewise by concentrated thinking on the topic and, as it were, placing before his eyes the image of the things he conceives in meditation. Besides this, he will read attentively the places in Sacred Scripture which fit whatever he has thought out in his soul.

And since a sermon written by someone else's labor is of little value in moving souls, let him never use the fruits of the industry of another preacher in order to put himself into the proper frame of mind, but let him by his own inspiration conceive all of that and bring it forth. All the more strongly will he thereby affect first himself and then others. The food of teaching will generate the strongest movements of soul toward holiness when it is presented to the people only after having been digested, so to speak, by the preacher's own mind.

Therefore let the preacher not brazenly regurgitate other preachers' homilies. It will be more than adequate to arrange and put them together with material from the homilies, sermons and treatises of the holy doctors of the Church, Gregory the Great, Ambrose, Augustine, Chrysostom and other holy fathers.

...

Concerning the rites of the one preaching

It is the ancient rule to preach a sermon within the celebration of Mass, namely after the recitation of the Gospel.

…

When a bishop gives the sermon in a solemn Mass, he shall be vested in miter and full episcopal insignia. He will make use of attending ministers in sacred vestments, placed on either side of him. Where possible, let there be seven ministers according to the ancient canon, and if not, fewer. There should also be a minister vested in cope, at the left side, to hold the pastoral staff before him.

…

On the times for preaching

Christ the Lord did not limit the task of preaching with any defined time and place, nor did the Apostles, who disseminated the most holy Gospel in every place and in every time.

…

Therefore on every occasion which presents itself, always and everywhere, the bishop will feed his flock with the word of God and saving teachings, to fulfill his pastoral office, since his words and very deeds should administer and provide the people with something like a perpetual sermon.

…

Parish pastors likewise, and all who have care of souls, should do likewise every Sunday and solemn feast, and every day in Lent and Advent.

…

Let them likewise preach as often as they administer the Sacraments, and let them do this, in the first place, with the Roman Catechism. Likewise in the days leading up to the administration of the Sacrament of Confirmation by the bishop, let there be preaching most especially about this Sacrament, so that the people will be more religiously instructed when they receive it.

…

The subject matter of preaching

First of all, the preacher will compose his sermon from the doctrine of the Gospel, which Christ the Lord and Teacher of life ordered to be preached to every creature, among all peoples and in all lands. But in order to compose such a sermon in the most excellent way, he will also apply, in a right and appropriate manner, the divine law and the other testimonies and examples of the divinely inspired Scriptures, the sacred traditions of the Church, the holiest interpretations and his knowledge of the whole of ecclesiastical antiquity, as the case may call for.

Therefore he will never fail to call the Gospel passage to mind, and let him not base his argument on something else (which too often is done), unless the character of the season, the feast, or the Office being carried out should occasionally require otherwise, or if he judges it more advantageous to treat of some other parts of the Mass.

He should sometimes join a clear explanation of the Epistle prescribed for the Mass, to his explanation of the Gospel.

He will likewise, and often, expound to the faithful whatever it is the Church of God is praying for that day, whatever is the most special object of her petitions. Therefore he will sometimes expound, accurately and devoutly, the prayers and orations which are called "collects," especially those[3] near the beginning of the Mass. And he will diligently explain to his listeners the mysteries of the sacrifice of the Mass, the Divine Offices, and of solemn seasons and yearly solemnities, so that rightly instructed by their Mother, the children of the Church will not only live in accord with such great mysteries which are being celebrated, but will be more ardently inspired to the veneration of the holy realities, and so draw an even richer spiritual fruit from divine things.

…

The preacher will not omit to call to mind the life of the saint whose feast day is being celebrated, and what he says about the saint needs to be accurate and serious, offering some attractiveness of examples to which the faithful can conform their own souls in right and holy living.

He will sometimes digress, as the occasion and subject matter permit, to an explanation of the Creed, the Lord's Prayer, the Angelical Salutation, the Ten Commandments, and the sacraments.

Next, in every subject matter and kind of sermon and treatise, he will avoid the following:

…

He will not twist the Sacred Scripture to his own meanings, contrary to that sense which Holy Mother Church has held and holds, or against the unanimous consent of the Fathers, as the Tridentine Synod wisely warned.

---

[3] The plural here reflects the fact that in St. Charles' time the liturgy very frequently added one or two commemorations after the Collect of the day's principal office, according to the season, an octave or a vigil.

...

He should not touch on the more subtle questions before an untrained audience.

...

Let him not bring recent teachers and authors into his sermon. The authority of the exalted pulpit is such that it calls for the Sacred Scripture in the first place, and the doctrine of the holy and ancient Fathers.

...

Let him not tear into anyone by name, or in words depict a person in such a way that the listener will easily be aware of who is being spoken about.

He must not grumble against any religious order, state of life, or way of life which is received and accepted in the Church.

Nor should he bitterly rebuke bishops, or other prelates, or civil magistrates in his sermon, but if and when the occasion presents itself, he should rather admonish them with respect.

And when he rebukes, let him not do it through hatred of men, but of sins, or better, from zeal for piety and charity.

When he censures vices, let him not get into a white heat and fury of anger, and let him not pronounce injurious or ignominious words. And he should not respond from the pulpit to the detractions and accusations that will sometimes come his way.

...

Charles Borromeo

Will you risk your life for the flock?

Sermon to superiors of monasteries and other religious priests at the time of the plague, 1576

Were I to try and explain to you, brothers, the miserable and mournful condition of our city, I could only do it poorly. For there is no one who does not have such great miseries constantly before his eyes. Moreover, I do not consider anyone so hardhearted as not to be shattered in soul with pity [when he sees][4] people bereft of the presence of their most beloved heads of the city and of all help, pushed out of their own sweet familiar homes, sick and only half-alive, with all their goods left behind; and finally led on deathly, sordid carts to those enclosed areas which are much more like stables than civilized dwellings, and from which there is little or no hope of ever returning. In short, they are as if tightly held in the jaws of death. These things are utterly miserable for human weakness to bear, but since they nevertheless concern time and this life only, they can appear tolerable, especially if someone is lifted up with hope for the life to come. But what shall we say about being deprived of those most helpful good things which lead above all to the happiness of the next life and eternal goods, and which, if someone loses them now, he also risks losing the good things which are to come and remain forever? That is most miserable, indeed grave and dangerous, both for those who suffer and for us, to whom the care and power of these things has been divinely given.

We know and see that as the body is wasting away by pestilence, so the devout souls of our brethren languish with desire for divine things. With voices only half-living, or by a gesture only, they request the Sacraments and implore mercy, but we with hard hearts delay or look away. As you know, we have kept the parish pastors in their post, but they are not enough for the multitude, as we know, unless each of them had the strength of many. In general, those who are led off to the quarantined houses are too far away to be helped by their own parish pastors. Not to mention the fact that parish pastors are often turned away by their subjects, if they have already ministered to the afflicted, until the passage of time can show that they themselves are healthy. And so it happens that even the residents of that priest's neighborhood need the service of other priests. I have sought outside priests, and not in vain, but we still need more, for the multitude

---

[4]This phrase seems inserted by Sax.

of people led off to quarantine still lies helpless. I do not find other priests willing to help, and I cannot force them, nor should I. I have recourse to you, whose condition and state in life manifests a disdain for all human things so that you aim exclusively at the worship of God and concern for the salvation of men. If there is anyone whom we could expect to come and save others and imitate the Lord in this way, it would be you first of all. I will certainly say that the sick do not need our assistance in such a way that without it they would have no hope of salvation, but often our services are necessary. Besides, it is indisputably clear that we all understand how much they benefit not only the bad but also the good, and how much alleviation they usually bring to the sick body and above all to the soul solicitous for its salvation.

But how can those upon whom mercy has been given and liberally poured out be so tightly limited with theirs, and measure it out in accord with temporal and external necessities? The same Son of God, who for the sake of the salvation of all men, including his enemies and the impious, was fixed to the cross and died in the greatest shame and the bitterest torment, invites us to go forward into the danger of a quiet and glorious death for devout brethren. He to whom we owe as much repayment as we could not obtain by dying a thousand times without end, does not even request this pathetic life of ours, but only that we put it at risk. We see many go through these dangers without escaping death. Moreover, we even see many who are free from fear but still die. But if we do not escape it, this will not be death; rather it will be a quicker attainment of blessed glory, which is true life. For what does our poor life find in human things so as to be grateful for them instead of the most precious and immortal benefits of God should we lose this opportunity? And why do we spare our life which in spite of everything we must lose after a few years, or days, or indeed hours, as the human condition dictates? It is rather the case that with this disaster of our city, the danger and risk which charity toward our brethren may not demand, will inexorably be required of us by the contagion. Just like almost countless others, who nevertheless looked out for themselves with all diligence, we are going to die. How much more beautiful it is in this affair, if we anticipate what is necessary in any case and provide a victim most pleasing to God for our sins and for everything we owe to his immense goodness and majesty? Alas! We daily see many who undertake these same dangers, led on by the hope of some utterly meager reward, which indeed they often do not obtain. Are we going to delay, though we have such good reasons and such great rewards offered to us? Look to the law of obedience, by the strength of which you rightly wish your actions to be fortified in view of your salvation. I know you are not unaware that the Supreme Pontiff, common father and bishop of all, placed that in our hand. You also heard the reading of his letter, in which he vehemently exhorts us to this glorious and holy ministry of aiding the brethren. In that regard there is no question for anyone of looking to the will of the bishop or fearing his interdict, when it is the first one among all the bishops who both declared it to be his will and added his own exhortations.

I wish, brothers, for you to show this service to God, which, as I hope, you will accept. But you will also affect us with this very great benefit, which no forgetfulness shall ever wipe away. If my very great worry and sorrow is alleviated by your virtue, when I see some of you here ready to go ahead and offer your life to God and to me in this blessed test for the sake of this most holy work, then I do not doubt that with the open entrance into these ranks of several or even only a few of you, many others who are now terrified and as it were paralyzed by their apprehension of something so unusual, will follow the joyful example of going in the way now opened wide. Therefore the man who goes first offers himself as an authority and a guide for others, and will greatly increase the weight of his merit. Nor do I present you with any really ardor of charity. Our Fathers, incited by the spirit of God, did the same in similar circumstances. They taught that this is what should be done, as one can see clearly enough in the writings of the ancients collected and edited by our command. Moreover, they extolled a work of this kind because it has the greatest power to motivate our souls to confirm that they are the stuff of martyrs. It is indeed a desirable time now when without the cruelty of the tyrant, without the rack, without fire, without beasts, and in the complete absence of harsh tortures which are usually the most frightful to human weakness, we can obtain the crown of martyrdom. What is even more, we can do so without the terrible hardship which always tends to accompany a disease of this type, in which the sick are abandoned by everyone and given no support or help from anyone. What we shall give to any sick man, we certainly shall not deny to the father of the sick, and it will be to our benefit when the example we have given is imitated by others. Anyone can hope that he will come out safe, and all the more so than almost innumerable others whom we see continuously going about their business in the middle of this raging pestilence with no precautions and no self-control. But if someone does contract the disease, and others are no longer there, then I myself, who will be going about among you every day on account of the sick, will be there. I shall be charged with caring for your health in both body and soul. I will willingly come to your aid. I offer myself to you right now as a minister of the Sacraments if that should be necessary. Relying indeed on divine help, I have decided to spare no labors or dangers in order to fulfill my pastoral office and to serve the flock committed to me in any way I can for their salvation.

Charles Borromeo

A face humble and free from vanity

Letter on shaving the beard. From the archiepiscopal palace, the thirtieth of November 1576.

To our beloved clergy of the city and diocese of Milan
Greetings and Blessings
From Our Lord Jesus Christ
It will not be necessary, most dearly beloved brethren, for me to write too many words either to persuade you on behalf of a practice you have already promptly begun to embrace, nor to commend to you a practice which, although practically lost nearly everywhere in Italy, has yet somehow been retained among you, so that one can say it is not something foreign. It is rather an ancient usage belonging especially to you, which is being reinstated, or rather protected so it is not lost entirely. I mean the practice that ecclesiastical persons not grow, but rather shave the beard.[5] Truly this custom comes to us replete with mystical meanings, for the purpose of making us realize both the excellence of our state, how different it is from that of the laity, and the unique way of life, so different from theirs, which our vocation requires. And as Venerable Bede declares, this custom also signifies holy humility, for although we are ministers of God, we do not raise ourselves up in pride, but cast away every vain confidence we might have on account of our valor, our good sense, or any other virtue which may be in us. And then it signifies that all our virtues, no matter how numerous and great they may appear to be, are often mixed with defects and vices, so that if they were to be challenged with the examination of divine justice, they would turn out to be few and small or of little importance.

This was a custom of our Fathers, almost perpetually retained in the Church, as ancient depictions give testimony of it as well. Even if it was later given up by some, starting a few years ago in a few places, it was always retained in Milan by some good priests who were lovers of that ancient discipline.

---

[5]The customary or prescribed clerical codes of distinctive appearance, including being clean shaven or having a beard, have varied greatly across the ages and between the different ritual Churches (Latin, Greek etc.). The basic intention of keeping past manners of dress and appearance has been to provide a help to humility and sobriety and to safeguard against vanity and worldliness.

And now with a visitation from God like this plague he has sent us, we are motivated to start pondering and reforming our ways with great care, bringing back good observances and holy customs which have grown cold or have been abandoned over the course of time. So in this matter too, after presenting it to many prelates and persons distinguished for piety and doctrine, we have set ourselves to bring about the design we have had in mind for a long time: the renewal, restoration and protection of this custom.

But our intention had hardly become known, when many of you anticipated its announcement and our exhortation … So there is no need for long persuasive discourses, but only to complete what is already well begun of this practice of which I am not the first. I at least have the consolation, just as a father is consoled to see his children to be advanced in good things, to be informed about your obedience and diligence in what I initially desired and thought about.

And those of you who have not yet put this into practice, take consolation from the fact that you have committed no fault of negligence if you now promptly start observing this usage, according to the announcement and the example of your Pastor.

And what, dear brethren, will be able to chill your ardor and consolation in restoring such an ancient usage of our Church, which is so fitting to our state? What of human respect and embarrassment in the eyes of worldly people, who with no thought of the holiness and antiquity of this custom and the mystical religious meanings it contains, either make jokes or at least do not esteem it as much as they should? Please God, that just as David happily endured the derision of his wife, a daughter of Saul, for honoring God by dancing before the ark, we too may in this way have by his grace an occasion of meriting something with him, and of blotting out our sins with this expiation he will give us, suffering some abuse from the tongues and opinions of men of the world, on account of our doing something that fits our state and vocation, and was therefore observed by the Fathers and our elders in the priesthood.

How little this would be for those who are obliged, like we are, to spend our blood and life itself when necessary for love of the Lord, for him who loved us so much that he emptied himself, taking the form of a servant (Phil. 2:7); who as it were laid down his grandeur, and hid his wisdom in the foolishness of the cross, and humbled himself unto death (Phil. 2:8), and such a shameful death; who for our life gave blood and his own life, offering his entire self for us. As the Prince of the Apostles said, *But let none of you suffer as a murderer, or a thief, or a railer, or a coveter of other men's things* (1 Pet. 4:15). For us it should be a joy and a consolation to suffer scorn and injury for love of Christ, for professing externally what we must have in our heart, and for being outwardly conformed to the internal obligations of our vocation.

May the Lord be blessed when he will give us what the Apostle referred to: *not only to believe in him, but also to suffer for him* (Phil. 1:29). In our time especially, when his divine majesty is now revealing so many signs of his anger upon us, we can easily understand what a need there is in us for amendment of life and reform in all things, even where that might occasion a little embarrassment for us.

But how can there be any embarrassment in this personal appearance of being clean-shaven, which rather manifests in part the grandeur and seriousness of our state and the vocation that distinguishes us from other men? Perhaps this distinction from the laity in personal appearance will make us low and ignoble? On the contrary, our radiance and true glory is maintained by everything which serves to manifest to us, or to everyone else, that difference between their state and ours which the Holy Spirit strives to teach us in so many other ways.

For this reason, together with our other observances, let us maintain the crown or tonsure on our head.[6] In this and in so many other ways, our clothing is different from those of laypeople, just as our studies, conversations, activities and every service must be different since that time, when by receiving the clerical character, we obtained God as our portion and special inheritance, were set apart from others and enrolled in this ecclesiastical militia in order to be a particular society of his divine majesty, consecrated for the ministries of his holy worship. But let us not be offended in being different from those from whom God has set us apart in order to be especially his.

---

[6]Before the introduction of the revised forms of the Roman Rite and the 1983 Code of Canon Law, which states that someone becomes a cleric through reception of the diaconate, first clerical tonsure at the hands of the bishop made a baptized man a cleric with a right to sustenance from the Church for his services, so that the Lord became his "portion." Hair has been snipped or trimmed for clerics in various ways and to various extents over the centuries, including the *corona* appearance mentioned here by St. Charles, and some form of the cross in memory of Christ's call to the apostles. Tonsured clerics are deputed to the divine praises in the liturgical choir, and their condition is seen by the Church as one of preparation for minor and major orders, if and when the conditions are met. Tonsure and ordination to the minor orders are continued today for those clerical institutes which come under the oversight of the Pontifical Commission *Ecclesia Dei*.

It should not be considered such a great novelty if, with this custom now being restored, we appear different from many others who are also in the ecclesiastical state. For in accordance with provincial decrees approved by the holy Apostolic See, we have embraced the custom of being different from the laity in other things as well. For example, we have stripped our houses of gold, silver, silk and precious decoration for beds and other furniture. We have moderated our table and culinary expenses, the number of our servants and their dress. We have taken care every day to practice moderation with the simplicity and style of ecclesiastical dress, restoring the old usages and observances of our Church. If in all this we have not allowed human respect to hold us back from being different in this or that thing from many others, then it should also be permitted that we do likewise in this matter of the beard, which is also an aspect of exterior appearance. And let us do so in order to conform ourselves to the ancient observance, which belongs not only to our Church, but one could say is common, even alive today in so many other provinces.

And let that be enough for you to know that even the world ought to be satisfied with you, if indeed a man who wants to please Christ is going to pay any attention to the world, and seek to please it. I should not be the servant of Christ if I yet pleased men (Gal. 1:19), as the holy Apostle says.

But what is more important, and what I principally wish from you on this occasion, brethren, is that this shaving of the beard shall be accompanied by a true resolution to execute and put into practice the things which are signified to us by this custom we are taking up again. It will be a source of shame to us to have an external appearance different from laymen, if we are then going to be no different in our habits from worldly people. Every external testimony of the dignity of our vocation above laymen will be a source of shame to us and not of glory, if we are then going to be inferior to many of them in virtues.

Separation and distinction in dress will be of little importance if we are going to persevere in secular and worldly practices and conversations. It would not be a very fruitful practice, brethren, to shave off facial hair, and remain full of anxiety and solicitude in temporal concerns which impede the studies necessary for our profession and the ministries owed to the souls who are sent to us. Such concerns envelop us in a thousand tangles and ties of the devil, and in the end submerge us in the abyss of our perdition.

These secular concerns are those that often make us contemptible in the eyes of the people. These earthly desires render us hateful to the world.

Please God that this worldly glory we show off does not in the end cause us to lose the true glory.

These bitter roots, dearly beloved brethren, are those which expand in our hearts and extend their branches, producing the bitterest fruits of a life in every way undisciplined; fruits of bad example, and of ignorance utterly pernicious for us and for others; fruits of negligence and sordid avarice in our ministries.

When someone allows a place in his heart for these disordered affections, it comes as no surprise if he no longer has the taste for the things of God, if he is dry in prayer, lacking in devotion in choir, unable to bear persevering in church for the Divine Office; if he is bored with the word of God and abhors the study of sacred things; if he goes almost without preparation, as if by sheer habit, to the tremendous sacrifice of the Mass, and receives no fruit from frequenting the holy Sacraments.

This is the reason why both in general and particular tribulations, no matter how much we have recourse to God, he often does not answer us. This is why even though the holy sacrifice of the Mass and other prayers, sacred actions and offices which we do as public ministers of Holy Church, in the person of Christ the High Priest or of the Church his Spouse cannot be refused or be of little effect, it is still true to say that Holy Church, we ourselves, and all those for whom we offer Masses and prayers, remain deprived of that particular fruit which would result from our own disposition and devotion in those sacred actions.

Since so much can be lacking in us, dear brethren, how often do you realize that when God gazes upon us, he speaks about us, and to us, in the words which he once said through Isaiah the prophet to that people of Israel on the occasion of their sacrifices and oblations: *To what purpose do you offer me the multitude of your victims? I am full, I desire them not. Who required these things at your hands, that you should walk in my courts? Offer sacrifice no more in vain: incense is an abomination to me. Your festivals I will not abide, your assemblies are wicked. My soul hates your solemnities: they are become troublesome to me, I am weary of bearing them. And when you stretch forth your hands, I will turn away my eyes from you: and when you multiply prayer, I will not hear you* (Isa. 1:11–15).

May God grant, brethren, that not one of us may ever have such a fault as to provoke God to words such as those, or to vent his anger upon us with the scourge of the pestilence with which he we know he has begun a visitation, passing through the ranks both of us, who are priests, and of the people. While he holds back his hand and proceeds slowly in this pestilence yet without removing its scourge from our backs entirely, it does indeed appear that on the one hand, he desires not to have to avenge our iniquities, his one desire being instead that we amend and return to him in truth. On the other hand he appears to want to make us clearly understand that until now we have not really done enough to placate him.

It seems to me, that when we now have recourse to him, insistently begging for liberation from the night of these present tribulations, he answers with the words of the same Prophet: *If you seek me, seek* (Isa. 21:12), so as to tell us, "Yes, seek my friendship, seek it through the means by which I offer it to you. If you seek me with words, seek me also with deeds, and if externally, then seek me internally as well. If you wish life, will to give obedience to the precepts, the obedience through which life is gained. If you seek me, seek me with diligence, solicitude, true desire, and resolutely, and not with a double heart and no longer teetering on the fence. You priests, if you are going to seek the grandeur and honor to which you are called, seek it with humility, despising the world; with disciplined habits of life, with holiness of life, with zeal for souls and my honor, and the other means which are proper to our vocation."

So, dear brethren, let us take up again and restore with our whole heart our ancient custom of shaving the beard with this true resolution: that as we leave off from having a beard, we will at the same time and from now on lay aside all ostentation and vain confidence of worldly prudence and strength, all esteem of ourselves and every other type of pride. Let us cut straight away and remove our attachment to the things of this earth. Let us throw aside all the tangled snares of worldly affairs. Let us entirely banish superfluous expenses. With an external dress and appearance different from other men, let us follow a singular and unique way of life worthy of our state and our profession. With our disdain for this common decoration of the face, let us renounce vain human adornments and glories. In this way we will all take care to render ourselves every day less unworthy of our ministry. We priests especially will be less unworthy of the tremendous mystery we handle daily, the mystery of the most holy sacrifice of the Mass. If on our part we join this holy interior and exterior fittingness for our vocation to the sacrifice of the Mass, then no words come to me to explain how many graces we will impetrate from the goodness of God, for our good, for the good of this people and for good of the entire Holy Church.

May God grant us all that through his mercy, and with this, we bless you and beg every blessing for you and for us, from his divine majesty.

Charles Borromeo

Come with the right intention

Homily to the Ordinands
Given the Saturday after Pentecost
June 1, 1577

My dearest brethren, whenever I must confer sacred orders, it is certainly not without a certain great wonder of soul, knowing that among all other pastoral activities, this is the most sublime and excellent above all others. For even though the ministry of any priest is the highest, and nearly divine, especially when he consecrates the Sacrament of the Most Holy Eucharist, surpassing the ministry of the angels themselves, still, who could deny that it is greater and more desirable to confer on others the very power and authority to confect this Sacrament? I confess indeed that I am struck with awe and filled with admiration when I approach such an arduous and sublime ministry, thinking myself a most unworthy minister of Jesus Christ, I who am about to administer such great Sacraments today with impure heart and tainted hands. And what will I say about that diligent and exacting investigation which is to be made concerning the morals and doctrine of each man who is to be promoted? For it is an investigation which I must carry out with the greatest possible exactitude and thoroughness, warned as I am by that word given by the Apostle: *Impose not hands lightly upon any man* (1 Tim. 5:22). In such a matter, even slight negligence on my part can render me guilty of a very grave fault. Although generally this examination is left to the strict verdict of the Supreme Judge, in whose courtroom the secrets of hearts will be revealed and an account will have to be rendered for every action. Nevertheless, in the meantime, bishops do well to be aware that this kind of fault, which we will expiate at the end of our lives, will receive a heavy sentence in them by the manifest judgment of God. For they promoted men whom they failed to examine adequately. Even though the bishops considered that they would be perfectly suitable coadjutors, able to help in bearing the pastoral burden, and I would even say they might have done so in good faith, still, I say, those men later showed themselves to be not only useless, but also self-serving and obstacles to the service of God.

From all that, we can draw the conclusion that it is not enough to look into the morals and doctrine of each one with a certain superficial investigation, but we must also be most diligent in examining even their intentions, to the degree that is possible. And after applying all possible diligence for that purpose, it will be necessary to seek and beg from the most good God, with fervent and abundant prayers, that he himself would choose and promote the ministers he already knows to be good. For that reason, on this very day you will hear us chant this devout prayer from the depths of the Church's heart in this ceremony of conferring sacred orders: *We who are only men, and ignorant of divine understanding and supreme reason, judge as best we can; but things unknown to us do not slip by you, Lord; hidden things do not deceive you, for you are the one who knows what is secret and scrutinizes hearts; you shall be able to examine the lives of these men by that heavenly judgment in which you always prevail, in which you both pardon sins and grant to men to now do the things they must to please you.*[7]

But to what end do we go on about all this, dearly beloved brethren? It is so you may understand how dangerous and how difficult this our pastoral ministry is; always difficult in other things, but difficult also in this action of today. And moved by pious sentiments of mercy toward you, we will insistently beseech God for you, that he may follow you with divine favor of his clemency and bathe your hearts with the light and dew of his Holy Spirit. You should likewise think about and ponder on this in your souls, namely that if it is necessary for us to take precautions in this great affair, so as not to be negligent in your regard, and to implore the help of the Holy Spirit with devout and fervent prayers, then how much more necessary is it for you to labor to obtain divine help, you, who will be found guilty if you accept Sacred Orders with anything other than that pure intention of soul we mentioned earlier.

It is indeed a most excellent and outstanding ministry to which you aspire today, and would that you consider with the intimate thoughts of your souls how excellent and outstanding your rank is going to be. Nevertheless, if you are going to avoid making yourselves unworthy of it, then not only must your life be characterized by the holiness and doctrine, faith and prudence with which you will be able to worthily bear the weight of so great an office, but then you must consider to what end you are seeking it. For if you have come here with the idea of providing yourselves with everything necessary for keeping fed and clothed, then your purpose is nothing other than financial advantage, no different from a sordid business deal. Then the best thing for you to do would be to turn around and go far away from here. For just as it is the greatest sacrilege to approach the altar for the sake of gain and profit, so no one will hesitate

---

[7]This prayer is said by the bishop in the ceremonies for the ordination of deacons.

to acknowledge that it is no light sacrilege to receive this Sacrament of Order, which prepares us for the ministry of the altar, for the sake of gain. Although according to a judgment of the Apostle, which is conformable to both divine law and natural right, the one who serves the altar should live by the altar, still, everyone recognizes that it is never permissible to place any personal need whatsoever before the worship owed to God.

But if any of you have been led to seek this station in life by ambition and desire for gain, then I beg you, *depart*; again I say, *depart* (Isa. 52:11). For the Holy Spirit, who infused this excellent Sacrament in the souls of those who receive it rightly with the greatest favor and graces, does not rest upon the proud and puffed up, but upon the meek and humble, as we read in the prophet: *Upon whom does the Spirit of the Lord rest? Upon the meek, devout and humble of heart.* Therefore, those who desire their enrollment or promotion because they have been led here by some other reason than serving, honoring and adoring the majesty of the good God, I want to warn again and again, so that they thoroughly understand how much more fitting it would be for them to have a millstone hung around their neck as they are cast into the depth of the sea (cf. Mt. 18:6), rather than enter the sheepfold of Christ by this way, a way other than the gate, which Christ himself in the Gospel testifies is the way of thieves and robbers (cf. Jn 10:11). Do not, I beg you, so sadden this Holy Spirit, the Spirit who is indeed gentle, but also angered by those who offend him and sin gravely. For clerics and priests of this type, who receive sacred orders so unworthily and with such a lack of holy intention, not only do not receive the grace of the Holy Spirit, but are also such that nothing can be more unhappy, miserable and disastrous for the Church of God than them. They are always the object of contempt and disdain from the faithful and deserted by God himself in this world. They also prepare for themselves an eternal damnation in the next.

So as to avoid that supreme unhappiness and misery, most dearly beloved, you must have the greatest concern and zeal, and leave no effort or labor undone. Therefore be strong in spirit. If anything sordid has perhaps crept in sideways into your hearts on account of your having come here with something less than the zeal and diligence demanded, may it all be cleansed and put back in order by the power of the Holy Spirit, whose gifts are to be most lavishly poured into your souls, provided of course that you yourselves do not place any obstacle. For as regards those who are restricted by some grave sin or ecclesiastical censures, or those who will approach stained by some blot on their soul, I do not even want to think that there might be some like that. Therefore may we undertake this holy and utterly divine work well, for it is of the Holy Spirit, whose octave we are still celebrating. And let us implore him: *Come, Holy Spirit, and emit a ray of your heavenly light; wash what is sordid, bend what is rigid, set right what is disordered*; To those *faithful* who this day supplicate you, *give the sevenfold gift; Give the reward of virtue, and the goal of salvation, give perennial joy*.[8] Amen.

---

[8]Borromeo is quoting from the liturgical sequence of Pentecost, *Veni Sante Spiritus*.

Charles Borromeo

Be holy or be struck down

To the Ordinands
Given on the Saturday of Embertide of Lent[9]
February 22, 1578

The greater and more excellent the dignity to which you have come to be promoted this day, most beloved brethren, the more you must weigh how great a danger hangs over you, and how strict the judgment of divine anger is, if you have not approached with the requisite sanctity of soul. Although that can be easily proved with many passages of Sacred Scripture and with many clear arguments, I nevertheless judge it right to place before your minds this one reason, which if rightly perceived by you, will be quite sufficient to terrify the souls of those who aspire to this sublime ministry either listlessly, or (what is worse) from ambition, or for filthy gain, or for any other reason whatever, which is not the faithful worship of God. For this ministry is what we find in *Exodus: The priests also that come to the Lord, let them be sanctified, lest he strike them* (Exod. 19:22).

In that command there are two words especially worthy of our consideration, the first one a word of honor and incredible glory, and the other a symbol of the most frightful calamity and hardship. These words are *sanctificentur* (let them be sanctified) and *percutiat* (lest he strike them). If I were to expound their force and strength to you even superficially, I would consider that I had done my duty by you, since I am obliged to rouse your souls in every way to the contemplation of such a sublime and profound mystery. In this brief period of time, I will pass over the manner in which one approaches God, namely that it is not only with bodily steps forward, but also with advances in the life of the soul. I judge it sufficient that you will already know this, you who aspire to the most holy Sacrament of Orders

---

[9]The Roman Church, followed by the rest of the Latin Church, gradually established four weeks or "four times," *Quatuor Tempora* (from which the English *"Ember*-tide" is believed to be derived) for a spiritual rejuvenation with fasting, on Wednesday, Friday and Saturday. According to the liturgist Blessed Ildefonso Schuster, O.S.B. (1880–1954), who was Archbishop of Milan from 1929 to 1954, the practice originated with a December fast in connection with ordinations, following the example of the Apostles' prayer and fasting in Acts 7 before ordaining the first deacons. A week around the beginning of spring, the week after Pentecost, and a week in September were gradually added, even though the Lenten Ember days only reinforce Lent itself. These days are also liturgical days with added orations and readings, especially on the Saturday (cf. Ildefonso Schuster, O.S.B., *The Sacramentary (Liber Sacramentorum): Historical and Liturgical Notes on the Roman Mass*, trans. Arthur Levelis-Marke, volume 1 [New York: Benziger, 1924], 329).

(in which indeed the grace of the Holy Spirit is conferred on those who rightly receive it), and that you know you will be approaching the very King of Heaven and Earth (before whom all choirs of angels cast themselves down in great humility, concelebrating him with perpetual praises, the God, indeed, of tremendous majesty and infinite power).

What wonder is it, therefore, if those who approach him must be *sanctified*, so the eyes of his most pure majesty are not offended by anything stained or sordid? And if indeed men about to be brought forth into the sight of an earthly king are accustomed to dress in more luxurious clothing so as to shine before their prince with all possible splendor, taking care that nothing should appear out of order or unfitting in their bearing and outward gestures, then how much more concerned must you be, brethren (if you are not utterly thick and stupid, brothers) so as to stand before our most great and high Lord and God with the adornment of the most precious interior virtues of soul. Indeed all adornment and beauty of soul is from within, as the psalmist says: *All the glory of the king's daughter is within in golden borders* (Ps. 44:14), that is to say, in ornaments of the most distinguished virtues, which are excellent like gold among the other kinds of metals. And they are holy humility, obedience, patience, abstinence, chastity, forbearance, piety and charity, which is the most perfect of all. The souls of the faithful, when interiorly girded about with the beauteous variety of these, shall be immediately ready to be led to the King and most closely joined to him, appearing rightly, in security and in sanctity in his sight.

You then who are about to approach the Lord must *be sanctified*; otherwise it is to be feared that you will *be struck* most severely by his avenging hand. But let no one think that this terrifying warning has been directed to priests alone, and not to all churchmen, since we read in another place: *be sanctified, you that carry the vessels of the Lord* (Isa. 52:11).[10] From this passage it is sufficiently clear that not only priests but also those who serve the priests must be sanctified. Therefore, let those who serve as ministers in the principal or conventual Mass[11] (as it is called), learn that even though they themselves do not confect the Sacrament, they nevertheless *carry*

---

[10]The Vulgate reads *mundamini* (be clean) while St. Charles uses *sanctificamini*, presumably to show the connection to the primary passage in Exodus he is commenting on.

[11]A conventual Mass is the daily Mass in a church where the Divine Office is publically said or chanted. Thus a conventual Mass is said or sung in all monasteries, cathedrals and collegiate churches that have a chapter. A conventual Mass assembles the members of a religious house or group of clergy, either in choir or serving in the sanctuary. Depending on the degree of solemnity for the Mass on a particular day, the celebrating priest would be assisted by deacon and subdeacon, as well as lector and acolytes.

the vessels of the Lord, since they touch them, approaching the altar and attending the priest who consecrates, and that they too must be sanctified if they wish to avoid that most grave danger, the danger of *being struck* by the Lord. I do not consider that any churchman, even the most learned, will ever come close to expressing how much power, and how much energy there is in that verb. For we cannot conceive of anything harsher that could have befallen the Egyptians from the avenging right hand of almighty God than those tremendous and utterly terrifying scourges which are so well known. I mean the horrible change of the waters into blood, the disgusting boiling up of frogs filling their houses, the heaviest and most irritating hosts of flies of every kind, the ravaging pestilence in the herds of the Egyptians, the immense and most voracious armies of locusts consuming everything, the oppressive and innumerable ranks of horseflies, the densest cloud of palpable darkness at midday; then the cruelest slaughter of all the firstborn. But then after having been despoiled of all precious things, they were horribly drowned in the Red Sea. All these things the Lord has signified with this one word, when he said, *I will strike Egypt with all my wonders* (Exod. 3:20). Who can turn his thoughts to the devastating angel decimating seventy thousand men from morning to evening with an unheard of plague (cf. 2 Sam. 24:15), or with incredible power utterly destroying the whole army of Sennacherib (cf. 2 Kgs 19:35), and not feel horror and trembling?

Let anyone recall that word of the prophet, *I will strike the shepherd, and the sheep of the flock shall be dispersed* (Mt. 26:31; cf. Zech. 13:7), and in the same moment call to mind how much and how pitifully the shepherd of our souls Christ Jesus was struck, when, utterly stained with blood, he was seen afflicted and pierced through with wounds on the cross, so that *From the sole of the foot unto the top of the head, there is no soundness therein* (Isa. 1:6). Who, I ask, will contemplate Christ Jesus so struck down, and not perceive in the depths of his mind and soul how grievous and how fearful it is to be struck down by the Lord? But he indeed, the Only-Begotten Son of God, was called "struck down" by the justice of the Father because he willed it, burning with that inextinguishable fire of charity, that he might expiate our sins and crimes and satisfy the divine justice for us, and he was struck down only in body, though most frightfully. But the Egyptians, and all others who are struck down for their crimes, crushed under the whole weight of the bitterest calamities, are not afflicted in their bodies alone but also afflicted in soul with eternal pains and tortures.

In the very same way, priests and other ministers of God will be struck down if they dare to approach the Lord impurely. Therefore if someone has come here not sanctified, or without having rightly cleared out the secret places of grave sin in his conscience, I now ask him to withdraw, and beg him to choose instead to blush for a short time rather than be struck by the angry right hand of the Lord and consumed by eternal fires. And then, as often as he approaches the altar, let each one always remember this terrible sentence which sounded with such severity on this very day, I mean the day of his promotion: The priests, or any other minister, also that come to the Lord, even to the altar of the Lord, let them be sanctified, lest the Lord strike them. Likewise let them remember the miserable and unhappy Oza, who when he placed his hand under the ark of God about to slip and fall to the ground, was struck by the Lord right there and immediately expired with withered hand (2 Sam. 6:7). But if Oza himself, inspired by his good zeal and carrying the ark of the covenant because of his office, was so harshly struck down for touching with his hand that ark which prefigured our altar, then how liable to damnation will they be who, not sanctified and not truly prepared, dare to touch the altar of God, which is far more noble and excellent, prefigured as it was by that ark?

Therefore I beg of you, dearly beloved, through the profound depths of mercy of our Lord Jesus Christ, diligently think on what you do here today, and take care with all effort of soul to flee the anger and fury of God. In the first place I am looking out for your own good, but I am also thinking of the other faithful of Christ who earnestly ask to be enlightened by you, as by light in the world, and who must also be seasoned, as if with apostolic salt, as you have so often heard it put to you by Christ the Lord: *You are the light of the world; You are the salt of the earth* (Mt. 5:14, 13). That indeed is what I insistently ask of Almighty God, namely that you rightly and perfectly give light and salt to the faithful. From him alone is every good and best gift, and may he pour forth upon you the salutary dew of all heavenly graces, and ever impart to you, now and always, the most lavish blessings in the name of the Father, and of the Son, and of the Holy Spirit. Amen.

Charles Borromeo

Spiritual deformity or integrity

To the Ordinands
Given on the Saturday after Pentecost
May 24, 1578

Most dearly beloved brethren,

If you should look diligently into what was written in the Old Law about the excellence and purity of priests and other ministers serving the altar, and what was written about external cleanliness of body, it will surely enough become clear to you how much more excellent and pure, and how much more free from all stain and blemish of body, and even more of soul, the ministers and priests of the Law of the Gospel must be. For if we compare the New Law's most holy sacrifice of the immaculate Lamb, the sacrifice of the Son of our God and Lord offered daily on the altar to God the Father for our sins, with those irrational victims slaughtered in the Temple of Solomon on prescribed days, what else will that be, if not to compare shadow to reality, darkness to light, earth to heaven, or rather brute animals to the most high God of gods, our savior Jesus Christ? Moreover, since our Lord himself was the giver of both the Old and the New Law, the Almighty and most wise Creator and Founder of all things, who will not see that everything then prescribed in the Old Law, was prescribed not so much to induce that rough and fleshly people to more zealous reverence in divine worship, but mainly for us, so that we who are the worshipers of the New Law could be instructed through those mystical figures about the great piety and veneration we owe to his Divine Majesty? His Divine Majesty does not now rescue us from slavery in Egypt, nor does he lead us by Moses dry shod through the Red Sea so as to bring us into a land flowing with milk and honey. For from the harshest empire of the devil, to whom we were subjected most miserably, serving him with no prospect of redemption by anyone else, God has liberated us for the freedom of grace. Through the most turbulent waves of this stormy age, as we cross it with dry steps under the banner of his only-begotten Son, who in the assumed flesh of our humanity has now undergone the punishment of the cross, he is leading us into the most delightful harbor of salvation.

And so now that the shadows have fled, the night has passed away, the day has come and the true sense of the Scriptures is now clear, let us attentively and briefly inquire what that most celebrated prophet and most faithful interpreter of the divine oracles, Moses, wrote concerning the ministers of the altar in the Book of Leviticus, in the following passage, where he spoke at the divine command about this to Aaron the priest: *Whosoever of your seed throughout their families, has a blemish, he shall not offer bread to his God. Neither shall he approach to minister to him: if he be blind, if he be lame, if he have a little, or a great, or a crooked nose, if his foot, or if his hand be broken, if he be crookbacked, or blear eyed, or have a pearl in his eye, or a continual scab, or a dry scurf in his body, or a rupture: Whosoever of the seed of Aaron the priest has a blemish, he shall not approach to offer sacrifices to the Lord, nor bread to his God* (Lev. 21:17–21).

Certainly in our time as well, those who approach the ministry of the altar must be free of such flaws and defects of body, unless they have obtained a dispensation from one who has the faculty.[12] Nevertheless it is with far greater zeal and diligence that we must be careful that the souls of those who are to be promoted are not polluted by the stains revealing vices. If we look rightly into the reality itself, what could *blindness* mean if not the darkness of ignorance by which our mind is so bound that it can in no way discern the things which should be seen? What could be meant by *lame*, if not that unsteadiness of spirit by which those who labor under such a vice are easily swept this way and that, like dust by the wind, carried off, bent and almost impelled to first one thing and then another? And by *nose*, which by a wonderful and most subtle power discerns the varieties of all odors, can anyone deny that the virtue of discretion is being signified, since those who lack the help of this virtue are found going now slack, now to excess, now to disorder in what they do, and sin in such a way that they weaken and corrupt even the acts of their remaining virtues, if they have any? And what is meant by the *feet* by which we walk or by the *hands* by which we work when these are called *broken*, if not the man who is not progressing rightly on the path of virtue, nor really bringing his virtuous works to completion? Likewise, what is represented by a *crookedness* in the shoulders but a man bent down to the ground, or by a *crookedness* in the chest but a man with his face lifted up against heaven? Is it not the man bent over earthly occupations, or the man raised up by worldly pomp or ambition? And then we have a *bleary eye*. If someone considers what vice drips forth from overflowing and bad bodily humors, he will indeed understand the *bleary*

---

[12]For decorum for the Sacraments, and respect for the natural sensibilities of the faithful in a formal, liturgical setting, ecclesiastical practice has generally prohibited men with grave physical deformities from ordination, unless a dispensation has been granted, as Borromeo indicates. His point, by way of allegorical interpretation, is to highlight the far worse condition of interior deformity of the soul.

eye to represent the man who is so wrapped up in carnal desires that he is barely free to turn the intention of his mind to doing anything right. And whoever contemplates *a pearl in the eye*, which is a thin, white membrane or film preventing vision, will be aware that it signifies practically nothing else except the man who takes too much credit for the brightness of his own righteousness. But what is meant by that *continual scab*, from which, once contracted, a man's members are never freed? Who would not affirm that this signifies the filth of longstanding lusts, which render the men they infect similar to pigs lying in a perpetual slough of mud, and that without some great force of divine grace to aid them, it is almost to be despaired that they will ever escape that most tenacious of all filth? Nor should it sound strange if we say that *dry scurf* signifies avarice, since just as a skin eruption can indeed attack the body without any pain yet greatly disfigures its beauty, and then usually ends in the incurable and abominable disease of leprosy, so avarice seduces the soul with the sweet desire of riches, and then gradually invades and infects all the powers of the soul, so as to end in that detestable vice *which is a serving of idols* (Eph. 5:5), as the apostle Paul testifies.

Nor should anyone judge it amiss if we say that a man with a *rupture*, such a burden to himself when the intestines have broken the peritoneum and descended, means the man of base thoughts and earthly concerns weighed down with cares, whose heart is in such drudgery that he can in no way lift his mind to contemplation of heavenly things. There is no one who would doubt that all these crimes and vices, which are grave in any Christian, are extremely grave both in priests and in everyone else assigned to the sacred ministry. For these men must so shine before all other men with splendor of doctrine and integrity of morals, so that having been instituted and elevated by Christ the Lord for the office of a light-bearing lamp, they may fulfill that office with a minimum of earthly cares without being held back in any way by allurements of the flesh, nor puffed up by worldly pomp, nor held bound or deflected by any of these passing or ephemeral goods (which are not truly good), nor subject to agitations of soul, but well-disposed to their neighbors, resting in the Lord, and having souls so perpetually fixed on the thought of divine mysteries, that they always *seek and mind the things that are above, not the things that are upon the earth* (Col. 3:1–2).

But neither should we pass over what Moses prescribed in the same place to those same priests, namely that they *not incur an uncleanness at the death of their citizens* (Lev. 21:1). By this priests are mystically ordered to avoid above all else, any connection whatsoever with other men's sins which lead souls into spiritual death, whether the connection be deliberate or on account of negligence or ignorance. *They*, therefore, *shall be holy to their God,* says the same lawgiver (Lev. 21:6), which means pure and immune from all stain of sin.

You, too, be holy, dearly beloved! Not blind, not limping in spirit, not indiscrete, not with broken feet or hands, not a crooked heart, nor bleary-eyed, nor laboring with the vice of presumption or the scab of lust, or the dry scurf of avarice; not dissolving yourselves completely in loose desires, nor ever cooperating with the lethal crimes of others; but rather entirely holy in heart, and mouth and deed, and with such integrity on every side that now rightly receiving the most Holy Sacrament of Orders, you may be filled with divine grace and the gifts of the Holy Spirit. Nor should you be proceeding from virtue to virtue always by yourselves, but also making others holy by your word and example. In pursuing the course of your whole life with eagerness to the mountain of God, may you finally arrive in the holy Jerusalem to enjoy the most blessed sight of the Most High God forever, with which he himself gives beatitude to his ministers who serve him faithfully, and with all other good things in abundance he fills them up in good measure, pressed down, shaken together and running over forever and ever (cf. Lk. 6:38). Amen.

Charles Borromeo

My portion is you, O Lord

To the Ordinands
Given in the evening at the Archbishop's House Chapel, Milan
Ember Friday of Pentecost
June 3, 1583

Dearly beloved brothers in Christ, great is the investigation and examination of life and morals which Holy Church's ministers, the bishops and pastors of souls, undertake concerning those who are to be authorized for carrying out the worship of God. But they are held back from proceeding by those thoroughly terrifying words of the apostle Paul: *Impose not hands lightly upon any man* (1 Tim. 5:22). Many things were decreed in this regard by sacred councils and the holy Fathers, which even if they were observed to the letter would still leave out many necessary things. We, who have been called by the Lord God to this pastoral office for your souls, shall employ all possible care and diligence in this regard. But since we are men, we are often mistaken and not unaware of the fact, we have the greatest sorrow of soul on account of it. But now, since nothing that was required has been omitted, either by us or by our delegates in that investigation of the morals, the age, the circumstances of birth, the learning, habits of life and ecclesiastical ministries of each one of you, and since we have attained certainty also from public documents and the testimonies of the proper people, we therefore turn to the Lord God who *is the searcher of hearts and reins* (Ps. 7:10), and we say, "To you, Lord, who know them rightly, we present these men."[13]

Therefore, corresponding to the great diligence we have employed in examining you, it is only right for you to bring an excellent disposition and due preparation for the reception of these sacred orders (here I mean not only the major orders; I am calling all of them sacred in the wide sense).[14] But first of all, and as I presume all of you know, the first disposition required is that you sincerely confess all your sins in the holy Sacrament of Penance, and that in approaching to receive the Most Holy Body and Blood of Christ, not being sullied by the stain of any mortal sin. It is not necessary that I go on at length about this disposition.

---

[13]From the Roman Pontifical.
[14]St. Charles here includes the minor orders of the western Church as well: porter, lector, exorcist and acolyte. Major or sacred orders are the orders of subdeacon, deacon, priest (simple priest and high priest or bishop).

There is another disposition which the Lord demands of you, and which I wish you diligently to consider today. This disposition consists in that diligent examination by which each of you shall scrutinize the intention and purpose you have for wanting to be numbered among the ministers of the altar. Look and see, all of you, whether it can be truly be said of you that, in the words employed by Holy Mother Church, *This is the generation of them that seek the Lord* (Ps. 23:6). Let each of you think carefully about why he is giving himself over to this divine service. Let him ask himself whether it is in order to escape poverty, to attain high ecclesiastical and clerical ranks, to become a parish pastor, to raise up indigent parents, to take life easy in leisure afterward, or for other reasons like those. If anyone among you is like that, let him hold back on this, I beg you through the mercies of our Lord Jesus Christ, so he does not bring such great insult and injury upon this most noble Sacrament. Let him beware of directing such a noble dignity to such an ignoble end. Otherwise woe to him; woe to him whose aim is not good. These are not the things to seek with such noble means, but the Lord alone is to be sought. You must be a generation of men seeking the Lord, so that from your heart you may be able to say to your God: My portion is you, O Lord (cf. Ps. 118:57). If there is anyone like that, and his sight and aim are pure and simple, then your whole body will be light (cf. Lk. 11:34). For you will find the Lord whom you seek, since he himself, who is infallible truth, has promised it: *seek, and you shall find* (Mt. 7:7).

Meditate, therefore, on how great a thing it is to be called into the Lord's portion, to be distinguished as a minister of the Lord. Consider, I ask of you, how much the Lord required the ministers of the old covenant to be selected from the whole people, and how much he required them to be separated out from the entire mass of people, when he said to them: *I have given you your brethren the Levites from among the children of Israel* (Num. 18:6), and in another place: *be holy because I am holy* (Lev. 11:44). Those ministers only handled sheep, oxen and lambs as victims. Is it not therefore proper that you, who are to be priests of the new covenant and to handle the Most Holy Body and Blood of Christ, should be more outstanding than them, and in sum superior to them in holiness of life? Get with it then, most beloved brothers in God; recognize the sublimity of your future office and ministry, the excellence of your order, and approach with the sole aim which we have mentioned, with this pure intention to not offend your God and Lord. And so you may be strong enough for what is required of you, flee to the Holy Spirit, the One who bestows graces and gifts, and whose descent upon the apostles we recall in these days. Implore the aid of him who stands ready to help all who invoke him. Ask strength of him *who gives to all men abundantly* (Jas 1:5); so that serving God and his altar most agreeably, you may rightly receive the reward of the ministry carried out, from the Supreme Priest and Pontiff who is Christ in Heaven. Amen.

Priestly anointing reflected in a virtuous life

To the Ordinands
During the celebration of Mass in the Cathedral of Milan
Ember Saturday of Pentecost
June 4, 1583

Among other things, beloved brothers and sons in the Lord, the supreme wisdom of the eternal God shines out wonderfully in this most admirable Order, which we know he instituted himself in his holy Church. In this very distribution of orders, which we celebrate today, who would not admire such a great variety in them of conferrals, anointings, offices and dignities, and the diversity of grades between the authorities? The Holy Spirit is always present to all these authorities, so he always works wonderful effects interiorly on those who are initiated or promoted in these orders, and then in others through them. These things are most manifest indications of his ineffable wisdom and are clearer than the light of the sun. If such a great diversity of created things proclaims the infinite wisdom of God, how much more, in the spiritual order does this multifaceted order testify to us of his goodness and the providence by which he gently disposes all things? Indeed, it should rightly amaze us or rather bring us to tears if in the face of so many and such great reasons for the most worthy admiration, someone could be found who in the midst of all these things was not astounded or even simply in admiration and as it were drawn out of himself and exclaiming with his whole feeling and mind, *O the depth of the riches of the wisdom and of the knowledge of God!* (Rom. 11:33).

That most wise queen of Sheba was amazed when, having entered the grand house of King Solomon, she contemplated the number and nobility of his ministers, his store of gold, the variety of gifts, the noble disposition of everything, and the administration not only of his most excellent household but of the whole kingdom. She burst forth into these words: *Blessed are your servants* (1 Kgs 10:8), since she seemed to be quite beside herself.

But how much greater than Solomon is God? How much does the Church of God excel Solomon's house? And how much greater reason does each one here have for admiration, amazement and even being beside himself? O how much those words of David apply to this vast Spouse and Church of Christ: *The queen stood on your right hand, in gilded clothing; surrounded with variety* (Ps. 44:10), so filled with treasures, so endowed with the gifts, the graces and the most holy Sacraments of the Holy Spirit, embellished with such a great multitude of porters, lectors, exorcists, acolytes, subdeacons, deacons, priests and bishops, with so many outstanding dignities, so many illustrious offices and functions. How excellent is the Church in distributions of graces which this same Holy Spirit (whose visible descent in fiery tongues upon the apostles we recall and celebrate this week) *dividing to every one according as he will* (1 Cor. 12:11, from the epistle for the Mass of the octave of Pentecost). Great indeed is the ornate beauty of this queen, the beauty of this variety of orders.

But there is also something else, far more important, which is required; namely, that her many ministers be distinguished for those virtues which each one's order and dignity requires, so that, to the same degree that they are distinct by their order from the rest of humanity, they should likewise be superior to all others by the example of their life and their praiseworthy habits and customs. Hear, brothers what our Savior Jesus Christ said to the apostles when he was about to send them the Holy Spirit: *stay you in the city till you be endued with power from on high* (Lk. 24:49). What do these words have to do with the promise of the Spirit? It was not without a great mystery that the Son of God pronounced these words, in order to show that the interior anointing of the Holy Spirit must be followed by an external clothing in all the virtues. What does it mean to *be endued with power from on high*? It means to shine with the external Christian and priestly virtues, to be an example to others, to lead the ecclesiastical life, which is the angelic life on earth; in sum to so order all your actions, *that they may see your good works*, and from your works be able to guess in what ecclesiastical order you have been established, *and glorify your Father who is in heaven* (Mt. 5:16), so that the ministry of Christ is not blamed in you, but instead the gravity of your way of life attracts people of the world to respect the ecclesiastical state. For woe shall it be to you, if through you comes scandal, and if on account of you the name of God is blasphemed among the Gentiles, and the majesty of our Most Holy Mother the Church is brought into contempt! Live, dear brothers and sons, as I hope with the grace of God you will indeed live, and order your life according to the rule of your orders, the rule which we have set forth briefly in the very words of Holy Church, and which all of you who are to be ordained have heard. Living in this way, may you finally possess and enjoy the eternal priesthood in heaven, and by the innocence and example of your life gain many on earth for Christ, to whom together with the Father and the Holy Spirit be honor and glory through infinite ages of ages. Amen.

Seeking greater holiness

Homily to the canons[15] of the major church and collegiate churches of Milan, given in the Archbishop's House Chapel
January 2, 1584

This renewal and beginning of a year, most beloved brothers, is usually a goad and prod for everyone in every condition of life for deciding on a new life, acquiring new habits, in fine for devising and doing new things. But if this newness of the year normally has such great power for everyone else, how much more should it rightly have that power for priests and for all who profess the clerical life? And among the clergy, that should be especially true for those who are preeminent and like lamps for the others, such as you are in the churches of this city and diocese. And for those who are contemplating and undertaking new things, who could doubt the necessity of first examining the old things? For if up until now you have led a life conformable to the law of God and fitting to your rank, it would be superfluous to treat of a new life, unless it were for increasing zeal and fervor for piety and religion. If on the other hand you have until now kept up habits of living out of keeping with your vocation, it will be quite useful for all of you and for us if each one of us takes stock of the past year and asks himself seriously how worthily he has walked before the Lord God. To this we have been invited by Jeremiah saying to each of us: *Set you up a watchtower, make to yourselves bitterness: direct your heart into the right way, wherein you have walked: return, O virgin of Israel, return to these your cities* (Jer. 31:21). That is to say, scrutinize your past life, go over the years of your life, place your past ways of acting before your gaze; as if *from a watchtower* carefully consider the year just completed. Inspect and evaluate your black spots and faults. Certainly anyone among us who decides to look upon himself from this watchtower, starts examining his errors not perfunctorily but seriously, will necessarily *make to himself bitterness,*

---

[15]Canons are clerics or priests belonging as a body (or "college") to a cathedral or other important church. Their principal task is the daily chanting of the Divine Office at fixed hours (the "canonical" hours). In many eras and places, the college of canons has had authority, power or influence in certain aspects of diocesan life and enjoyed certain rights, privileges and responsibilities attached to their position. Throughout the history of the Church various Popes and Councils, the Council of Trent included, deemed it necessary to enact disciplinary reforms of canons.

find causes for tears, and will be constrained to go over his years of life in bitterness (cf. Isa. 38:15).

But already I hear many priests silently responding: "By the grace of God the clergy is quite reformed; no longer does one see those old abuses, those old scandals; the sins and the corruption which used to thrive no longer thrive. O how much the clergy has been changed from what it was before! So many provincial councils have been celebrated, so many diocesan synods have been held; so many evils have been dealt with, that nothing any longer appears in need of emendation." Indeed the state of the clergy has changed, O brothers; the life of priests has been reformed; many abuses and scandals have been taken away. May there be endless thanks to God the author of all good things. But believe me, there still remain bitter weeds. There are many things that must be brought into a better condition. There is still reason for tears. That is what I wish all of us, who have come together as one for this purpose, to consider and recognize today. Concerning this, we shall see some things which can be so bitter for us, that we will need to correct them, and I will need to enkindle my zeal together with you this day as we begin a new year with a newly conceived resolution to start improving our life.

As you have heard, the state of our clergy is such as to offer us occasion both for thanksgiving to God and for tears at the same time; thanks indeed for the amendment of life already established, but tears indeed for the errors still allowed to pass. This morning I was asking myself, to what can the present condition of the priests be likened, and finally it occurred to me that it is like the state of the Israelite people beloved of God, which was therefore a sort of type and most manifest figure of us. The people, liberated from Egyptian servitude, *marched from Haseroth, and pitched their tents in the desert of Pharan. And there the Lord spoke to Moses, saying: Send men to view the land of Canaan, which I will give to the children of Israel* (Num. 13:1–3). *Moses therefore sent* some men *who returned after forty days, having gone round all the country, and came to Moses and Aaron and to all the assembly of the children of Israel to the desert of Pharan, which is in Cades. And speaking to them and to all the multitude, they showed them the fruits of the land: And they related and said: We came into the land to which you sent us, which in very deed flows with milk and honey as may be known by these fruits: But it has very strong inhabitants, and the cities are great and walled. We saw there the race of Enac* (Num. 13:26–29). *In the meantime Caleb, to still the murmuring of the people that rose against Moses, said: Let us go up and possess the land, for we shall be able to conquer it. But the others, that had been with him, said: No, we are not able to go up to this people, because they are stronger than we. And they spoke ill of the land, which they had viewed, before the children of Israel, saying: The land which we have viewed, devours its inhabitants: the people, that we beheld, are of a tall stature. There we saw certain monsters of the sons of Enac, of the giant kind: in comparison of whom, we seemed like locusts* (Num. 13:31–34). *Wherefore the whole multitude crying wept that night. And all the children of Israel murmured against Moses and Aaron* (Num. 14:1–2).

You have heard the account. How can there be anyone who does not see that it concerns us as well? The people had gone forth from Egypt, and had fixed its tents in Haseroth. The Hebrews were on their way to the promised land, and still they were nevertheless broken and struck down in spirit, were weeping, speaking badly about the Land, afraid and murmuring. They are the priests of the present time. They have indeed gone forth from Egypt and been rescued from harsh servitude, because the more grave and enormous sins are no longer found among them. They are in Haseroth, which means *vestibule*, because if they will it they are close to attaining the height of virtue, already in the entryway of the Promised Land, that is ecclesiastical perfection. They can attain the summit of piety and religion, which is truly a land *flowing with milk and honey*, because nowhere does God allow true consolation and an overflowing of all graces to be truly found except in those men who cultivate those virtues. And O how sorrowful things still are! When they hear the synodal decrees, and when the things which concern them are set forth, they are struck down and broken in spirit, they weep, they are frightened off, and they assert how hard it is to be always in church, to stand for so many hours in choir, to recite such long offices, never to refresh oneself! O how long is this work, how unremitting it is, and what giants the Canaanites are! How shall we be able to go up to these cities; how will we fight these monsters, compared to whom we are like ants? All things seem heavy, laborious and difficult. Moreover, some also speak badly about the Promised Land, criticize the constitutions, the decrees and this now established way for them to live. Perhaps some also murmur against Moses and Aaron, against their superiors. O how much this faintheartedness displeases the Lord! The Lord had thought of punishing all those people with raging pestilence and death. But by the prayers of Moses, although they had to persuade him in a way, God yet willed for a punishment that none of those who had spoken badly and murmured would enter the Promised Land.

And who knows, most dearly beloved, if this very great tepidity in sacred things, which is so strong among the clergy, is not the punishment for their faintheartedness and murmuring? Many vows of devotion are made, many resolve to do good works, but what progress in the way of the Lord is then seen? What kind of actual birth for these desires, what uprooting and separation from the cares and anxious solicitude of temporal things? One thing I certainly consider to be most reprehensible in the clergy: the fact that there are so many burning quarrels, so many court cases, so much time spent at the tribunals, so many suits between churchmen which are constantly being litigated before alien judges.[16] Alas, what are all these things if not the clearest signs of tepidity in divine things? O what a great and fearful sickness this is, the tepidity that is found in men consecrated to God! *I know your works* (Rev. 3:1), the Spirit says to the bishop of the Church of Sardis, *that you have the name of being alive: and you are dead.* O how many seem to be alive to others, but are close to death! They are indeed a little reformed outwardly, but interiorly they are cold, tepid, dead. Great is the battle of the Spirit against the tepid, brothers. In a wondrous way he hates and detests them. To the bishop of the Church of Laodicea God says: *I know your works, that you are neither cold, nor hot. I would you were cold, or hot. But because you are lukewarm, and neither cold, not hot, I will begin to vomit you out of my mouth* (Rev. 3:15). This is not because someone cold (by which a sinner is to be understood) is better than someone tepid, but because he is more disposed to receive warmth and health. For the one who is tepid, since he does not recognize his infirmity, is less solicitous for recovering his health. Therefore he dies in his sin, and little by little he weakens and ends as cold as can be. Perhaps many of us are like this, they are not *extortioners*, nor are they *adulterers*, or fornicators, or murderers, or drunkards, or lacking self-control. They are not stained by those very grave sins, sins for which that Pharisee (who nevertheless left condemned) was not answerable (Lk. 18:11–12). Nevertheless, who among us is advanced in virtues and well along in the way of the Lord? What fervor of charity is there, what piety in religion, what constancy in working, what light in the example of life we give, what sacerdotal majesty in our habits and ways of acting, what attention in the recitation of the ecclesiastical offices? These things we see nowhere; we have none of that. The Holy Spirit adds, *because*

---

[16]In an age in which Church tribunals still judged many types of disputes that today would go before civil authorities, judges could be called "alien" when men consecrated to the service of the Church took their disputes to the civil tribunals, rather than to the ecclesiastical. St. Charles probably did not intend the clergy to transfer all their suits to ecclesiastical tribunals, but rather to drop most of them as altogether unworthy for them to litigate since they are indicative of spiritual tepidity.

you say: I am rich, and made wealthy, and have need of nothing: and know not, that you are wretched, and miserable, and poor, and blind, and naked (Rev. 3:17). O my brothers, these words wound us, especially those who because they consider themselves to have accomplished enough, stand still, not at all solicitous for progress. The *miserable, and poor, and blind, and naked* are those who consider themselves rich and in need of nothing. The Lord adds, *I counsel you to buy of me gold fire tried, that you may be made rich* (Rev. 3:18). O how holy a counsel, truly divine and paternal! We are counseled to buy gold, not the resemblance or likeness of gold; gold, I say, *fire tried.* And what is this *gold*, if not perfect charity in intention and deed; to seek God's glory always, with everything else put in second place; to direct all one's efforts and actions to this end, whether someone is saying or chanting psalms, or praying, or giving a sermon; whether he is with God or with his neighbor, whether he is at home or in church? He who always has this end in view *may be rich.* If he is going to say or chant psalms, it will be with attention; if he is going to pray, it will be done fervently; if he is going to be with God, he will obtain whatever he asks; if with his neighbor, he will bring him around to whatever he is proposing; if he stays at home, he will enjoy secure tranquility of soul; if he is going to remain in church, it will seem to him that he is sojourning in a paradise of delights. This kind of intention is worth a great deal in all priestly actions and in the priest's way of life. *If your eye be single, your whole body shall be lightsome* (Mt. 6:22).

But since we have made mention of the attention regarding psalmody, which is so necessary also in other services and sacred functions, take this one thing for most certain, brothers: nothing in your offices and psalmody can be pleasing to God if an accompanying attention of the heart is not continually present. Hear what the Lord said to the priests through Malachi: *Cursed is the deceitful man that has in his flock a male, and making a vow offers in sacrifice that which is feeble to the Lord: for I am a great King, says the Lord of hosts, and my name is dreadful among the Gentiles* (Mal. 1:14). And a little before: *If you offer the blind for sacrifice, is it not evil? and if you offer the lame and the sick, is it not evil? offer it to your prince, if he will be pleased with it, or if he will regard your face, says the Lord of hosts* (Mal. 1:8). Do you do the same as those who offer *that which is feeble* to God? Certainly, those who show him merely external worship, who say the psalms only with their lips and voice; those who in body are indeed standing in church, but in soul are wandering in the marketplace and city squares. They sing the divine praises with their mouth, but in their heart turn over worldly and secular business. Is not the body weaker than the soul; is not the flesh weaker than the spirit? Why therefore do some only offer God the weaker things that they would not dare offer to men? Let them beware of the anger of God, since he is *a great King and his name is dreadful among the Gentiles*. He will not give his honor to anyone else, nor will he suffer anyone to delude him, to prefer someone else to him, or to put him in second place with impunity. Is not a weakling being offered to God when a priest involves himself in secular concerns at fixed and regular times, but only deals perfunctorily with ecclesiastical services, in fact considering the former things to be the most important, but the latter as things he can do at his leisure? Believe me, as long as this admonition is not carved most firmly into your heart, namely that priests are to dwell at their churches alone, say the psalms, pray and study, but that the other things do not concern you, then all your duties will seem onerous to you, and the offices too long, choir a sheer bother, and the church itself like hell. Or is it not the case that when you recite the psalms with the mouth, but with the heart think about quarrels, household cares, relatives or other similar things, you are giving the heart, which is the nobler part of man, to those things, and only bone and flesh, which are weaker, to God? Beware, brethren, beware, because a great King is God. He looks and sees far ahead, and wherever he wills he extends his rod; and at an hour when you are not thinking of it, he will protect his honor, inflicting the penalties you deserve. His is not the memory of a man, who can easily forget an injury. Beware, so that of you he will not rightly say, *this people honors me with their lips: but their heart is far from me* (Mt. 15:8). But when you pray, let the heart pray with the mouth, let the spirit say the psalm with the lips, and pay attention to what you are saying as you pray. There is a book of perfect devotion entitled *Treasury of Devout and Christian Practices*[17] and recently printed at Verona at our request. This book contains many excellent things pertaining to your state, but most important is its teaching on the sins one can commit in the recitation of the psalter, and how to chant the psalms well. I strongly exhort each of you to have a copy of it and frequently read through it.

But I beg you, let us investigate the cause of this sickness, namely the reason why priests do not chant the psalms attentively in choir, why their minds are deluged at that time by all their private and family concerns. Certainly all that mental wandering comes from the fact that they have not sufficiently disposed themselves for what they are doing, and they have approached it with no prior recollection of soul. Perhaps they head up toward

---

[17]Sax notes that this book was authored by a certain Giovanni Perelli.

the steps of the choir still full of worldly conversations, and they think they can suddenly have a mind fixed on God, as often as they please, and that they can automatically obtain from him, just by asking, whatever is necessary for their religious service. Certainly these men tempt God, and they are very similar to those who uselessly and thoughtlessly request miracles of him. Therefore the Wise man most prudently warns, *Before prayer prepare your soul: and be not as a man that tempts God* (Sir. 18:23). For this purpose sacristies have been set up in the churches, where the canons and priests have been accustomed to gather before choir, so that, thinking about where they are about to approach, they may dispose themselves for rightly chanting the psalms. If someone is going to address some king or the Supreme Pontiff, will he not diligently think over in advance what he is going to orally put before him, so he does not end up embarrassed and banished from his sight on account of an ill-considered stream of words before such a great prince? If therefore on account of men we are very careful, and speak only after mature consideration of the things that should be said, then should we not do the same in advance when we are going to speak with God? But in spite of everything, to our supreme sorrow, the order of things is entirely twisted here. No longer do people recollect themselves in the sacristy or prepare themselves for the divine colloquium; but they let themselves go with course, trifling and worldly discussions. Indeed the mere name of sacristy should inspire in us the greatest veneration of God, and discourage us from all these things. It is a sacred place, a place of prayer, a place of silence. Nevertheless it is generally reserved for useless conversations or even talk that is entirely out of place there. Prayer is the last thing we find people doing there, nothing is less observed than silence, and this place of silence becomes a public forum of quarrels, contention and secular affairs. On the door of the sacristy, and on tablets on the walls, in all places and according to the constitutions of apostolic visitations and councils, SILENCE is written in big letters, and it seems that silence is practically banned from the place. On the breast of the High Priest, on the breastpiece,[18] there was written: *Doctrine and Truth* (Lev. 8:8), in order to indicate that works must correspond to teaching and preaching, and what was preached or said must be done. Writing SILENCE is a type of *teaching*. Those letters teach that here we must refrain from speaking, give our attention to God alone, and bid farewell to all worldly concerns. *Doctrine* is present, but where is *truth*? Therefore realize how

---

[18]The Douay-Rheims provides a Latinate translation "the rational"; here we have used the Revised Standard Version translation "breastpiece."

much you fail in your office and how similar you are to the hypocrites when you do not do what you teach.

But why should we talk about the sacristy only? Even in the choir the divine praises are sometimes joined with profane speech, and a new kind of confusion of tongues is instituted, which brings no light insult to God. For who would turn his back or dare to converse with others as well while addressing someone whose power and dignity he knew? Let the appointed *punctatores* be diligently aware of how they are exercising their office; for they will give a strict account to God.[19] For this purpose *censores* are instituted, so that through their zealous work and diligent observation of the delinquent, at least this kind of external fault can be removed, since interior wandering of minds is known to God alone. Believe me, this is no light matter. There is another censure, another correction, another admonition than man's: God's. In any case, to speak truly, the indication of what lies within is exterior composure or the lack of it. A wine jar does not put forth any other odor than what it contains, and *for out of the abundance of the heart the mouth speaks* (Mt. 12:34). Consequently an exterior lack of composure is a manifest sign of interior disorders and wanderings in the mind. Hear what the Holy Spirit says in speaking about these external signs: *The attire of the body, and the laughter of the teeth, and the gait of the man, show what he is* (Sir. 19:27); that is, these things clearly show how anyone is interiorly. Our most blessed father Ambrose attached great importance to these external gestures and motions of the body; so it will be very helpful for me to bring before you a passage from his words in the first book *On Duties*, and they pertain to prayer and the disposition necessary for prayer:

Paul also bids that prayer be offered up with modesty and sobriety. He desires that this should be first, and, as it were, lead the way of prayers to come, so that the sinner's prayer may not be boastful, but veiled, as it were, with the blush of shame, may merit a far greater degree of grace, in giving way to modesty at the remembrance of its fault. Modesty must further be guarded in our very movements and gestures and gait. For the condition of the mind is often seen in the attitude of the body. For this reason, the hidden man of our heart is considered to be either frivolous, boastful, or boisterous, or, on the other hand, steady, firm, pure, and dependable. Thus the movement

---

[19] *Punctator* was the official who kept a record, with points on a tablet, of absences from choir.

of the body is a sort of voice of the soul. You remember, my children, that a friend of ours who seemed to recommend himself by his assiduity in his duties, yet was not admitted by me into the number of the clergy, because his gestures were too unseemly. Also that I bade one, whom I found already among the clergy, never to go in front of me, because he actually pained me by the seeming arrogance of his gait. That is what I said after he returned to his duty after an offence committed. This alone I would not allow, nor did my mind deceive me. For both have left the Church. What their gait betrayed them to be, such were they proved to be by the faithlessness of their hearts. The one forsook his faith at the time of the Arian troubles; the other, through love of money, denied that he belonged to us, so that he might not have to undergo sentence at the hands of the Church.[20] In their gait was discernible the semblance of wickedness, the appearance, as it were, of wandering buffoons.[21]

From these words you will easily gather how carefully we ought to avoid disorderly comportment of body.

O may the disorderly comportment of priests not become so great as to extinguish all devotion, piety and religion in the people as well! The mass of people who are weak, seeing such bad example, little by little comes to have contempt for divine things. And so those who never lose their recollection of mind and spirit when outside of choir, easily find themselves composed when they are in choir, and those who are not accustomed to engaging in dissolute talk when they are far from the church, easily show forth the dignity and majesty of religion when they are in church. It will be most helpful to you if a frequent suggestion of ours is constantly observed, namely that on occasion all the canons and priests of each church gather together for discussion of spiritual things, for in this way mutual charity will be increased among you, and you will add new motives daily for your devotion, and you will attract the people to religion by your example. But if these things are interrupted, then your fervor will necessarily grow tepid, and from there you will begin to neglect divine worship. After that, many will even be so careless and thoughtless in their

---

[20]"[S]entence at the hands of the Church" could be translated more literally as "priestly judgment," which is probably an allusion to the judicial powers of the bishop's tribunal, in contrast with civil tribunals.

[21]St. Ambrose, *On the Duties of the Clergy*. Book I, chapter 18, translated by H. De Romestin, in *A Select Library of Nicene and Post-Nicene Fathers of the Christian Church*, second series, volume 10 (Edinburgh: T&T Clark, 1989), 13. [translation slightly modified]

treatment of divine things that they will give the impression that they are in no way doing the weightiest thing that has been committed to them.

Indeed nothing worse can be imagined than this negligence, since God is so irritated as to have said through his prophet, *And now, O priests, this commandment is to you. If you will not hear, and if you will not lay it to heart, to give glory to my name, says the Lord of hosts: I will send poverty upon you, and will curse your blessings, yea I will curse them, because you have not laid it to heart* (Mal. 2:1–2). But is it any wonder that priests of that kind *have not laid to heart* the sacred things of their ministry, if they have become the kind of people about which in another place we read, *as a dove that is decoyed, not having a heart* (Hos. 7:11)? Therefore David exhorts us so often to *sing you wisely* (Ps. 46:8), so that the heart is in harmony with what is said, and that we treat divine things with the whole affection of our heart. What a shame it is, brothers, when one has been set apart from people in general, distinguished from them in bearing and dress, and has received the crown on one's head; when one has said at his first orders, *the Lord is the portion of my inheritance* (Ps. 15:5) and therefore goes before others in dignity—if nevertheless, in spite of all that, he in no way differs from the people in his manner of life. There may be *a kingly priesthood, a holy nation, a purchased people* (1 Pet. 2:9), but when the life of the priest is brought into consideration, it is necessary to say, *as with the people, so with the priest* (Isa. 24:2).

It is something blameworthy in you, if you are satisfied by having the virtues of the common people, thinking it is enough to be like the most perfect and holy among them. And what must be said if you do not attain their level of virtues? If you are not equal to them in the virtues of religion, piety and sincere devotion? Certainly there will be no place for excuses in that case, nor should anyone say: "I am a man like the rest, fragile, weak, infirm," for though you are a man like the rest, unlike the rest you have received the indelible character. The just Lord, who has raised you up to this state, has provided you with sufficient helps whereby you can satisfy the demands of your office and ministry. And no one doubts that this is most true, for if we did not firmly believe it, we would be accusing God of injustice.

Therefore let each one of you today most diligently make out the payment to God, and first of all, according to the amount he has received; and then let him consider the manner in which he responds and satisfies his duty. How many convenient resources for studying are spread about before you, for there is nothing more to be desired in any other city at all, except Rome, the mother of all cities. If therefore I neglect studying (as any one of you should say), who will not blame me? I have been placed in this sublime degree of dignity, as *I am made a spectacle to the world, and to angels, and to men* (1 Cor. 4:9). Therefore in what manner should I order my life and habits? Are not my defects and mistakes like ugly spots on the face, which are picked up immediately at first glance and cannot be hidden? Why should I not serve God, who has conferred such nobility on me, with all my heart? Why do I not hurry to choir, to give due praise to him from whom I have received so many things, instead of delaying my arrival in choir as long as I can without getting a black mark from the Censor? Does that not indicate that I am going to show service to God on account of gaining something from the distribution or to get some return, and not for the sake of him who is my inheritance?[22] O what a sordid goal that would be, how disgraceful it is even to mention serving God for earthly things and casting such a noble ministry so low!

I admonish you, brothers, with Paul, *that you stir up the grace of God which is in you, by the imposition of my hands. For God has not given us the spirit of fear: but of power, and of love, and of sobriety* (1 Tim. 1:6–7). The things which have been commanded you, do not carry them out from fear of punishment, or *to the eye* (Eph. 6:6, Col. 3:22), for this servile and ignoble fear is not fitting for your soul since you have received *a spirit of power, and of love, and of sobriety.* And we can hardly say how much *sobriety* in food, speech, gait, clothing and life in general is required in you to *live soberly, and justly, and godly* (Tit. 2:12), so you do not offend those observing you in word or any other way! All eyes are upon you. Your errors lead others into heresies; the bad life of priests has caused many to apostatize from faith. This we ourselves learned by experience, when we arrived in some locations in Raetia on a visitation.[23] Many heretics from there come here, and anything they take note of in you, which does not correspond to your exalted honor, they immediately tell once they have departed from Milan: "The priests in Milan, who are examples for everyone else, do such and such, live in such and such a way, speak in such and such a way; and so they are allowed to be much worse than us." Therefore beware, that *the name of God through you is not blasphemed* (cf. Isa. 52:5, Rom. 2:24); but *set up a watchtower* today, and bewailing these *bitternesses* (Jer. 31:21), take care that in future no one shall find in you any reason for bitterness, no occasion for tears and weeping. Amen.

---

[22]St. Charles may be recalling the Antiphon *Tu es, Domine, qui restitues haereditatem mihi,* which is sung by the choir in the ceremony of tonsure of clerics, and then pronounced by the ordinand himself during the actual snipping of a bit of his hair by the bishop.

[23]Raetia was a region that included eastern and central parts of modern day Switzerland.

Charles Borromeo

Vigilant shepherds

Homily to parish pastors, confessors and secular preachers[24]
of the city of Milan given in the Archbishop's House Chapel
January 3, 1584
What will we have accomplished, most beloved brethren, once these most
sacred feast days have elapsed? I do not know. Perhaps you are wondering
why I speak in the plural: what will *we* have done! The reason is ready to
hand, since I observe these Reverend priests, our collaborators, gathered
together here. Whenever there is mention of the clergy, the bishop is also
spoken of as the chief cleric and head of the clergy. The discipline of the
clergy is the discipline of the bishop, and the instruction of the clergy also
pertains to the bishop. Since today I am speaking to not just anyone in
the clergy, but to the priests who hear confessions, who are ministers of
the word of God, and have care of souls, and to those who by their office
and properly speaking are our coadjutors and cooperators in the rule of
souls committed to us and in the principal pastoral tasks; what shall I say
to you that I would not wish said first to myself? Since you are sharers of
our solicitude and have a share with us in our cares and labors, exhortation
to you is exhortation to us; your danger is our danger; your offices ours;
finally you will be sharers of our joys and the fruits of our labor, and of the
rewards of blessed hope, which are rendered to the pastors by the Prince
of all Pastors, Christ the Lord. Therefore, when we are dealing with you, it
concerns us as well.

I will say again: I do not know what we will have accomplished in these
sacred days. I do not know how we will have used the occasion offered us
for rousing ourselves. I do not know whether we will have contemplated
those shepherds, their vigils and keeping watch over their flock, the angels'
appearances, the joyful announcement of the birth of Christ, the hastening
of the shepherds to the manger, their joy at finding the signs which they
had heard from the angel, the glory which they gave to God, the admiration
with which they were filled, and the amazement they all shared in such
newness. These things are most fittingly applied at the beginning of the
new year. Therefore we have all gathered here today so that warmth and
fervor of spirit may be renewed in us. Those shepherds point to us, pastors
of souls. I beg you to see that what appears in those shepherds has become
characteristic of ourselves.

---

[24]These would be clerics who are not members of a religious order and have a mandate to preach.

First, what immediately captures our attention is the keeping vigil of those shepherds. Not content with having said that *there were in the same country shepherds watching*, Luke adds: *and keeping the night watches over their flock* (Lk. 2:8), in order to show their perseverance in vigil. Indeed night was divided into four vigils, all of which were kept by the shepherds. Thus Christ our Lord, speaking about the vigilance of spiritual shepherds and having the same perseverance in mind, indicated this when he said: *Let your loins be girt, and lamps burning in your hands. And you yourselves like to men who wait for their lord, when he shall return from the wedding; that when he comes and knocks, they may open to him immediately. Blessed are those servants, whom the Lord when he comes, shall find watching. Amen I say to you, that he will gird himself, and make them sit down to meat, and passing will minister unto them. And if he shall come in the second watch, or come in the third watch, and find them so, blessed are those servants* (Lk. 12:35–38). O how often does a priest begin to employ a little diligence in carrying out his office; but when he encounters some obstacle, he little by little loses fervor and all that effort comes to nothing! The Lord wishes assiduity in a good work, constancy in keeping vigil. In this way *the shepherds were keeping the night watches.*

But the evangelist adds something else, which I know could not be more pertinent to us. He submits that they were *keeping the night watches over their flock* so that we might recognize that pastors of souls often keep vigil, but not the kind of vigil which pleases the Lord and which he requires. They keep vigil in temporal affairs, but in spiritual affairs they fall asleep, slumbering under heavy eyes. Take someone, a priest, who most diligently looks after the monetary returns from his priesthood, allows nothing to be lost, most skillfully defends the rights of his church, recovers things which have been lost and is always zealous for new and increased revenues. Such achievements are not evil, for he is carrying out his sworn duty. But being asleep where the salvation of souls is concerned in order to pay attention to temporal goods: this is not the right way, this is not the vigilance pleasing to God. One should pay attention with moderation and sobriety to these things. More care must be given to souls than to lawsuits, to spiritual than to temporal affairs. That type of vigilance must be exercised only out of necessity. Those affairs should not be dealt with willingly but under constraint.

And because we have come this far, brethren, let us rouse each other to keep vigil and to execute our duties solicitously. So I would like all of us to consider today what sleep we need to guard against; what sort of sleep is pernicious to ourselves and our steps, and therefore most assuredly ought to be driven away, since our most particular office and duty in life is to keep vigil.

Concerning the various and different spiritual slumbers, Sacred Scripture reminds us to avoid all of them. The first of them is ignorance. O ignorance, the enemy of priests, how shameful it is in them, and how deadly! The priest holds souls in his hands, so he must discern between the different kinds of leprosy. It is for him to lead to pasture the people committed to the care of his teaching and example, for him to teach the Law of God, to give milk and solid food, and to hand to each one the nourishment which is suitable for him. O what an impediment ignorance is to all of those duties! What a strict account shall be rendered by the uneducated priest who is not fit for accomplishing any of them! For sure, nobody is entirely sufficient in wisdom to bear worthily the weight of his duty. But if this is true of anyone who must know things for himself and himself alone, what shall be said of those who must have knowledge both for themselves and others? *The lips of the priest*, says the Lord through the prophet, *shall keep knowledge* (Mal. 2:7). God required of his priests knowledge so easy and quick that they seemed to have an understanding of everything, which was kept and guarded on their *lips*; for the peoples *shall seek the Law at his mouth* (Mal. 2:7), demanding it as if it was something owed to them, belonging to them.

But those who are ignorant, how will they acquit themselves of a debt such as this? I want this to be considered by you above all and repeatedly. You must always place these words before your eyes, weigh them and ruminate on them. Concerning this, I am sorry not a little for myself. But on the other hand I am more afraid for you, when I contemplate so many resources for study you have available in this City, when I call to mind so many teachers, lectures and Colleges, and nevertheless perceive so much negligence in many priests who refuse to avail themselves of the divine mercies shown them, thinking they have already studied more than enough and made progress. Paul wrote to Timothy, a bishop most learned and accomplished in sacred studies, but still he urged him on to study even more, in words most grave, saying: *But continue in those things which you have learned, and which have been committed to you: knowing of whom you have learned them; And because from your infancy you have known the holy scriptures, which can instruct you to salvation, by the faith which is in Christ Jesus. All scripture, inspired of God, is profitable to teach, to reprove, to correct, to instruct in justice, that the man of God may be perfect, furnished to every good work* (2 Tim. 3:14–17). And someone will think it is enough for him to have been examined and approved for the care of souls, and that his priesthood gets him enough to live on, when Paul inculcated this to the very learned Bishop: *Continue in those things* (2 Tim. 3:14), even though he was also saying to him that *from infancy he had known the holy scriptures*? O how much should priests be marked by devotion to studies and progressing in them always! This slumber of ignorance, brothers, is something we very much need to flee.

This slumber was detested by the prophet saying *His watchmen are all blind, they are all ignorant* (Isa. 56:10), and then: *the shepherds themselves knew no understanding* (Isa. 56:11); *they themselves*, I say to those who are duty-bound to see, placed as they are on the watchtower as lookouts for approaching disasters; *they themselves*, whose task it is to show others the way, *they themselves* are *blind*. And how will they teach others the right way when they are ignorant of it in their own lives? *The shepherds themselves*, who must open the Scriptures to others, and from whom others *seek the Law* (Mal. 2:7)—*they themselves knew no understanding*. Far be it from you, therefore, that there should be someone in your number of such base soul and darkened mind as to say within himself: "I have gotten myself ordained a priest, what further reason do I have to spend time on studies?" By experience we have at times come to know of those who took the exam for their studies and were admitted to the care of souls because they had received a sufficient grade. It happened that after a certain number of months and years it was once again necessary for them to be tested on their knowledge of doctrine; and then we learned that they knew less than when they took the first exam, despite the fact that in addition to the knowledge they had showed, they have now added a long time in care of souls and the practice of what they had learned, despite the fact that they have preached the word of God, despite the fact of having many occasions to make progress in learning. Despite all of this, it was found that they had unlearned, because, satisfied with what they knew, they stopped all studying. O most ignoble and base souls! Without a doubt they show that when previously they studied, it was mechanical, in order to get the priesthood, not for love of studies and of virtue. Dearly beloved, do not quickly dismiss the opportunities offered to you by God. Do not be ungrateful to the divine clemency in your regard. Show forth by your deeds the character and liberality of your souls, and that you delight in virtues and desire to progress in studies.

There is another sleep full of dangers which Isaiah expresses in this way: *dumb dogs not able to bark, seeing vain things, sleeping and loving dreams* (Isa. 56:10). They dream vain things and delight in those vain things. Who these sleepers are, the same prophet declares in another place, saying: *And as he that is hungry dreams, and eats, but when he is awake, his soul is empty: and as he that is thirsty dreams, and drinks, and after he is awake, is yet faint with thirst, and his soul is empty: so shall be the multitude of all the Gentiles, that have fought against mount Sion* (Isa. 29:8). O priests, do you know who these sleeping and dreaming ones are? They are those who immerse their hearts entirely in the world, who have no other intention except to increase their worldly means, to enrich their relatives, and to provide for their own old age. And how miserable they are! Where does all this end? Death suddenly comes upon them, *and they shall leave their riches to strangers: And their sepulchers shall be their houses forever* (Ps. 48:11–12). How miserable it is to say it! Ecclesiastes appears to paint a living portrait of such priests: *Considering I found also another vanity under the sun: There is but one, and he has not a second, no child, no brother, and yet he ceases not to labor, neither are his eyes satisfied with riches, neither does he reflect, saying: For whom do I labor, and defraud my soul of good things? in this also is vanity, and a grievous vexation* (Eccl. 4:7–8). This is the calamity of most priests, and into this they often fall. So what if a priest has many and poor relatives. Is that reason for him to make such sordid use of his priesthood? Indeed it is not without the greatest sadness of soul that we sometimes hear of the unworthy words and complaints of priests concerning alms, tapers and candles owed them when they come to do funerals and recite the Offices of the Dead. What then will such miserable priests gain for themselves? They will heap up money, and they will display their ignoble soul to all. Death will come, *and another will squander away his goods in rioting* (Sir. 14:4). And not rarely will it happen that once they are dead, their relatives and heirs will not provide even one Sacrifice of the Mass for them. This avarice of priests is utterly pernicious. When this pestilence has invaded their hearts, they fall into the abyss of all calamities. About these most unhappy men the Prophet complains, that *every one has turned aside into his own way* (Isa. 53:6). These are the ones mentioned by Paul the Apostle, *for all seek the things that are their own; not the things that are Jesus Christ's* (Phil. 2:21).

When a priest yields ground to this accursed spirit, everything is ruined. He steers everything to this end, profit and riches. He is silent, when he should rebuke. He tolerates, is indulgent and dissembles about people's sins. He absolves people whom he cannot actually absolve. He is all effort whenever opportunity is at hand for getting money. He brings the jurisdiction of the Keys into ill repute with this ignoble and vile purpose. At length he perverts all sanctions. But from that point on, badly directed men grow hard skin in their sins. They grow old in concubinage and in usury. Nevertheless this kind of minister of the altars has his excuses ready. They say, we have already related their names in Easter time to higher authority:[25] we have fulfilled our duty, what more are we supposed to do? Rightly Bernard says: *The son dies, and will the mother take consolation over him, whom she now sees dead, because she knows that in everything possible to her, she was there, and applied every remedy that he not perish? Maternal love will in no way at all allow for such a consolation.* That kind of a priest should say to himself: "I too have a son, a parishioner, dead and ruined in sins. Am I going to console myself and consider that I did enough because I made this misfortune known to the superior or the bishop? Is zeal for the honor of God and the salvation of this soul burning in my heart?" O if this zeal pressed even a little upon a priest, my dear brothers, how anguished he would be, how bound up with sorrow! Indeed it would never cease. He would pass sleepless nights. He would never hold back tears. No effort and diligence would he spare until he restored the life of the soul to his son. But what sorrow instead! It happens that frequently in villages several will be found who, living in sin for many years, have nevertheless confessed and approached the Sacred Table, and some also who in their sinful persistence have done neither. And all these things are caused by the avarice of priests. *Astonishing*, says Jeremiah, *and wonderful things have been done in the land. The prophets prophesied falsehood, and the priests clapped their hands: and my people loved such things: what then shall be done in the end thereof* (Jer. 5:30–31)? *For from the least of them even to the greatest, all are given to covetousness: and from the prophet even to the priest, all are guilty of deceit. And they healed the breach of the daughter of my people disgracefully, saying: Peace, peace: and there was no peace* (Jer. 6:13–14). The avaricious priest says: "The friendship of this one can still be profitable to me; I attach

---

[25]According to the Sax edition of 1746, St. Charles decreed that parish pastors, in dealing with those who did not receive Holy Communion at Easter time, should first warn them with a prescribed formula, at the altar, on the following feast day. If a parishioner persisted in his obstinacy, the parish pastor would then inform the archiepiscopal court. The person would be prohibited from entering the church unless and until he made his Easter duty; Christian burial would be denied to someone persisting in this recalcitrance until death. Moreover, names of offenders in this matter would be posted on the door of the church.

great value to it. Therefore I will be silent and pretend everything is fine." *How Astonishing! What Wonder!* They strive to justify illicit contracts, *sew cushions under every elbow: and make pillows for the heads* (Ezek. 13:18). They excuse, *and my people loved such things* (Jer. 5:31), saying: "In this matter I do not feel that sting of conscience which another, more strict priest tried to inspire in me. Too rigid himself, he tried to inflict an empty fear on me. I have found a priest to absolve me, even though I keep a concubine in the house. It is enough if I promise not to sin anymore with her." And *what then shall be done in the end thereof* (Jer. 5:31)? Adding nothing further, he ends this paragraph. So I ask, what is in store when death comes for the priest, and for the penitent deceived by a wicked priest? You yourselves, think what it will be. Certainly if the blind lead the blind, both will fall into the pit (Mt. 15:14). What is the reason for all this dissimulation, laxity and fraud and killing of souls, if not the fact that *all have turned aside into their own way, every one after his own gain, from the first even to the last* (Isa. 56:11). By his own mouth eternal Truth taught us to utterly flee this sleep, when he said: *And take heed to yourselves*, and beware, *lest perhaps your hearts be overcharged with surfeiting and drunkenness, and the cares of this life* (Lk. 21:34).

Brothers, is there any other pernicious sleep for priests in addition to this one? Indeed there is, gluttony and drunkenness, as you have just now heard from Christ. For lack of moderation in food weighs down the heart no less than it does the body. There are some who say: *Come, let us take wine, and be filled with drunkenness: and it shall be as today, so also tomorrow, and much more* (Isa. 56:12). Let us enjoy the world, as habit dictates. Why should we uselessly attempt to renew the world? The whole purpose of these people is to eat, drink and relax. And will there be found priests who have accepted the care of souls just in order to relax? O brothers, this is not is the purpose of your vocation. This is not the intention of him who elevates you to this duty.

When Christ called Peter and Andrew to be Apostles, he used these words: *Come after me, and I will make you to be fishers of men* (Mt. 4:19). The life of fishermen is full of labors and dangers. Night and day they mend their nets. They are not frightened away from fishing by the hot or cold weather, nor do they stop because they are feeling the cold, even though often they catch nothing. By the example he made of those brothers, the Lord showed that he whom he calls to rule souls is not called to quiet or ease, but perpetual labor and fishing. The rule of souls is an exceedingly laborious thing, and nevertheless there are some so ignorant of their duty as to tell themselves: "I have acquired the priesthood. I can grow fat on it, copious returns I gain, resources for living comfortably I now possess; therefore, I will relax." A surpassing and most wicked spirit is this, unworthy even of a gentleman, and even more so of a priest! Such a priest is moved by that spirit which said: *Soul, you have much goods laid up for many years take your rest; eat, drink, make good cheer. But God said to him: You fool, this night do they require your soul of you: and whose shall those things be which you have provided?* (Lk. 12:19–20).

Not a few fix limits to their labors and care, saying: "After being called, I went to the sick man. I heard his confession. I gave to him the Most Holy Sacrament of the Eucharist. In Eastertide I refreshed my subjects with Holy Communion. On feast days, I kept at it, even after the noon meal, in order to explain Christian doctrine. Nothing more is required of me." Why are you saying, "nothing"? O how much and how many things are required by the care of souls! Do you, minister of sacramental Penance, think you have done enough if you heard the confession of a sinner? Alas! Your office demands much more than that. You have to warn him in season and out of season, impress upon him the pains of hell, expose to him the ugliness of sin, set forth the Passion of Christ, borne for the extermination of sin, repeatedly exhort, ask, instruct, invite and direct him to frequent the Sacraments. When Christ has been born in his heart through grace, he still has to be educated and sustained in that by you. Will the pastor of a parish, who has received souls like a deposit from the Lord, think he has accomplished enough if he only took the time to fulfill his Easter duty? O how much more care remains for him to show! *He that rules*, says St. Paul, *with carefulness* (Rom. 12:8).

The omission of this carefulness is most pernicious; for from here results the ruin of his subjects and the souls committed to his rule. *I passed by the field*, says the wise man, *of the slothful man, and by the vineyard of the foolish man: And behold it was all filled with nettles, and thorns had covered the face thereof, and the stone wall was broken down* (Prov. 24:30–31). If fervor becomes even a little bit remiss in the care of souls, all evils immediately begin to grow up. This we have learned most clearly by experience. *The field* of the priest is the parish; *the vines* are the souls committed to him. If the pastor is *slothful* and sleeps, immediately *nettles and thorns fill* the parish. A thousand abuses, corrupt practices and scandals grow and increase, and *the stone wall was broken down*. Indeed the observance of the commandments, by which souls were guarded as by a *wall*, is destroyed. From that point on, the pastor stands accused of laziness and slumber by a disordered parish, by subjects given to license and wanting in discipline. Such sloth in us, O brethren, is generally a most grave and deadly sin, although it can be excused a little in others upon whom this weight of responsibility does not weigh. Let them at last hear the spirit of the Lord rousing them and saying, *How long will you sleep, O sluggard? when will you rise out of your sleep?* (Prov. 6:9).

Such were not the holy shepherds, as related in today's Gospel, *who kept vigil by night.* Therefore the Lord showed them such great honor and filled them with such light, for God illumines those who are vigilant in their ministry. Anyone among us must keep watch with expectation for the Judge, and say: "I will have to render an account for these souls. The Lord has entrusted them to me for safekeeping. I do not know at what hour *the Son of Man will come* (Lk. 12:40) and settle accounts with me. Therefore I will be always ready, so that *that when he comes and knocks, I may open to him immediately* (Lk. 12:36)."

Here there is another, most grave type of sleep, namely, that one is not in expectation of the Lord at each hour and moment. The kind of preparation he expects from us, he himself teaches, saying: *Let your loins be girt, and lamps burning in your hands* (Lk. 12:35). You will have *loins girded* if you are not involved in worldly cares, but free and unshackled by them; and *lamps burning in your hands* (Lk. 12:35) certainly mean purity of life and deeds in accord with doctrine. O what a life, what a decent lifestyle, what gestures and speech must characterize priests! But how much greater must be the splendor and light in the works of those who have the care of souls, who are set before the people entrusted to them as examples, and according to whose example those people for the most part model their lives!

And with what care should be avoided a frequenting of, and excessive familiarity with, people of the world, which generally turns out to be the downfall of all clerics! Through this excessive familiarity they are dragged to feasts and banquets, and from this point on, they are rendered contemptible and turn out worse than people of the world, taking on all of their habits, *And they were mingled among the heathens, and learned their works* (Ps. 105:35). But if the priest or pastor, who is the eye of his parish, is in the dark, what will the whole household be like (cf. Mt. 6:23; Lk. 11:34)? If salt loses its savor, with what will it be salted (cf. Mt. 5:13)? If the man through whom others should be seasoned, taught, illumined, and directed, is himself affected for the worse, how will it be with his miserable subjects?

Therefore those who keep vigil with that spirit of expectation you have just heard are the ones who avoid this sleep, and they are the ones whom the Lord consoles most delightfully. Indeed while the shepherds were keeping watch *the brightness of God shone round about them* (Lk. 2:9). With the announcement by the angel, they heard that Christ had been born, and afterward also saw him. And the pastor keeping watch, sees a sinner repent through his own example and labor, sees another break illicit contracts, sees another approaching the Sacraments frequently. In all these things he understands that Christ is born and he is filled with wondrous joy.

The shepherds themselves went with haste to the manger, and perceived the sign given them by the angel, namely, *the infant wrapped in swaddling clothes, and laid in a manger* (Lk. 2:12). If we too, brethren, have in these last days approached the manger with them, O my! What did we see? There we saw God made man, in the middle of winter, in the middle of the night, amid cold and freezing, born in a stable, having *no room in the inn* (Lk. 12:7), lying in straw between two animals, getting cold, trembling, wailing. Why, O most holy Infant, do you suffer all these things, if not on account of souls? Will we ourselves get tired of bearing up under effort, labor, suffering and a little poverty for the sake of those same souls?

The high priest had inscribed on his humeral veil the names of the children of Israel, in precious stones and gold (cf. Exod. 28:17–21), signifying that Christ, as the Supreme High Priest, would have carved upon his heart the souls of all men as most precious to him. By this we too were taught by Christ's example to consider as precious in our eyes the souls committed to us. To redeem them the Son of God poured forth all his blood, and will we judge even one soul to be of little worth? Will we see the people all sprinkled with the most precious blood of Christ and not offer our very lives for them if necessary? Will we not teach them, admonish and direct them, and will we not protect souls redeemed at such a high price? Most beloved brethren, this is the foundation I wish to lay firmly in our hearts at the beginning of this year. Three days ago, at the most fitting time, Christ began to shed his blood at his Circumcision while still an infant.[26] And we are going to be idle and slothful? Should we not rather be expending ourselves, and beyond measure, when all the mysteries of Christ we have seen so far arouse us with such ardent flames?

---

[26]Borromeo is referring to the liturgical feast of the Circumcision of the Lord, which in his time was celebrated on January 1st, the eighth day after his birth, which according to Jewish tradition was when a male child was circumcised and given his name.

Once they had seen Christ, the shepherds thus returned to their homes full of admiration, wonder and joy, *glorifying and praising God* (Lk. 2:20). O what will be the consolation of a priest at the end of his life, if he sees as many souls as possible having been given back to God through his labor! How much tranquility of conscience to be able to say: "I gained this soul for Christ. That soul I pulled out of concubinage. That other soul I frightened off from illicit contracts. These are my spoils. He *was lost, and is found; was dead and* through me *is come to life again* (Lk. 15:24)." *My brethern*, says St. James, *if any of you err from the truth, and one convert him: He must know that he who causes a sinner to be converted from the error of his way, shall save his soul from death, and shall cover a multitude of sins* (Jas 5:19). Holy Job remembers the poor whom he himself clothed and their gratitude to him in these words: *If I have despised him that was perishing for want of clothing, and the poor man that had no covering: If his sides have not blessed me, and if he were not warmed with the fleece of my sheep* (Job 31:19–20). Therefore, if the very *sides* and bodies of the poor, covered and *warmed* as they were with clothes from the holy man, were thanking Job not with words but with sensation and warmth, how much more will souls called back from sins bless good priests, since when they were naked, they were clothed with grace and warmed by the fire of charity through the diligence and effort of those priests! Absolutely no consolation can be found which compares to this one.

On that account, brothers, remember that this most excellent duty is ours; ours I say, because I mean to exclude no one here. It is my duty, but also the duty of the pastors of parishes, of priests who hear confessions, and also of those who preach the word of God. Therefore we must all be vigilant. The care of souls is like hunting. The apostles were hunters, and as many as have succeeded to them, as well as their coworkers, are hunters. The Lord said about them, through the Prophet, *and after this I will send them many hunters, and they shall hunt them from every mountain, and from every hill, and out of the holes of the rocks* (Jer. 16:16). Two kinds of dog are usually employed in hunting. Certain dogs are sent into the woods to terrify the animals, compel them to come out, and then drive them to flight. But other dogs pursue the fleeing animals and capture them. It is the same in spiritual hunting. Preachers move the hearts of sinners, threaten them with the punishments of hell, show them the ugliness of sin and strike terror. The sinner now terrified and going over these things in his mind realizes: "O how great was the danger I was in! If I had died, I would have been immediately consigned to Hell, to be tortured by that horrendous perpetual fire." He hastens to a confessor, and immediately the prey is captured for Christ. He opens his conscience to him, uncovers his sins, seeks remedies, and by the prudent priest's admonitions, exhortations and salutary precepts, the meat of the hunt is prepared (cf. Gen. 27:7) for Christ.

Here is where all of you, therefore, must be, you who are like the nerves of the spiritual life of this people. Let us catch flame, I beg you, at the beginning of this year. Let us rouse each other. Let us resolve most firmly to be Ministers of God, called not to peace and idleness, but to labor. Let us recognize our vocation. Let us consider what zeal for souls really is. Let us truly embrace so great a province as this one. Let us aim at being truly beneficial to souls, in example, exhortations, precepts, rule and right administration of the Church. Let the people be aroused to a strict rectitude of life, not only seeing in us a lifestyle free of blame, but also how we carry ourselves in a becoming manner, in external actions sealed with respect and tact. May they see our ministry pleasing to God. May they see us worthily serving at the altars, loving to maintain the church—the house of God—full of decorum and adorned, with all the sacred vessels kept clean and bright. Brothers, we are going to visit your churches, altars and sacristies without advance notice. When you least expect it, we will suddenly be upon you. Do what is needed, I beg you, so that we will not be forced to apply severe discipline. We have been prevented these last months from fulfilling this duty, as you know, in order to obey the most holy Vicar of Christ, who had entrusted to us the visitation of the Province of Raetia. After this, until the solemnity of Corpus Christi, we shall make ourselves much more available. In the meantime make a note of whatever you may think worthy to bring to our attention when we come, especially concerning those who spend immoderate sums on banquets or who become dissolute beyond measure in these most miserable and Bacchanalian times, so that we may bring some remedy in the Lord for their infirmities. Furthermore be especially diligent, according to the instructions you were given, that people do not go about masked in the city on Sundays and feast days. Be heartfelt in your attachment to a holy comportment by the faithful in the house of God, namely that men pray separately from the women in the churches, and that the women be there with heads veiled at all times. And be responsible for the clerics serving you, so that they not wander about the city. And if in anything you need our help, let us know. But on Tuesday of next week let the pastor of each parish bring us the books of the year that just finished, 1583, in which the baptized, the confirmed, the deceased, and those who contracted marriage, are written down separately. Finally, live in such a way that you may with joy render an account of yourselves and your subjects to God who requires it of you. Amen.

You are the pattern of the flock

Third Oration to the clergy at the Eleventh Diocesan Synod
April 20, 1584

And she cried travailing in birth, and was in pain to be delivered (Rev. 12:2), said John in the Apocalypse concerning the woman about whom we are going to say more. O what sorrow and what a cry we hear from holy Church! She calls out both before God with her prayers, and through my mouth, pronouncing divine words to you. I seem to hear her say to her Spouse, our Lord Jesus Christ, what Rachel of old had said to her husband Jacob: *Give me children, otherwise I shall die* (Gen. 30:1). I am still yearning to give birth, indeed I still dread the thought of sterility, and unless you, O Christ, come to my aid and give me many children, then truly I am about to die. This is the spirit of our most loving mother. In this spirit above all are we gathered together. She desires in the first place that we too should have this spirit.

I must hope, most beloved brothers, that amidst so many voices raised so high and so many tears, many people suffering along with mother Church and grateful for so many graces most generously communicated to us by God, will receive within themselves the most fertile seed of the divine word, warming and fostering it with the ardor of charity, and finally conceive Christ in the secret womb of their hearts. May there be many who sense the strongest movements coming about in their souls and the greatest possible flame burning. But what then? What about us? The Lord is not going to say about us, is he, what was once predicted to men of old by the Lord through Isaiah: that *You shall conceive heat, and you shall bring forth stubble?* (Isa. 33:11). We are now inflamed and ardent; we are now near to the birth. But when the time of birth arrives, we are not going to give birth to straw, are we? We are not going to be languid and tepid, are we? O dearly beloved, this is not the goal of the Church; this is not her so vehement desire. She desires children. She wills the newborn to come forth into the light. It is not enough for her if we have good desires, but she desires that we also bring them forth in our midst by our works. For this reason she cries out giving birth. This is the principal goal of her labors, her sorrow and her torments.

Therefore having first set forth this most firm hope, that each and every one of us here should conceive and be near the moment of birth, what remains except for us to see what kind of birth the Lord God, together with Holy Mother Church, requires of us? For births are of different kinds: in the bodily order, they are male or female, but in the spiritual, perfect or imperfect. Therefore we will consider in what way our future act of giving birth can be perfect. For nature also intends this always, namely that a male and perfect offspring be generated, but it is through the infirmity and weakness of the generating male that a female is often produced.[27] Therefore how much more will grace desire the same. Therefore let us consider how these types of birth differ between themselves. And because it is not enough to give birth and give birth to a male, but it is necessary to guard and to educate the offspring until he grows into a perfect man, *unto the measure of the age of the fulness of Christ* (Eph. 4:13), we shall, therefore, in the second part, treat of spiritual guarding and educating.

Admirable, reverend priests, was the example given by Gideon, that great leader and commander in the people of God, by whom God showed what kind of works and what kind of births he demands from his ministers and his Church. About to go up against the Midianites, he had assembled a very large army and contracted a massive number of troops. But many of these men here (the Lord tells him) are not suitable for my intention or for carrying out my works. Therefore those who are timid should be the first to depart, for I require only men who are strong, constant and of firm will. Gideon did this, and out of the greatest multitude of soldiers, he kept only ten thousand men with him. And not content with this, the Lord went on to send them to a river, and he indicated to Gideon what kind of test to which he wanted the men submitted: *The people are still too many* (he said), *bring them to the waters, and there I will try them: and of whom I shall say to you, This shall go with you, let him go: whom I shall forbid to go, let him return.*

---

[27]This analogy that St. Charles presents requires some explanation. Rather than dismiss St. Charles as misogynist, it is important to note that his allegorical application of male births (perfect) and female births (imperfect) here reflects not only the scientific understanding of procreation at the time, which we now know as inaccurate, but also an attentiveness to Scripture and the sexual differentiation of human nature as an image of God. The Aristotelian and Thomistic vision of male and female in human nature, part of the background of St. Charles' homilies, contains true metaphysical insights in the midst of biological inaccuracies, and implies no lack of appreciation for woman. For some of the most recent exposition of St. Thomas Aquinas on this issue, see Francisco J. Romero Carrasquillo and Hilaire K. Troyer de Romero, "Aquinas on the Inferiority of Women," *American Catholic Philosophical Quarterly* 87.4 (2013): 685–710; Eric M. Johnston, "The Biology of Woman in Thomas Aquinas," *The Thomist* 77.4 (2013): 577–616. On the order of grace in this whole question, Johnston recommends Charles de Koninck, "Ego sapientia: The Wisdom That Is Mary," in *The Writings of Charles de Koninck*, volume 2, trans. Ralph McInerny (Notre Dame: University of Notre Dame Press, 2009), 1–62.

And when the people were come down to the waters, the Lord said to Gideon: They that shall lap the water with their tongues, as dogs are wont to lap, you shall set apart by themselves: but they that shall drink bowing down their knees, shall be on the other side. And the number of them that had lapped water, casting it with the hand to their mouth, was three hundred men: and all the rest of the multitude had drunk kneeling. And the Lord said to Gideon: By the three hundred men, that lapped water, I will save you, and deliver Midian into your hand: but let all the rest of the people return to their place (Judg. 7:4–7). Therefore Gideon went forth against the Midianites: *And he divided the three hundred men into three parts, and gave them trumpets in their hands, and empty pitchers, and lamps within the pitchers. And he said to them: What you shall see me do, do you the same: I will go into one part of the camp, and do you as I shall do. When the trumpet shall sound in my hand, do you also blow the trumpets on every side of the camp. And Gideon, and the three hundred men that were with him, went into part of the camp, at the beginning of the midnight watch, and the watchmen being alarmed, they began to sound their trumpets, and to clap the pitchers one against another. And when they sounded their trumpets in three places round about the camp, and had broken their pitchers, they held their lamps in their left hands, and with their right hands the trumpets which they blew, and they cried out: The sword of the Lord and of Gideon* (Judg. 7:16–20), and in this way they carried off the victory over their enemies. O what kind of mystery is this: the Lord rejects the timid and wants only those who lap up water, have trumpets, earthen vessels and lights hidden, and in this way a notable victory followed. What do these things mean?

Here let us learn directly who gives birth spiritually to males and who to females. Those who are fearful, those who fear poverty, mountain churches, difficult places: these are not apt soldiers for the army of God. He who bends the knee toward the water, who wants his comforts, who seeks his own interests, who strives to satisfy himself in all things: such a one is not a worthy soldier. But those of intrepid spirit, who drink standing, who do not lower themselves with terrestrial desire: these are ecclesiastical ministers, ready to set out for the conquest of glorious provinces. O how gloriously did the most holy apostles put this into practice, so constantly tearing themselves away from all worldly things and human respect, and with such strength of soul depriving themselves of all things, not only comforts, but even things necessary for sustaining nature: breaking the clay vessels and pots which were their bodies, as they exposed themselves to sword, tortures, fire and death. These are they who triumph over the world, the demon, and themselves, who carry off glorious victories for Christ, who give birth to males, that is to heroic and perfect works.

Who therefore are those who bring forth a perfect birth, and who are they who bring forth an imperfect one? They differ between themselves in various ways. First of all, some are languid, thinking it is enough for them to be good like other people, content with the common virtue of others. These are indeed an imperfect birth, far from what their vocation calls for. But a perfect birth is the churchman, whether canon, parish pastor or priest, who recognizes the excellence of his vocation, and its pre-eminence over the state of laymen, even good ones. He understands that from him is required another humility, another charity, another devotion, and other virtues from those of other men, as he assiduously turns over in his mind those words of the Savior: *unless your justice abound more than that of the scribes and Pharisees, you shall not enter into the kingdom of heaven* (Mt. 5:20). In these words the Savior compares our justice not to the sins, but to the justice of the Pharisees, a justice of which they considered themselves to be most observant, and the greatest practitioners and promoters. St. Gregory exclaims, "What is there in common between the shepherd and the flock? In virtue he must stand out, and surpass those whom he has received to rule, as much as the shepherd too, because he is a man, is ahead of the sheep in dignity of nature, because they are brute animals lacking reason."[28]

Therefore the difference between a churchman's virtues and those of a layman, and the priest's excellence in virtue, must be as great as the difference between man made to the image of God, and the beasts, whose souls perish with their bodies. Such and so great is the position of a churchman! How notable his dignity to handle souls most precious, the Sacraments, the very Body of Christ; to be the instrument of divine operations in souls; to be able to forgive sins; to have rightful authority over souls, an authority much more excellent than that of emperors over bodies. And someone who has a dignity like that is going to think a commonplace life is enough for him? Will he be content with commonplace virtue? Alas, this mistake is beyond measure. Therefore, those who surpass those limits and daily strive to conquer themselves by virtue—these are the male births, the perfect births.

I have already passed over the fact that sins which are light in others are proportionately more serious in a churchman; and those which are mortal

---

[28]Again, St. Charles has been inspired by the great Latin Doctor: St. Gregory the Great, *Pastoral Rule*, Book II, chapter 1 (cf. note 53 above).

in others, are sacrilegious in them for they sully a person consecrated to God. For if this very place has the power, because it is sacred, to make a simple theft or some other crime a sacrilege as well, how much more will that be the case with a living dwelling and temple of the Holy Spirit, O priest? Which is more sacred to God? Those walls or the priest himself? Certainly it is on account of the priest and the duties he will carry out that the walls are consecrated. Passing over these things that are certain, let us at least understand that in the degree we excel others in dignity, to that degree also must we excel everyone in virtue.

Nor is it for us to congratulate ourselves with this mistaken standard, by which we assess our virtues with the common virtues of other men; but we must apply *good measure, pressed down and shaken together* (Lk. 6:38). Indeed there are some who have come to know this true standard, yet they measure not themselves but others with it. They want to direct others to a perfection in the direction of which they themselves will not lift a foot. These are those who *say, and do not* (Mt. 23:3), who show others the way into which they themselves do not wish to enter. They build an ark for Noah and his children, but not going into it themselves are submerged in the waters of the flood. Concerning these measures and standards, the Lord says: *Diverse weights and diverse measures, both are abominable before God* (Prov. 20:10). That is to say, with one weight, the lighter one, you weigh your own deeds, and with another, the heavier one, the deeds of others. With one short length you measure your virtues, but another, longer and more extended, for measuring those of others. This is abominable to God. Rather, if it is permitted to have weight and weight, measure and measure, then you should use the heavier weight and the longer unit of measure for weighing and measuring your own works. You are the form of the faithful, O priest. You have been constituted their example. You are the exemplar placed on a mountain, and according to that example the faithful must arrange the pattern of their habits and lives. What you take care to effect in others, you must first bring forth in yourself, in order to be *a pattern of the flock* (1 Pet. 5:3) in the Lord. But what I tell you, I say first of all to myself, and to all prelates, for we are placed as lights upon a candlestick (Mt. 5:14). But I also say it to you who have been called to a share in our care and solicitude.

And there are other priests who are utterly greedy and parsimonious with God, and in regard to him they are not afraid to construct the most subtle reasonings, not calling to mind that even if they did much more than what they do, they would nevertheless still be *unprofitable servants* (Lk. 17:10). They will examine something with the greatest possible diligence in this way: "Am I bound to do this by a prescription of the constitutions, or not? Is it a mortal sin, or not?" For unless they are held bound under danger of sin or the decree of a prelate, they do not wish to do it. They keep the strict letter of the law, but in fact they do not even succeed at that, since the law itself prescribes that we are to be generous with God, and *a cheerful giver*, the kind of people he *loves* above all (2 Cor. 9:7). O good God, who have been so generous to all creatures, but to men especially, and priests above all; who have given your gifts so copiously; who when you had nothing else to give, finally gave even yourself, and your blood: O how great an injury is brought upon you and your generosity, when we treat you so stingily.

This is certainly not the sacerdotal spirit, brothers; this spirit is not ecclesiastical. It is an utterly low and vile spirit, which has nevertheless gotten itself marked with the royal dignity. So is such stinginess with God fitting for heroic men, so noble and sublime? Far from us, far from us be this low indignity. O how miserable and unhappy we would be if God treated us in this way, and when we have sinned, by what law is he bound at once to start awaiting our repentance? Why would he be unable to cast us immediately into Hell? What has he received from us, which would bind him to bestow his grace and gifts on us?

Beware, beware, brothers, so as not to provoke God's wrath upon us, so as not to persist in offending his majesty. For nothing is harder, even for men, than to be beneficial and utterly generous to someone from whom the only response is ingratitude. It is this kind of tight and stingy person that the Lord hates and detests the most. He taught us this most clearly by the example of that servant to whom he had remitted his entire debt, but who then held and throttled his fellow servant. The master willed him to be bound by punishment and chains and to stay there until he paid back the debt down to the last fraction. And which of us could ever repay our infinite debts with God, if we were bound to that? If even a single mortal crime should be punished by eternal death? Therefore let us be liberal with God, so that he can be more liberal with us; for this will be a sowing of blessings, and likewise a reaping of blessings afterward.

There is another variety of giving birth spiritually, for there are some who have good will and good desires only up to a certain degree, as long as religious service and devotion to God bring advantages with them, for as long as there is peace and tranquility. As long as the whole affair consisted in the celebration of Masses and frequent reception of the Holy Eucharist, these people follow God and Christ in themselves and bring him to birth in others. But when they come to contradictions and persecutions which must be borne, to extreme poverty which must be endured, to the shedding of their blood for souls and their neighbors, then right away they fall away from God, even though at another time they were priests of upright life, praiseworthy morals and sufficient learning, but no more. The harvest indeed is great, brothers, but workers who would be willing to bear the weight and heat of the day are few (cf. Lk. 10:2; Mt. 20:12). In the morning and evening hours, many will gladly labor, but when the sun begins to shoot forth its rays and heat, these immediately leave the work behind and flee to leisure and quiet.

Paul was the kind of worker in this field of the Lord who could say that just having food to eat and clothes to wear would be enough for him (cf. 1 Tim. 6:8), and still, even in those bare necessities, he suffered great want. Can we conceive what kind of want that was, since when he was rich by his own estimation, he barely had enough to sustain him? Who could ever imagine the hunger, thirst, labors and troubles that Paul endured in the preaching of the Gospel? When he found himself in the greatest poverty, he did not want to ask people for anything so that the Gospel would not be rendered a burden for them. And we miserable ones indeed wish to labor in the vineyard of the Lord, but only as much as, and for as long as we like— and still we think we are something? O how far we stray from the truth; for he who does not have the spirit of Paul, and is not prepared to serve God *In labor and painfulness, in much watchings, in hunger and thirst, in fastings often, in cold and nakedness* (2 Cor. 11:27) and calumnies, what this man brings to birth is entirely imperfect and female.

A different mind, a different soul is required in us, so that we may be ready to bear all labors; *for* (says the Apostle) *we are appointed thereunto* (1 Thess. 3:3). To our first parent Eve, God said: *in sorrow shall you bring forth children* (Gen. 3:16); and you, O priest, think you can bring Christ to birth in yourself and in others without pain or trouble of any kind? Christ brought forth children for the Father with such great pain and shedding of blood, and death; and you are going to consider yourself to be of a higher class than the Son of God? You are wrong, you are wrong: *A woman, when she is in labor, has sorrow* (Jn 16:21), and has pain, and you will in no way be able to give birth without pain.

But do not be terrified, brothers, by this necessity for pain and labor. Certainly the greatest happiness is joined to it. If we understand things by human calculation, the life of a priest is indeed the most miserable, for together with Paul I will say that *If in this life only we have hope in Christ, we are of all men most miserable* (1 Cor. 15:19). But a different spirit is required if we are to consider all those things which have been said or prescribed to us. Thus among the Hebrews who murmured upon hearing from the explorers that giants lived in the land of Canaan, the Lord had this to say about Caleb, who checked the people's murmuring and exhorted them to complete the journey: *My servant Caleb, who being full of another spirit has followed me, I will bring into this land which he hath gone round: and his seed shall possess it* (Num. 14:24). Therefore these things are not to be weighed with the spirit of the flesh, for in testifying to Peter that he had confessed rightly concerning him, the Lord said that *flesh and blood had not revealed* it to him (Mt. 16:17).

Therefore the priest with a priestly spirit, when he takes in all these things, will find them all quite easy and sweet but to the priest who does not have the priestly spirit, those same things will seem laborious, onerous, heavy and unbearable: *Youths shall faint* (says Isaiah) *and labor, and young men shall fall by infirmity* (Isa. 40:30). Such are adhering only to the spirit of the flesh: *But they that hope in the Lord shall renew their strength* (Isa. 40:31). And how will they change? Indeed they will be filled with divine strength, of him, I say, who assuming our infirmity, communicated to us his strength: *they shall take wings as eagles, they shall run and not be weary, they shall walk and not faint* (Isa. 40:31). O how wonderfully does it lighten the load if we consider the utterly abundant reward prepared for the priest who conducts his ministry faithfully, whether in ruling souls or in the celebration of Mass. How utterly divine it is to cooperate with God in the salvation of souls. This will entirely bring it about, that good priests will run and not feel burdened; walk and not fall faint; bring to birth, and barely feel the torments. Let sorrows come, let labors come, let dangers come, together with poverty and infamy. Let there be the peaks of the highest mountains to conquer, let it be necessary to separate ourselves as far as possible from kin and our own home, let there be a parish to accept in the poorest and most uncomfortable places. They will not flee any of these, but rather, like Christ's servant Andrew, they will go forth to meet the cross already so long desired.

But we must add that it is not in the future life alone that consolation is set forth to us by the Lord, but in the midst of the labors themselves the greatest joys are mixed in, and they are so vast that all human labor does not equal them. Who can express how great is the joy of that mind which sees one soul regained for Christ by his own work? He can say, "This man was a sinner; he had wandered away from the path; he was liable to eternal death, all tied up with the chains of a thousand sins. Through me he has now been made another man; I have rescued him from the jaws of both the devil and Hell. I have restored him to God; I have cleansed God's image in him which he had deformed." These joys are infinite. No human consolations, whether those of the most powerful kings or of the richest men or of youths dissipating themselves with all pleasures, can be compared with them.

The angels rejoice in heaven over this, O priest, whoever you may be, and they give credit for this joy of theirs in part to you. They hope for thrones left vacant among them to be filled, and for that ruin among their ranks, which came from sin, to be repaired by your work.[29] With what solicitude do you think they are ready to fly in protection to you, whom they see to be God's coworker and, if I may say so, their own consoler? This is a joy which easily tempers all the pains of birth. For just as *A woman, when she is in labor, has sorrow, because her hour is come; but when she has brought forth the child, she remembers no more the anguish, for joy that a man is born into the world* (Jn 16:21), so priests like that, though they labor and suffer cruelly giving birth to Christ both in themselves and in others, nevertheless, when they see the newborn brought forth, will see their sorrows, their labors and their torments cease, and they will no longer remember the *anguish* which they had because Christ has been born in them and in others by their work.

Here, most beloved brothers, I must digress a little, although it will not be digression to narrate how many things God has done in us, and how wide the fields and harvests are, which he sets before us, and in which, if we so wish, we can by our labors bring forth the most abundant harvests. In our hands, reverend priests, we have the opportunity for doing heroic, priestly works. As you know, the regions of Raetia are nearby, concerning which I cannot begin to say how alienated they are from the true and living God; the enemy of faith and all good, the devil, had overcome them. Oratories, churches, and altars had been profaned; the Catholic religion had crumbled and was being more or less maintained only by a few and the very poorest, and it seemed that soon even the dim light of faith holding out in them was going to be extinguished. We have been in those parts out of obedience, sent by the most holy Vicar of Christ; and immediately upon arrival the Lord gave us such prompt obedience and wonderful dispositions from the people, and such great constancy under persecutions after our departure, that the grounds for praising the divine goodness were truly vast.

---

[29]Here Borromeo is following the position of St. Augustine, and others in the tradition like St. Bernard of Clairvaux, who held that the creation of man was in view of filling the ranks in Heaven made vacant by the rebellion of Lucifer and those angels who fell with him.

Among the priests there was no one who ministered the Sacraments legitimately, who aided those poor Catholics, who strengthened them; and immediately upon our arrival, they showed themselves so docile that as soon as they heard the voice of God through us, many were reconciled to God. Others returned to the bosom of Holy Mother Church, and when finally refreshed by the most holy Sacraments, they were so strengthened in their devout resolution that in these recent days they gave an admirable spectacle of constancy in religion, when they were so utterly afflicted, tested and harassed by the heretics over the mountains in Chur and others as well, heretics who destroyed the seminary of the Jesuit Fathers which had been established there. They freely professed with raised voice that they were ready to take up arms and risk their lives, rather than ever fall away from their newly conceived ardor of soul. And their firmness and constancy of faith has grown so much, that when we consider our own coldness, we are red with shame, seeing how those rough and uncultured peoples, so alien to all religion and city life, acquiesced so readily to our admonitions, and were so capable of receiving the help we left them through a few priests we left behind and others we later sent.

O happy are those priests who have begun to expend and exhaust themselves in a project so pleasing to God. How happy too, those who themselves *She has put out her hand to strong things* (Prov. 31:19). The way is open, brothers, for reaping the most abundant fruits. Help the work along with your prayers. Who knows, perhaps you clergy here present will be the instrument of divine mercy among those most numerous peoples for directing them in the way of salvation, just like in those times of our most blessed Father St. Ambrose. Almighty God has prepared this mercy for this clergy, but only if we are present to accept it. Therefore as much as I can, I commend this great work to your Most Holy Sacrifices and prayers. If we want perfect and male births, then we must help these souls. I myself testify to you before our Lord Jesus Christ, that most of the calamities of that people come from lack of good and legitimate priests. And if we are going to be able to bring the remedy to such evils, will we be afraid of poverty? Labor? Deaths? Are we going to see such an abundant harvest ready for reaping, and still have a legitimate excuse before God if we refuse to cooperate out of fear of the inconveniences? O priests, brothers, O you Oblates first of all, whose principal mandate is to be excellent in all ecclesiastical ministries and to fulfill in a certain more excellent and perfect manner those things which the whole clergy is bound to do. How great is the occasion which opens up for you. Therefore what are you doing, why are you delaying, instead of all of you crying out to the Lord with "Here we are, Lord, send us"? (cf. Isa. 6:8). I pray the good and great God, that he efficaciously show all here present how pleasing this whole work shall be to him; and that he inflame the hearts of many, so that, freely desiring to serve God alone, they may approach and apply with all their hearts to join the Oblates.

...

Those poor Christians ask with the greatest insistence that priests be sent from here. They themselves attest that in very great measure their calamities arose from the scandals given by priests who went back to those parts from here and apostatized from the faith. Therefore we owe them a lot more; for whatever sin the wicked heretics saw among us, who are the closest neighbors to those parts, they straightaway exaggerated from their platforms and pulpits in front of those unfortunate people, and in this way seduced innumerable simple souls. Or do you not reckon that many come from those regions daily, even to this very church, in order to spy on our every action and then report it back to their own? I know that is a fact; and on this account I firmly hold that we are also bound in conscience to repair those ruinous conditions, which in great measure were brought upon them from us.

But since we are on the topic of those regions at a distance from us, brothers, we might also call to mind so many peoples who are abandoned in our diocese, so many people deprived of priests, so many little ones hungering for the word of God and the most holy Sacraments. But I know what many will say: "Who will want to remove himself there, where the poverty is the worst there can be? Where there is nothing but protruding mountains and places difficult of access? Where day and night you have to labor and endure the greatest hardships?" And on that account, brothers, souls redeemed by the most precious blood of Christ will perish so that we can be comfortable? Shall our delights be preferred to the salvation of souls? This, my dearly beloved, is what I find intolerable, what I can hardly endure: that we have here not a few men who, when some church is offered to them to serve, immediately respond that it is not satisfactory to them, or is too distant from their blood relatives and close friends. O would that we had none of that spirit in this whole assembly of clerics. The things I am proposing to you today, brothers, are heroic works, male and perfect births. Or rather, these churches should be willingly accepted just because they are what they are, and involve so much labor. They are the very ones which we should willingly embrace since more glory is given to God.

But do you know what it is that makes us tepid in our ministry? Certainly nothing else than our not considering what souls, Hell and Paradise really are. Why therefore should we wonder at holy men filled with charity, who were so zealous to acquire souls? Who will not admire the zeal of the great Roman Pontiff Gregory?[30] One day, when on account of traveling businessmen great markets were being held in the Roman Forum, and many had streamed from all sides into one place for buying goods, it happened that Gregory, still a monk, passed by. He saw, among other things up for sale, slave-boys light in color, well-formed, of handsome face and very blond hair, and he asked the merchant what country he had brought them from. He responded: "From the island of Britain, where all the inhabitants' faces shine brightly like these." Gregory said: "Are those islanders Christians, or are they still tied up with pagan errors?" The merchant responded: "They are not Christians, but enmeshed in the traps of paganism." Then Gregory said, with a heavy sigh: "O, for grief, what splendid faces are presently in the possession of the prince of darkness, and how their splendid appearance up front carries a mind empty of the internal grace of God!" Then approaching the Pontiff Benedict,[31] he succeeded, with powerful petitions, in getting his request to be sent to that island, in order to rescue souls most precious from the power of the demon. Once the favor had been granted, and he had been on his way for three days, he was called back to Rome by the same pontiff, since the Romans were all complaining and reacting with the greatest bitterness to the permission for such a servant of God to leave the city of Rome.

But that most ardent desire of helping souls lodged in his soul and cast the deepest roots into his breast. For afterward, having been raised to the pontificate, he most clearly showed how much value he attached to souls. When his turbulent thoughts pressed upon him, for converting the Anglo-Saxons, as when he was still a monk, and when he had begun the fourth year of his pontificate, he sent Augustine[32] on mission to evangelize Britain, together with two other monks of his monastery. But after some days of the long journey they had undertaken, weighed down with weariness, they decided

---

[30]Pope St. Gregory the Great (590–604).

[31]Pope Benedict I (575–79).

[32]St. Augustine of Canterbury (d. 604), Benedictine monk of St. Andrew monastery in Rome and first Archbishop of Canterbury, who was sent by Pope St. Gregory the Great to evangelize the Angles.

to return home rather than go to a barbarous, savage and unbelieving nation whose language they did not even understand. For this they sent Augustine back to Rome, asking the supreme Prelate to cancel such an uncertain and dangerous journey as the one he had just imposed upon them. But not only did the most holy Gregory not grant their requests, but he also exhorted them to proceed, using the gravest words, and also indicating how strongly he himself was held by the desire of having a share in their work.

With how much zeal for souls did that most holy virgin Catherine of Siena not burn? Since she had received from the Lord, among other extraordinary gifts, the gift also of seeing the pains both of Hell and purgatory, and the joys of Heaven, and likewise the beauty of the souls of men. Thirsting with such ardor for their salvation, like the apostle Paul, she desired to become anathema for her brothers. For some persons heard her thus expressing herself in prayer during an ecstasy: "My Lord, how shall I be able to bear the fact that beings formed after your image perish for eternity? Would it not bring greater increase to your glory if, charity remaining, I alone perished, putting up my body as a block to Hell's entrance, so that I would endure all the torments of Gehenna, instead of so many thousands of souls who would be excluded from the company of your blessedness?"

But to this petition the Lord responded (as afterward she revealed to her confessor), that it was in no way possible for charity to be found in Hell. For the force and power of charity are so great that it would extinguish the flames of Gehenna, rather than suffer any harm from them. O what zeal she had, so truly and utterly worthy of all Christians. O if only we could see what it is to liberate one soul from the jaws of Hell, I do not doubt that today many would come here to us and petition to become Oblates. And they would not only cross mountains, but also expose themselves to all the greatest and most obvious dangers to life, wherever there might be hope for recovering even one soul. *How beautiful are the feet of them that preach the gospel of peace* (Rom. 10:15). Why should we wonder at the fact that the most holy virgin of Siena used to immediately kiss the ground wherever some preacher had passed, because the feet of Christ's coworkers had trod over it? Nothing is more pleasing to God than for us to become helpers of his Son. Nothing is more delightful to Christ than to find men who will bear this yoke with him. Nothing refreshes Holy Mother Church more than to see her sons giving birth in this way. In sum, these men despoil Hell, lay the demon low, exterminate sin, open paradise, fill the empty thrones of heaven, give joy to the angels, glorify the most holy Trinity, and prepare themselves eternal and unfading crowns.

Second part

And she cried travailing in birth, and was in pain to be delivered (Rev. 12:4). It is necessary, most dearly beloved, to *cry out*, to make our voices loud. If we do not come to the aid of our Church, who will? Who will do this? Who will reform the peoples? Behold, only people like these are good examples for the people, the ministers, the leaders, the spiritual mothers and fathers. For who will minister the divine graces to the peoples? Those here present. Will we finally bring this birth about? With God's goodness favoring us, I hope we shall do it; and to this end we shall take care that you be supplied with everything necessary.

But once the newborn has been brought forth, do torments and cries cease? Not at all. Rather a new reason for solicitude presents itself again: it is necessary to nurse, feed, and diligently guard this newborn. The woman about whom the above cited words in the Apocalypse were written, she who *cried travailing in birth, and was in pain to be delivered*, gave birth to a son. But the huge dragon was waiting so that with mouth opened, and tormented with rabid hunger, he could immediately swallow the newborn. Wherefore she who before the birth was tormented with stern sorrows, is constrained to feel new pains after the birth. All women who have borne children will not dispute that. Most certainly great diligence and solicitude must be employed in feeding and guarding little children, as that most tender age is always exposed to a thousand dangers.

But the invisible birth requires a much greater level of care than the bodily and visible one. O accursed dragon and devil, how much I see you lying in wait always for these delicate offspring just born; how much you delight in these tender souls. With reason indeed did Jeremiah lament with tears, saying, *he has filled his belly with my delicate meats* (Jer. 51:34). You have devoured so many little ones; you have filled the infernal prisons with many little infants. This has been done by your ministers at your suggestion. Thus Pharaoh, at your instigation, drowned the little boys. Thus Herod, at your persuasion, ordered all the innocent little boys killed. How many times does a man decide to change his life, giving serious consideration to a complete reformation of his ways; but when he then sets out do something, immediately the demon swallows up the offspring.

A high degree of care is indeed required from you, brothers, so you do not lose the ardor of spirit which you have conceived here, nor permit the delicate offspring you have brought forth to be devoured, whether by losing the devout sentiment with which you have been filled, or by permitting the good things you will bring forth in others immediately to perish. What a sorrow it is. How many parish priests having care of souls bring Christ forth in not a few people, and then fail to care for them. When the greatest care and diligence must be employed, they interrupt all their work, thinking they already have done more than enough. What kind of impiety is this? Not even beasts and brute animals do this, rather they nurse their newborns, foster, feed and protect them from all possible adversities with their beaks, their teeth, their claws or in whatever ways they can. And so where is that care and solicitude required for the education of the child who has been born? And are you going to abandon the delicate little one? When effort and sweat are needed all the more, will you take your leisure and remain inert? When his soul is more flexible, and more disposed to receiving and carrying out salutary admonitions, will you wash your hands of him, as they say, and involve yourself no more in care for him?

Brothers, this is a great fault. It is great laziness, and a fierce cruelty to that soul. Concerning such things, a most exact account will have to be rendered to the Spouse of souls. If people have fallen ill, do they want to be deserted by the doctor before they have completely recovered? And if those who are held in sickness of the body demand such assiduous care from doctors, why is that they immediately abandon souls when they are barely healed of the pestilence of sin, and are still weak and infirm? The demon does not sleep, brothers. No, he does not sleep; rather he is laying traps constantly, mouth always open, prepared to devour. He is always seeking the death of our offspring. Therefore countermeasures must be employed, and we must be constantly anxious with solicitude, and protect what we gave birth to.

But protection is not to be provided only while the offspring is yet little. When he has matured and grown, he is still at risk; for never are we safe from sin, as long as we abide in this vale of tears. We are always surrounded by dangers, by traps, by enemies. Certainly it lies in wait in the first place, as we have said, for the tender offspring only recently born, but it does not cease on that account to attack those who are older, and adults. For the cruelty of Pharaoh as well could not be satisfied with the drowning of the little boys, and never did give up pursuing even the whole people, until, at the demand of the divine justice, it had to pay the due penalty of its temerity. Therefore protection is always necessary. Therefore holy Church always calls out and is tormented, daily thinks up and employs new plans, calls new synods and gatherings, and is visiting her ministers day by day.

And for this reason, both by us and by our visitators, we will visit you and your churches. He who considers himself safe is the one who is in greater danger, and he who thinks he needs nothing is the one worse off than the rest.

But there are two dangers which above all are much to be feared in the case of offspring already grown to adulthood, and especially churchmen.

The first danger is that malignant and burning wind of pride. O what a swirling storm is the pride which often forces shipwreck on pitiful ships, not only on the deep sea, but even in port, when they seem to be more safe. Take this priest who became quite learned, advanced in studies, is quite suitable for preaching, is endowed with a pleasing personality, especially when preaching, is very good likewise in hearing confessions, has come to know the value which should be attached to souls, and is most zealous for them. He is not avaricious, nor stained by lusts; he is a man of upright living, and of habits worthy of a churchman. But seeing himself in such a state, this miserable man begins to be blinded by the very light itself. He looks down on others as less learned than himself, considers himself above certain pitiful old priests who lacked all helps necessary for advancing in studies, places himself before others, presumes much about himself, vaunts himself and whatever is his. Miserable and unhappy man: he suddenly loses everything all at once. The wind of pride blows and dries up all those good things and virtues with which he used to shine.

O careless young man, has God conferred so much mercy on you that you should be born in these times, raised in wonderful surroundings, and have such great advantages for studying, all so you can turn proud? Lower yourself rather with everyone else, and with all submission and humility give thanks to God, who has not done so much for other priests who, if they had only had just a little help, most certainly would have progressed much more than you. Let there be no proud learning in this clergy; let there be no knowledge which puffs up among these priests; let there rather be less knowledge, but more humility. The greatest danger coming into port is that of dashing the ship against the rock of proud exaltation and so shipwreck, with the most sorrowful and red-faced loss of all the good things which had been brought forth with the greatest labor.

But why should another man become proud on account of having received an ecclesiastical dignity and some ministry or prelacy over many souls? This man should rather humble himself, for he is the servant of all those souls, and the more souls are committed to his faith and pastoral care, the more souls he is bound to serve. Wherefore the Roman Pontiff too, having the care of the whole Church, is rightly called not only servant, but servant of the servants.

And this other priest is going to be proud because he now knows that he knows a lot and is quite advanced in learning? What does he have which he did not receive? And if he received it, why does he glory as if he had not received it? (1 Cor. 4:7).

But neither are there lacking those who when they become aware that they have done some excellent and heroic work, become proud on account of it. Let this spirit be totally absent from all of you, my brothers. Peter after fishing all night had taken nothing, but in the morning, at the command of the Lord, lowering the nets, he filled them and dragged many fish to shore. He didn't become proud on that account, did he? On the contrary he was more humble, and turned to Jesus said, *Depart from me, for I am a sinful man, O Lord* (Lk. 5:8). O priest, be like that! So you have gained a thousand souls for Christ; granted, you have filled the nets. But always humble yourself more, saying, "O my God, who am I, through whom you have deigned to do so many things? I, a most pitiful little worm, was able to become in some way an instrument of such great works? Far from me, far from me be it, to ascribe this to myself; I acknowledge that I am nothing, but everything is yours. Only sins and infirmities are mine, but whatever good has been done through me came down in its entirety *from the Father of lights* (Jas 1:17), the author of every good."

And truly the more someone draws near to God, the more humble he will be, since the more we approach the light of the sun, the more we see even the slightest dark spots which were hidden before. Thus the priest, the more frequently he celebrates and becomes more united to God, rightly has the eyes of his mind enlightened, and comes to know and see his imperfections. This was true of all the saints. Thus Abraham, when the Lord appeared and spoke to him, was not for that reason exalted with pride, but rather humbled, saying, *I will speak to my Lord, whereas I am dust and ashes* (Gen. 18:27).

And a second danger also threatens the offspring once he is adult, a danger which is all the greater for being not being recognized and taken with sufficient seriousness. I mean the falling off of fervor in the works of God. This will perhaps appear a small thing to you, but believe me, it is a very great danger. I am not now speaking here about the tepid, about whom it is said, *you say: I am rich, and know not*; whom the Lord reproves, saying, *I would you were cold, or hot. But because you are lukewarm, and neither cold, not hot, I will begin to vomit you out of my mouth* (Rev. 3:15–16). Rather I am speaking about those who are perfect and advanced in the way of the Lord, entirely complete in purity of life and in all heroic kinds of virtues. I say that for such men as these, what they must avoid above all is a falling off, even a slight falling off, of their fervor and the first warmth of their charity. For in a short time, this can bring entire ruin upon them and cause them to lose every good thing.

Do not believe this from me, brethren, but believe the Holy Spirit saying through John, *Unto the angel of the church of Ephesus write: These things says he, who holds the seven stars in his right hand, who walks in the midst of the seven golden candlesticks: I know your works, and your labor, and your patience, and how you cannot bear them that are evil, and you have tried them, who say they are apostles, and are not, and have found them liars: And you have patience, and have endured for my name, and have not fainted. But I have somewhat against you* (Rev. 2:1–4). This bishop must have been truly great, brothers, in order to receive so many praises from God, and to hear so many virtues of his enumerated, but what does the Lord have against him? *Because* (he says) *you have left your first charity* (Rev. 2:4). He had not sinned mortally, but had only grown a little remiss in his first fervor. "There are not a few who over the course of time little by little suffer loss to their virtues."[33] So what did this bishop have to be afraid of? Listen: *Be mindful therefore from whence you are fallen: and do penance, and do the first works. Or else I come to you, and will move your candlestick out of its place, except you do penance* (Rev. 2:5); that is to say, I will take away your virtues and gifts, to which you will never afterward return, but you will remain darkened, ignoble, and low.

Therefore, most dearly beloved, let each of you think about the fervor he once had when he began to serve God, and let him make efforts to recover that fervor and accomplish its first works, for this is the rule of spiritual perfection: to promote the works of God in the same spirit in which they were begun. No matter how much he has advanced, let no one trust in himself, but let us always keep some fear, and let no one think himself unable to perish because he has brought offspring to birth and maturity, and has educated them. Even men who seemed most holy have sometimes fallen most shamefully, and those who began to take it easy, fell most miserably. Here I could present innumerable examples to you, but I will conclude with a single example, from which we shall learn not to trust in ourselves, and when we have sinned, to wipe out our sins by penitence.

Genebaldus the monk,[34] who had been consecrated bishop of Laon by the most holy Rémi, archbishop of Rheims, having left his wife who

---

[33]St. Gregory the Great, *Moralia in Job*, Book 19.

[34]Genebaldus was a Frankish bishop of Laon (France) during the fifth century. He had married, and later renounced conjugal life, either for the monastic state or the episcopate, both of which require continence. Ordination of married men to the priesthood was frequent in the early centuries, and historical sources mention the consent of the wife. Genebaldus' story is known to us from the tenth century chronicle of Flodoard. In his detailed history of clerical continence and celibacy, Christian Cochini, S.J., comments that the story "probably has a kernel of truth" (*The Apostolic Origins of Priestly Celibacy*, trans. Nelly Marans [San Francisco, CA: Ignatius Press, 1990], 111).

was a niece of blessed Rémi, became overconfident about his life up to that point and the sublimity of his position, when he should have been thinking that he was not wiser than either David or Solomon when they exposed themselves to the soft charms of women; he incautiously allowed his wife, whom he had renounced, to visit him frequently, as though she were only a sister of his, coming for salutary instruction. He forgot the passage of Scripture, *Waters wear away the stones, and with inundation the ground by little and little is washed away* (Job 14:19). And so it happened that the repeated visits and frequent sweet conversations of the woman incited the heart of the bishop to lust, and the thing did not stop there. The ardor of lust burst into flames, and he conceived a son of her who had once been his spouse. In utter shame, Genebaldus wanted to name him "Thief." But by a most imprudent decision, and wanting too much to maintain his honor, he ordered the woman to keep visiting him, so that no suspicion of a sin hidden to men, but not to God, would arise in the eyes of the people who would notice that suddenly he was now avoiding her. And so again he fell miserably into sin, and she bore him a daughter, whom he named "Little she-fox."

Finally, with a glance over at him who had looked upon Peter and brought him to the bitterest tears, Genebaldus acknowledged and bewailed his sin, and touched by the heaviest sorrow of heart, entreated Rémi to come to him as soon as possible. When Rémi had come, he opened the wound of his soul to him in a secret room, and with the greatest contrition, wanting to give back the stole and renounce the episcopate. But when both of them had wept for a long time, St. Rémi then began to console him and urge him not to despair of the divine mercy, but strive to wipe out the sin by penance. Then he enjoined penance upon him, closing him up in a little dwelling made in the manner of a tomb, for seven years, that he might do penance there, eating his bread with ashes and tears. When finally after seven years of continuous weeping and prayers, in the night vigil of Holy Thursday, which he had spent in prayer and in bewailing the fact that he who had been ordained to reconcile penitents to God on that day, had made himself unworthy even to stand among the penitents in church, in accordance with the gravity of his crimes, on that occasion an angel of the Lord appeared to him, announcing that his sin was remitted, and opening the doors despite the seal the archbishop had placed on them, ordering him to come out. But Genebaldus refused to come out until Rémi, who had enclosed him, should order him to, and also adding that even if he should see the Lord Jesus coming to him, he would not come out until he had seen Rémi. Then Rémi, informed by an angel, came and with the greatest joy restored him to the ministry he had once been given. He then lived a most holy life afterward.

Brothers, what do you think about such a man? How many things you can learn from him! But be sure you learn never to believe too much in yourselves, and learn how dangerous it is to live in close proximity with women, even relatives of one degree or another. Learn how dangerous it is to not remove the first beginnings of sin, and to persist in them. Learn how entirely you must obey your bishops and prelates. Finally, weep from to time, and lament over yourselves, since you have been ordained to justify and reconcile others to God, but have often made yourselves hateful to God by your sins.

May God all good and most high grant us, beloved brethren, to have these things we have said today inscribed with iron letters in our hearts, so they never depart our souls. But ever solicitous with fear and trembling, let us give birth, in ourselves and in our subjects, to the Lord Jesus, and keep him there. To him be honor and glory through unending ages. Amen.

CHAPTER 4
MAKING THE WORLD HOLY

Daily Christian living

A booklet of reminders for the people of the city and the diocese of Milan for living as a Christian, in what is common to every state in life, and in particular to fathers and mothers of families, masters and heads of workshops, and for workers.
December 20, 1577

...

Charles, Cardinal of S. Prassede, Archbishop, to his beloved people in the city and the diocese of Milan.

Greetings in the Lord.

The hand of God has been so kind to us in the scourge of pestilence with which he has visited us in these times, that we can also well understand how he seeks only our conversion and life, not our death.

His divine majesty had hardly unleashed the sword of his most just wrath against our sins, when he remembered that we are also his people and little children; and thus the depths of his mercies were moved on account of our affliction.

How right was the holy King and Prophet David to hope always for such testimonies of the goodness of God that with sweetest feelings of living hope he would say in the midst of his tribulations: *Will God forget to show mercy? Or will he in his anger shut up his mercies?* (Ps. 76:10). But at the same time he would again make his heart firm and renew his good intentions in the service of God, clearly recognizing his liberation by the divine hand from his every affliction and calamity, and so he added those words: *And I said, now have I begun: this is the change of the right hand of the most High* (Ps. 76:11).

O most beloved children, does it not seem to you, that such a special mercy of God as the liberation of this great city from the mass death which he was threatening from the beginning of this calamitous pestilence, deserves and requires from us a corresponding resolution of renewal of life and customs, praise and thanksgiving to his divine Majesty, in recognition of such a benefit? Let Milan fix in her heart and forever say in this remembrance: "This indeed has been a change of the right hand of the most high God. I reckon I will now begin to live for my God who has again given me life. I now and forever renounce sin, the old Adam, my licentious life, debaucheries, laziness, pride, my disordered self-displays and all other ingrained bad habits. Let there now be a beginning of that true spiritual renewal to which God has called and is calling me in so many ways."

You, Lord, who have the power to renew the heavens, the earth and all things, give to all of us that new heart, that new spirit which you promised us through the mouth of your prophet: *And I will give you a new heart, and put a new spirit within you* (Ezek. 36:26). Bestow it upon us, Lord, with such abundance of your grace that it will produce in us, efficaciously and constantly, new resolutions, new customs, a new way of life and in the end that eternal renewal which the new Adam, our Lord Jesus Christ, already came into the world to bring us.

With this help, when our heart shall be enlarged, the reforms will no longer appear hard, nor your service burdensome. But the yoke will be sweet and the weight of your holy commandments light to us.

Dear children, this is the sentiment with which we must all gratefully recognize both the health in which we find ourselves, thanks be to God, after such evident danger, and the life which, after such a terrifying threat of death, God has granted us, for a longer space of life in penitence, such as we need.

To this end, and with hope that those who still have not borne fruit in the last scourge, will now necessarily consider this liberation bestowed upon us even more strongly than the last one and which human reason persuaded us, we have brought together some reminders for Christian living, common to every state in life, and some others which are more particular to fathers of families, and yet others for heads and masters of workshops, their servants and workers. We have printed all of them in a booklet so that each and every person may have them ready at hand, often before their eyes and kept alive in his memory. He is not only to know them but above all to practice them, because the well-being of our lives consists in the observance and not just in thought of the will of God.

Dear children, this task of ours is always opportune as a help for your salvation which we desire so much. But certainly this present time has appeared most opportune…

So to this occasion we must add another, which we are already celebrating, in which the Church celebrates the solemn memorial of the holy Birth of our Lord Jesus Christ, and together with this all the fullness of grace and blessing which he has brought to us.

Before such grand liberality of the Lord, how could we his ministers not burn with ardor to make some special spiritual gift over to you our dear children, who are so much and so paternally loved by us.

…

What a gift it would be to help you spend time usefully in these feasts instead of card games, debaucheries and other pernicious activities with which, sometimes, those sacred days are unfortunately profaned and provoke the wrath of God upon us. Rather it would be to fruitfully spend your whole life with that gratitude that we owe immeasurably for those singular benefits which the goodness of God has always made over to us in this time.

It therefore remains for you, dear children, just as we with such affection exhort and beg you in the Lord, to seize, embrace and fruitfully put into practice these our reminders, in such a way that their execution may be abundant consolation for you and us.

In particular we lay this charge upon those who have others under their care. As much as possible we wish to efficaciously recommend the total and diligent observance of these reminders especially to you, fathers of families and other heads of households or workshops, in such a way that not only you observe and practice them exactly, but that you make sure they are studiously and fruitfully put into practice by your children, servants, stable boys, your whole family and by others who depend on you.

Nor is it we who give you this charge. God himself gave it to you when he commanded you to have care of them, and he has so many times given assurance that you must render a strict account in his tribunal at the point of your death and at the last judgment.

For this purpose we say to you in the same way that the apostle St. Paul said to his disciple Timothy (cf. 2 Tim. 4:1–2), namely, that before God, who is to judge the living and the dead, we seek that you spare no effort and be most solicitous to induce everyone under you to the practice and execution of these our reminders, and of all the things which concern the observance of the divine precepts.

Insist in season and out of season, beg, abjure, reprove, correct according to need. Where correction does not help, send away from your houses and workshops all bad and dissolute servants, shop-boys and workers, rather than make yourself partakers of their sins by your negligence or tolerance, and before they ruin the Christian discipline of your houses and workshops with their corrupt customs and bad habits. Otherwise you may draw upon yourselves, your children and your houses those temporal and spiritual curses which God in the Holy Scriptures threatens against those who do not observe his holy commandments and do not cause them to be observed.

Therefore, as God already said to that people of his of old: *Lay up these words in your hearts and minds, and hang them for a sign on your hands, and place them between your eyes. Teach your children that they meditate on them, when you sit in your house, and when you walk on the way, and when you lie down and rise up. You shall write them upon the posts and the doors of your house* (Deut. 11:18–20).

In the same way, when you are sitting by the fire with your family, standing and walking about the house, rising in the morning and retiring at night, and in a word always and everywhere, you must by good observance of God's precepts and rule of Christian life have at heart these reminders, having them at hand, teaching them to your children, recalling them often to their memory, keeping them before your eyes in your houses and workshops.

Let this collection of reminders be the mirror which your womenfolk place before themselves in the morning and every hour in order to see again and polish the face of the soul and their way of life, to please God and please the world in the right way; instead of those mirrors and pompous ornaments with which many of them have perhaps quite uselessly consumed so many hours in order to please the world in their vanity.

And in particular, you who are fathers, mothers and heads of households and dependents, have always before your eyes that dreadful example which we have in Holy Scripture of Eli, who even though he felt displeasure at the dissolute life of his sons, often reproved them and exhorted them to amendment; nevertheless, because he did not correct them efficaciously, received from God that severe punishment whereby on the same day his sons were massacred, the army scattered with the death of many thousands of men, the ark of God was taken, and he himself fell dead from his stool, his wife was lost and died, and his posterity was deprived of the priesthood.

May this example be light and a goad to all of you in your strict obligation to keep discipline in your families and others dependent on you. If you conduct yourselves such as we hope for from your goodness, in accordance with the table of reminders with which we instruct you, you will be able to expect from the Lord God, now and forever, upon yourselves and them, great blessings, which we continually beg for you from his divine Majesty.

From the Archdiocese, the twentieth day of December, 1577.

Reminders for Christian living for every state of life

Our nature is already damaged by sin and is of itself so inclined to evil that we easily neglect and refuse to do what is good.

Therefore we need assistance and incentives to live well, and someone to continually bring things to mind.

For this, various reminders gathered together here will be useful to be read often, each one as in a mirror to see in part the form of the Christian life and what is lacking and what should be done.

General reminders The principal thing we must acquire and have is the grace of God, without which one cannot live in a Christian way.

For this it will help to have the fear of God, which is the beginning of our salvation and every good, guarding ourselves against anything which would offend his most pure eyes.

Therefore always have God before your eyes, in whose sight you stand and who always sees you.

Consider often the end for which you have been created, which is to acquire heavenly glory, and that toward this goal you must set out. All creatures can be of service to you toward this end.

Think often about death, the strict judgment of God, and what must follow afterward.

Have zeal for the honor of God, and not merely that you yourself observe his holy commandments with all diligence, but that his name not be blasphemed and no irreverence be committed toward him by others.

Have great reverence for all the things of God, his saints, all the orders of Holy Church and your pastor, taking care to show entire respect and obedience.

Have great confidence in the Lord, who will always be everything for your greatest good.

Have your eye continually on the providence of God, thinking that nothing comes about without his will and that good is drawn out of everything.

Make a diligent effort for self-knowledge, for the knowledge of your own lowliness, baseness and misery, fleeing vanities and one's own reputation.

Never trust your own judgment and opinion, but defer easily to the opinion of others, seeking counsel frequently.

Take care to be grateful to God for his many benefits, recognizing them, thanking him and living well in order to show your gratitude.

Do not be concerned about pleasing men, provided you are pleasing to God, and always be looking out for what will be to his greater glory and service.

Await the reward for your every effort from Christ and not from the world.

In your affairs and works, have the intention never to will anything illicit, and to perform them all for love of the Lord so that all of them may be meritorious.

Know and recall that there is no greater wealth and treasure, nothing more excellent and fruitful, than to love God and serve him, and that everything else passes like smoke and shadow.

Obey all superiors promptly in upright things, temporal superiors included, and have due reverence and respect for them and to all who are greater than you.

For your part, take care to maintain the peace and quiet of your house when possible, living in charity with all, whether you are married or in any other state of life.

Take care with divine grace to restrain your anger over things which happen during the day at home or elsewhere, and not to start shouting so as not to burst out with something worse.

Remember to bear with the defects of others at home and elsewhere, as you wish others to bear with you.

Remember that you are a Christian and that you must therefore bear the injuries done to you patiently for love of Christ, and forgive, and return good for evil, and pray for your enemies.

In your tribulations and adverse circumstances, remember to have recourse to prayer, and accept all these scourgings and every adverse thing, whether commonplace or particular to you, as coming from the hand of the Lord.

Manage the things of the world as a servant of God, and not as an absolute owner. Make use of them according to need, not pleasure, and take care to pass through these temporal things in such a way as not to lose things eternal.

At the beginning of every action, make the sign of the holy cross with great confidence in its power.

Do not begin any important business without first praying, and also take counsel with your spiritual father or other prudent and devout persons.

From time to time through the year, ask someone you trust his impression of you, and think it over, whether you are on the right path to salvation.

Try to arrange and distribute the hours of the day well according to your various activities, such as prayer, hearing Mass, conducting business, eating; and thus you will not lose time.

Blasphemies and dirty words must be far from the mouth of a Christian.

Guard yourself against the bad habit of swearing to something often.

Flee every sort of superstition and black art.

Do not be easily willing to judge your neighbor, especially his intention, but keep your eyes on your own sins and defects.

Guard against the desire and curiosity to know other people's business and all the news, especially in matters of faith, and of speaking about things you do not know enough about.

Guard against murmuring and against talking too much, and never impugn anyone's good name.

Never share anything with others which could disturb their peace and quiet, or that of others, and cause dissension.

Guard yourself against dissolute words as well as useless conversations.

Guard yourself against dissolute ways of acting and behaving which offend God and man, and take care to be modest and reserved in all your actions.

Flee bad company more than you would the plague, and anyone who gives you evil memories, wicked advice or bad example; and thus you will flee all occasions and encouragements to sin.

Flee theater foyers, taverns, crossings, banquets, dances, parties, masked balls and vain performances, where God is offended, and guard yourself not only against participating in any way, but also from being present at them.

Guard yourself against laziness as the poison of the soul, but rather take care to stay occupied in pious works or at least useful things.

See to it that there be no profane image in your house, and even less immoral ones, neither in pictures or on the walls, in books or anywhere else, because this is harmful to yourself and gives scandal to others.

In conducting business, buying and selling, guard against any kind of deception, falsehood, lies and oaths and against desiring any of the possessions of others.

Flee the management of other people's money or goods, if you can, unless you are obligated to do so by charity or some other reason.

Not for gain, nor friendship or love of relatives or favors, should you ever do something unjust or against God.

Do not let yourself become excessively cheerful in times of prosperity which make the soul forget the miseries and dangers of this life.

Rather, recall now and again the calamities and vicissitudes of the things of the world, and for this reason it will be good at times to read some book on the contempt and vanity of human things, like a certain holy and learned man who was accustomed to read the Lamentations of the prophet Jeremiah in his times of prosperity.

In adversities do not lose heart nor become sad; rather you should rejoice, for this is the straight road to paradise and one of the favorable signs man can have of his salvation. Remember to occasionally read some spiritual treatise on tribulations.

Guarding the heart and the whole man Make a firm resolution to never offend God, especially by mortal sin, but rather to suffer any evil, even death, and to flee with all your strength any sin whatsoever, even venial.

Keep guard over your heart, so that no bad thought enters there. Resolve on this often and examine yourself if you are neglectful.

When some immoral passion or some bad thought stirs within you, seek to resist it from the beginning, allowing it no space but chasing it away so it does not lead you into sin.

Similarly take care so your eyes are not raised too easily, and do not fix your gaze on that which is not permissible to desire.

Restrain your tongue, and do not actually say everything which may be on the tip of your lips.

Remember that we are continually tempted and surrounded by the demons, always on the ready to make us turn traitor; nevertheless, stay on top of the situation.

Confession and communion Try to start out with a good general confession of your whole life if you have never done so, as it is the beginning and foundation of a new and good life.

Choose a learned and good confessor for your spiritual father and guide of your soul, in whom you must have great faith and with whom you should confer on all doubts and important affairs in which your conscience could be burdened, and govern yourself according to his counsel.

Go to confession often, the more often the better, every eight days or at least every month, and more often for the solemnities and principal feasts of the year.

With similar frequency approach Holy Communion, and when you cannot communicate, at least do not neglect to confess, in order to obtain the grace given through this Sacrament.

Try to never retire for sleep with some mortal sin on your soul, but confess it as soon as possible, and if that is not possible at the time, at least take care to have contrition and sorrow for it and weep over it bitterly.

Do some act of penance every week, such as fasting, the discipline, a hair shirt, sleeping on a hard surface and other things; but only with the advice of the spiritual father.

Prayer and spiritual exercises Have in your room some devout image of Christ, Our Lady or of some saint to whom you are particularly devoted.

You should also have in your room some holy water, and retiring and rising, entering and leaving the house, bless yourself with it against all the tricks of the enemy.

Take care to have and wear some *Agnus Dei*[1] image or medal with faith, devotion and reverence.

Have a special devotion and reverence to your Guardian Angel.

Also have a saint, or some saints, as your advocates, such as the saint whose name you received in holy Baptism. In particular take the glorious Virgin for your protector and have recourse especially to her in all your needs.

If you can, say the Little Office of the Blessed Virgin Mary[2] at least on feast days if you cannot the other days, and the rosary every day or as often as you can.

Never neglect prayer, at least morning and evening, but pray in every way necessary, whether accompanied by other people in your neighborhood at church, or the members of your household or workshop where you may be, or when you are alone. And when you cannot pray at the hour indicated by

---

[1] This is a very old expression of devotion; worn like a medal, it is a flat piece of wax stamped with the image of the Lamb and blessed.

[2] The Little Office of the Blessed Virgin is a short version of the daily Divine Office, with antiphons, readings and prayers of a Marian character, varied according to the season. Dating back to the eighth century, it became a popular way of prayer for lay people unable to pray or attend the full Divine Office used by clergy and religious.

the church bell, do so at another time. It would also be good to do mental prayer if you know how, otherwise at that time you should recite the seven penitential psalms, or litanies, or say the rosary or other vocal prayers.

Remember to pray not only for yourself, but for all manner of persons, and especially for the exaltation of Holy Church, for the Holy Father, for your pastor, for all the bishops, for the princes of Christendom, and especially for your king and his magistrates, and the souls of the departed.

You must be very devoted to the saints who are the protectors of this city and diocese, and observe their feasts and vigils, honoring their churches and relics, especially on the days of their festivals and solemn divine offices.

Every Friday, if you live in the city, or else whenever you come into the city, take care to visit the sacred nail of our Lord in the metropolitan church, and to obtain the many indulgences granted every day to those who pray before the most holy Sacrament in that church.

On Saturday evening, be at your parish church, or in the aforementioned metropolitan church, at the hour for singing the *Salve Regina* or other Marian antiphon.

You shall have great faith and devotion regarding indulgences ..., taking care to obtain them.

Be devoted to attending the stational churches[3] of this city on their appointed days, which follow those of Rome, and also to make frequent visits to the Seven Churches. Do not permit that such rare and singular graces and spiritual helps granted to this city and diocese should be given without fruit.

Be particularly devoted to attending all the public and solemn sacred actions of the place where you are, whether ordinary or extraordinary, and you yourself should participate in those mysteries. Thus when you are in the city, you should attend the solemnities of the cathedral church, the Mass and pontifical celebrations. Likewise during the Ember Days attend the sacred ordinations by the archbishop, praying God to grant him abundant light in an action of such importance as that, for the spiritual health and

---

[3]The ancient tradition of attending Mass at a "stational church" is one that St. Charles brought back to Milan from Rome. This spiritual practice has its roots dating back to the second and third centuries of the Bishop of Rome celebrating liturgies at particular churches in the city. Over time certain feast days became connected with certain churches (cf. John Baldovin, SJ, *The Urban Character of Christian Worship: the Origins, Development and Meaning of Stational Liturgy* [Rome: Pontifical Oriental Institute Press, 1987]). The tradition continues today in Rome during Lent (cf. George Weigel and Elizabeth Lev, *Roman Pilgrimage: The Station Churches* [New York: Basic Books, 2013]).

salvation of the whole people, and copious graces for those who at that hour are promoted in the ranks of sacred orders.

You should also be inspired by these holy rites that you see used and the respect and reverence that you should give to every ecclesiastical person.

…

Do not fail also to participate devotedly in all the general and particular processions of your parish and those in the vicinity.

In the same way, do not fail to participate in all the ordinary and extraordinary prayers, or the Forty Hours devotion, or any other devotions, which are offered in the metropolitan church or in your parish, never failing to take your turn when it falls to you.

When the sign is given that the Blessed Sacrament is being carried to the sick, you must not fail to go and devoutly accompany your Lord the King of the universe with your candle, giving glory and without being ashamed.

While doing so, pray for the sick person to whom it is being brought, and give thanks to God to have made us worthy of so great a gift, his having left himself to us in so great a Sacrament.

This same duty of accompanying the Blessed Sacrament you will do every time you encounter the Blessed Sacrament in the street at the time of its arrival, even dismounting your horse or carriage.

When the *Ave Maria* sounds at morning, noon and evening, say three Hail Marys kneeling down, along with the three verses which are found in the daily exercises of the Little Office of the Blessed Virgin Mary, calling to mind the Incarnation and Passion of Christ our Lord.

When at home or anywhere else you hear the bell ringing for the elevation of the Lord at the consecration at the principal Mass, you should call to mind the lifting up of the Lord on the cross, and while kneeling down lift your mind to adore your Savior, and offer a brief prayer as if you were present.

When the bell is rung for someone who has died, you should pray for him and remember that you too will soon follow him; and so resolve to be ready.

When the bell is rung indicating a storm, not only should you promptly start praying on account of that danger, either going immediately to a church or at least in the place you happen to be at the moment. You should also give some thought to the thunder, lightning and terror which will occur that day on which Christ will judge you.

Get into the habit of saying *ejaculatory* prayers frequently during the day in your mind or with your lips, quietly when you are with others. These would be some brief sentence from the Psalms, holy words or another brief prayer that illumines the intellect and renews your love for God in every occasion that presents itself.

At the beginning of anything: *Deus, in adiutorium meum intende; Domine, ad adiuvandum me festina* ("O God, come to my assistance; O Lord, make haste to help me.") (Ps. 69:2).[4]

In difficulties: *In te, Domine, speravi non confundar in aeternum* (In you, O Lord, have I hoped, let me never be confounded). (Ps. 30:2)

In affliction: *Salvum me fac, Domine, quoniam intraverunt aquae usque ad animam meam* (Save me, O God: for the waters are come in even unto my soul). (Ps. 68:2)

In temptations: *Adiutor meus esto, ne derelinquas me* (Be you my helper, forsake me not). (Ps. 26:9)

Considering your own weakness: *Miserere mei, Domine, quoniam infirmus sum* (Have mercy on me, O Lord, for I am weak). (Ps. 6:3)

Considering your own sins: *Sana me, Domine, et sanabor* (Heal me, O Lord, and I shall be healed). (Jer. 17:14)

Desiring to love the Lord: *Diligam te, Domine, fortitudo mea* (I will love you, O Lord, my strength). (Ps. 17:2)

In doubts: *Deus meus, illumina tenebras meas* (O my God, enlighten my darkness). (Ps. 5:20)

Desiring perseverance in doing good: *Deus meus es tu, ne discesseris a me* (You are my God; depart not from me). (Ps. 21:11–12)

And others similar to those as you can be instructed by your spiritual father. The Psalms and books of Holy Scripture, as well as the reflections of the saints, are full of them.

When you wake up at night and cannot sleep, think about God and spiritual things and do not give space in your thoughts for worldly things, but as your father Saint Ambrose reminds you, pray the Psalms and the Our Father with devotion.

When you go to bed, think that perhaps you will not be alive in the morning, and when you get up, that perhaps you will not make it to evening, and in this way you will be looking out for yourself.

---

[4]This is the opening verse when praying any of the hours of the Divine Office.

While conducting business or working, try to occupy the mind with something spiritual, like with what Christ our Lord said or did, or with some saint, or psalmody, or singing spiritual things.

Every time you leave or come back from doing anything, remember that your Guardian Angel accompanies you and is ready to help you, and counts your steps in your good works; or else imagine the presence of Christ our Lord and realize that you are in his presence.

From everything that is done, happens or which you see, seek to derive fruit and some spiritual insight. Just as with the cultivation of the soil, with what effort and diligence should we cultivate our soul, in order to give back good fruit to the Lord. On a beautiful sunny day, think how much seeing the eternal light will delight you, since this light causes such joy. On a dark and cloudy day, think how much pain there would be if you were in that eternal darkness, since you are so saddened by just a little bad weather. From a garden full of pretty flowers, think how beautiful and pleasing to God is a soul adorned with the flowers and varied colors of the virtues, and how great is the wisdom of God, since so great artistry is seen in a flower or a single leaf. And do likewise with everything.

Particular exercises for the morning When you get up in the morning, first of all turn to God, asking for his help, and pray before occupying your mind with other things. As your father St. Ambrose instructs you remember to say the Creed among other devout prayers.

To do this well, due diligence will be necessary. So in the morning you must get up on time and in the evening be over and done with your affairs so that you go to bed at a decent hour.

As soon as you wake up, occupy your mind with God, and realize that your Angel calls you at this hour, so praise the Lord with him.

While dressing, think about something spiritual, like how you were clothed in grace in Baptism, that you are a pilgrim on a journey, and that you must direct your paths toward the homeland.

Then, kneeling in the place set aside for prayer, first thank God that he watched over you during night and brought you to this hour, and then thank him for all his gifts.

Next, pray to him to watch over you during this day, and to keep you always free from every sin and from ever offending him.

Thirdly, pray that he give you the grace always to do his holy will and direct your every affair according to his good pleasure.

Fourthly, offer yourself to him and all that you will do, say or think, with a pure intention, all for his praise and glory.

Fifthly, entrust yourself to the glorious Virgin, your Guardian Angel, your patron saint and all the saints, and for this say some good and suitable prayer.

Then do some mental or vocal prayer for a certain amount of time, an hour or half an hour without strain, according to your ability.

Prayer and particular examen in the evening In the evening after supper, or at some other hour, if you can read, read a little from a spiritual book, lives of the saints, or something else, especially the saint of that day, reflecting a little on what you read or discussing it with others.

Before going to sleep, and kneeling before a sacred image, first of all thank God for all the benefits received in general and especially those of that day. Ask for both the grace and true light to know and detest sin. Then briefly examine your conscience on what you have done, said and thought that day. Humbly ask his divine Majesty for pardon of every offense and defect you find in yourself, firmly resolving, with God's help, to guard yourself from them and to confess them.

While undressing, be thinking that man has been stripped of grace through sin, and that it is necessary to strip oneself of bad habits; or else think some other good thought or prayer.

The manner of praying and behaving in church Take care to pray on your knees and with all the devotion of which you are capable.

When going to the place of prayer, consider that the Lord is present there and observes what you wish to do and whether you do it in the manner in which it should be done.

Hearing the bell ringing for Mass or the other divine offices to which you are going, lift up your mind to consider that you go to pray and attend the offering of the sacrifice of the Body and Blood of Christ our Lord for the remission of your sins or to praise God, and so you must go there with contrition and devotion.

Upon entering the church and blessing yourself with holy water, lift up your mind and remember the sacred font of Baptism and what you promised there. Take care to cleanse your soul of sins with tears and penitence, and resolve to keep yourself from them in the future.

In church, stand with reverence and fear of God; stand in your place, not the places for the clergy or set aside for persons of a different station in life.

Do not sit irreverently with your back to the Blessed Sacrament, and do not approach the gradual steps[5] or pass beyond the grill of the altars. Avoid all talking in church, and every irreverent or indecent motion, gesture and act.

Be attentive to the divine offices, and do not fix your gaze on anything except the most sacred mysteries being carried out there and other objects of devotion.

Always kneel at low Mass, standing only for the Gospel.

Particular exercises for feasts, liturgical seasons and vigils Guard yourself against passing feast days in vanities but rather in good works.

Take care at least on feast days to go to Mass in your parish as your own church, and there hear the good lessons which are given to you, to educate yourself about the things a Christian is obliged to know for his salvation, and to bring back into use the good old custom of making an offering.

Take care on feast days to hear Vespers and the divine offices.

Take care to hear preaching and sacred reading, not only on feasts but all other days on which you can attend, and this should be not out of curiosity but in order to draw fruit, going to hear them wherever you feel yourself more inspired, and looking attentively for ways to put them into practice.

When some feast or solemnity is approaching, like Advent, Septuagesima,[6] Lent or others, remember what your father Saint Ambrose taught that, in order to celebrate it, you must renew your entire way of life, preparing yourself with Confession, Holy Communion and spiritual exercises.

In Advent, if you do not fast during that entire season as instituted in the past as a holy practice, then at least take care to fast three days of the week, that is, Wednesday, Friday and Saturday.

You will also fast on the vigil of the patron saint of your parish.

---

[5]The gradual steps are the steps leading up to the sanctuary and the altar.

[6]This is the seventeen day pre-Lenten liturgical season that begins with Septuagesima Sunday. From at least the Council of Nicaea, a widespread practice in the Church prescribed roughly forty fast days in preparation for Easter (hence the Latin *Quadragesima*, the fortieth fast day before Easter), but there could be no fasting on Sundays, and the Greeks did not fast on Saturdays either. As a consequence, the Greeks extended the fasting season further back, to the Sunday the Latins would later call *Septuagesima*. The Roman Church added the four days beginning on Ash Wednesday to make up for some nonfasting Sundays, but the example of the many Greek-rite churches in the Eternal City also inspired the Roman Church to establish its own Septuagesima season. Cf. Schuster, Ildefonso O.S.B., *The Sacramentary (Liber Sacramentorum): Historical and Liturgical Notes on the Roman Mass*, trans. Arthur Levelis-Marke, volume 2 (New York: Benziger, 1925), 3–32.

Every Sunday of Advent, do what you are reminded to do by a holy Pontiff, namely that you receive communion in a holy manner, and strive to do the same on the Sundays of Lent.

On fast days, you will have to accompany the fast with more frequent prayer and with almsgiving if you are able.

If indeed you eat only once on a fast day, still you must not, as St. Augustine reminds you, load down your table with too much food.

It would be good to give to the poor what you would have spent for supper on a fast day out of love of God.

For the feasts which are proper and particular to this city and diocese, such as the feasts of St. Ambrose, the holy martyrs Gervasius and Protesius, Nazarius and Celsus, Nabor and Felix, you must remember the ancient devotion of the people of Milan, who with vigils, processions, more frequent prayers and with all sorts of holy practices celebrated them. With this example, you must participate in the worship of these feasts with ever-greater devotion.

Pious works Take delight in the works of mercy, in almsgiving, visiting hospitals, jails and the sick and helping the poor in every way possible, especially those in greater need.

Seek membership in some pious association for pious works, or some company of spiritual men, so as to perform some pious work and to keep yourself well occupied, especially on feast days.

With whatever little or much God has given you of resources, and with labors and your own sweat where resources are lacking, be prompt to help the churches, especially your parish which is your own church, for its adornment and every other need, so they may be decent and beautiful, as is fitting for the house of God.

When you see your neighbor in some manifest sin or about to fall, do your duty of fraternal correction or admonishment, with charity and discretion, so as to win him back.

Nobles, rich people, persons of rank and rulers, should be guides and examples to others in a good life and in every sort of good work.

If you are moved to undertake a holy pilgrimage, seek counsel from your Pastor and Spiritual Father. Do not fail to receive from this Pastor the blessing, conforming to the Church's ancient use.

If you go on a journey, pray those short prayers and passages called the *Itinerario*, which are printed in the Little Office of the Blessed Virgin Mary, first thing in the morning each day before leaving on foot.

So as to always stimulate your spirit to devotion and actually to put into practice with spiritual works that which the sacred rites and ceremonies holy mother Church urges upon you and teaches, when you see some ceremony in church for a solemnity or during one of the liturgical seasons or the administration of the holy Sacraments, such as the vesting of the newly baptized in the white garment, or something similar, make an effort to discern something of what those sacred ceremonies signify, not out of curiosity, but to draw spiritual fruit from it.

Food and dress Whenever you are at table to eat, you should be thinking that you are there out of necessity, and first say the blessing, the one in the Office of the Madonna, and afterward give thanks to the Lord. If you do not know those prayers, then say an Our Father and a Hail Mary, and make the sign of the holy cross over the food or the table.

When you eat or are at table, before you begin, remember the sin that our first parents committed by eating, which will help curb your appetite and to regulate it.

Be careful to be temperate in eating, drinking, sleeping and dressing up, being more inclined to make use of little rather than being self-indulgent.

Guard yourself against pompous fashions in clothing, and against every sort of vain beauty product or making yourself up, whether you are a man or a woman.

Reminders for fathers and mothers of families and all heads of households

The father and mother of the family, and every head of household, should keep well in mind the obligation that they have to impart Christian living to their children.

...

Number and quality of the household Hire and retain only that number of servants and similar help of which you have need and which you can comfortably sustain on your income and resources, without going into debt nor reducing them to salaries that are too low.

Be very careful, when you take on persons in your household that no blasphemers, nor men with mistresses, nor suspicious characters or persons given to dissolute living and other vices, are among them.

Vigilance Be solicitous and vigilant about everything, keeping informed about all their comings and goings, conservations and practices.

It will be very helpful to have a trustworthy and sure person of the house or neighborhood (if the household is small) who can be a discreet censor of lifestyles, observe everyone and inform you of all disorders and spiritual dangers which they see or hear about regarding the members of the household.

Correction When something bad in their regard is told to you, do not be too quick to believe everything you hear, but first examine well and find out the truth.

Where you find a fault, admonish the person who needs it in an appropriate way and make the necessary correction.

Those who after several warnings about important things do not change their ways, send them away if they are servants, or punish them if they are your children.

Do not tolerate in them blasphemy, pilfering, concubinage or other dissolute lifestyles, or anyone who does not confess and receive communion at Easter, or anyone who neither knows nor wishes to learn Christian doctrine, at least the more essential things.

Precautions and guidelines Make sure that children and servants, male and female, sleep separately and apart so there is no danger of anything improper, and make the necessary provision so that each has his own separate bed.

Married couples must not have their little boys and girls sleep with them, nor in the same room with them, but in another secure and separate place as much as possible.

See to it that in the house there are no bad books or indecent pictures, and let no lewd songs be sung, but rather let there be spiritual and Christian songs of praise and devout things.

For all of that and everything else necessary for a respectable household, you will have to visit the house unexpectedly three or four times a year, as well as storage and deposit places, keeping the house free of every vanity.

See to it that your people do not converse with bad company in your house or outside it, and that they flee every occasion of sin.

Let there be no one idle, but let everyone have some decent occupation.

Do not put up with the women standing above the doorways or at the windows, and even less using makeup and other vanities.

Also see to it that wives do not go wandering and running about here and there, but let them be quiet at home, each one solicitous toward her duties and holy and pious works; and let them go to their devotions in a holy manner.

They should not go outside the house anywhere at all without first veiling their heads with linen cloth, or some nontransparent veil, so that widows and married women will have their hair and a good part of their face covered. Daughters who are yet minors, and other girls should cover their faces even more.

All the more should these things be observed when they go to church, the stations, processions and other devotions.

Do not tolerate pomp and superfluous decking out in either the men or the women of your household.

Administration

Keep away from spending money on extra dogs or horses, that money which could give life to many of Christ's poor.

Keep away from other useless and superfluous expenses, remembering that if you have resources, you are their administrator and must give an account to God.

Give alms willingly to the poor and inculcate this virtue in your children, giving them permission and authorization to carry out that same duty.

Treatment of household members

Be charitable and prudent with all the members of the household, treating them and making sure they are treated well, with love, and seeing to it that they are not cheated of their wages or anything else.

Do not speak injurious language either to your children or to any other person.

Rather make an effort with divine grace to restrain anger and taking offence in adverse circumstances which arise during the day in the house or outside.

When your people are sick, exhort them to patience and to bring forth the good fruit of an amendment of life. Take care by all means that they confess within three days, as prescribed in the bull of Pius V, giving faith to the doctor.

Visit infirm servants and have them looked after with charity. Do not send them to the poorhouse, since you made use of their services when they were healthy.

Peace and concord

Take care to maintain peace and tranquility in the house, and that there be fraternal charity, showing no partiality to anyone and bearing with everyone patiently.

Do not permit that the people of your household do injury to anyone, nor have enemies or hatred. Rather whenever some disagreement arises, see to it that they are reconciled immediately, whether within or outside the house.

It would be good to never allow them to bear arms, except for needful defense or some requirement of their work, or other clear necessity.

Exhort them often to pardon those who offend or insult them in words or deeds, and not to take revenge or take a stand on some minor point of worldly honor.

Example With words and deeds give a good example to your people, seeing to it that you do not say or do anything in their presence which is out of order and from which they will learn or conceive the desire to do the same.

Teachings Always give your family good training and reminders, and never, merely for the sake of not making them feel bad or other such reason, cease admonishing and telling them the truth.

Among the other things, remind them often of the following as needed:

Not to deceive or defraud anyone ever, and not to take anything that belongs to another.Not to found one's judgments and estimations on the basis of nobility and the grandeur of this world, but rather Christian virtues and a good life, and not to be ambitious for rank and dignity and human glory.To flee the superficiality of temporal things, and to look down on them more readily and consider them low, rather than to fill oneself up on them.

…

Piety, exercises of prayer and other devotions Have devotion to all the customs of Holy Mother Church, and take care that in your house not one is missing.

At the Nativity of our Lord, or during other solemn seasons, when the Church customarily sprinkles the houses with holy water, see to it that you do not miss that blessing.

When the customary time comes for the priest to bless fruit, bread or other food, keep that good custom yourself.

Do not give your children names of pagans or famous people thought to be damned, but of saints, so they can imitate them and take them as their special advocates.

Do not permit any superstition, but make them have recourse to God in everything and confide in him, fleeing every black art or magic.

Teach them good behavior and Christian manners in deeds and in words, placing before them the example of Christian piety and not the impiety of nonbelievers and of the enemies of God.

Be aware of the need to have everyone confirmed at the proper time, your children and the whole household, so there is no one in the house who is not confirmed.

Do not block your daughters from entering a convent, nor prevent your sons from becoming religious should they so desire.

Take care that the children hear Mass in its entirety every day if possible, or at least on feast days.

…

See to it in every way that everyone in the house knows Christian doctrine, at least the most necessary things; therefore, send or take them on feast days to the schools of Christian doctrine, male and female, older and younger.

Those who are of the right age may be diligently instructed how to make a good confession.

Likewise, those who also are of the right age and capacity may be instructed concerning Holy Communion …

It would be a great help if the whole family had the same confessor, in such a way he will be more able to minister to spiritual needs and lead the family in the way of God; at least see to it that they go to the more qualified confessors.

Make sure in all ways that they observe the regulations on fasting from Holy Mother Church: Lent, the Ember Days and the vigils and the others of vows or custom.

That everyone may be well instructed to pray and to make an examination of conscience according to his capacity.

That they pray at least in the morning and in the evening and make their examination of conscience before going to bed.

Morning and evening at the sound of the church bell, or at least at some other hour more convenient for everyone, the whole family should be gathered together to pray as one, either in church or at least at home before some devout image.

To this end and others as well, it is in every way a good thing that each house have a place of prayer arranged and set apart in a decent place, for the use of the whole household.

Every head of household should sprinkle the whole family gathered together, either at the end of evening prayer or some other time before going to bed, so they go in silence to sleep with his blessing.

…

Have some spiritual book read at table during the meal, if you have someone who can do it, sons or others, at least for a little while.

That book should be approved by one's own parish pastor or confessor.

Every evening in place of entertainment one should read a little from some spiritual book, the life of a saint, even better that of the saint of the day, and reflect together for a moment about it in order to draw fruit, so that with zeal and care everyone will acquire some virtue from their example.

The evenings before a solemnity, the heads of households should exhort everyone in the family to live rightly and to celebrate rightly those feasts, and to frequent fruitfully the Sacraments, the prayers and the preaching and holy lessons.

It would be good if every first Sunday, or some other feast day of the month, the parish pastor would gather together all fathers of families in the parish church, so they may gain further light and advice for the good government of their households, in addition to the benefit of considering together the needs of the parish and its church …

Reminders for masters and heads of shops, their assistants and apprentices

Of the quality of assistants, apprentices and workers The master and head of a shop or work area should not employ any assistant, worker or apprentice who has not confessed and received Holy Communion that year at Easter.

Nor any blasphemer, or anyone living in concubinage, or otherwise scandalous, or who delights in consuming his wages in taverns, making his own family suffer, so long as they do not amend after proper fraternal correction.

Similarly do not employ any player of prohibited games, all the more so since along with these games there is often joined blasphemy, theft and many other evils.

Take care that all who work for you know Christian doctrine, at least the more necessary things …

Of the reciprocal duty between masters and apprentices Treat your assistants, apprentices and workers with charity, and promptly pay them the salary they have earned at the proper time.

They for their part should be loyal and faithful to their bosses, showing them proper honor and respect, taking good care of their employers' property as if it belonged to them.

Prayer and other devotions Keep in every shop a devout image of our Lord Jesus Christ or of Our Lady or of some other saint.

In the morning when first entering the shop, each one should genuflect before the sacred image which is placed there, saying an Our Father and a Hail Mary, and let them do the same in the evening when leaving.

At all the other times during the day when entering the shop or passing before that holy image, let them bow reverently.

When the bell rings the *Ave Maria*, let everyone kneel down and say it devoutly, and when the bells rings for the dead let them pray there for the dead.

When the bell rings at the consecration of the principal Mass in the metropolitan church, or another principal church in the area where one finds oneself, let everyone kneel down and in that place adore Our Lord and take a moment to pray.

…

Decency of lifestyle In the shops and work areas, indecent things must not be done or said, and even less in the presence of women or anyone else who comes or passes by on the street.

There must be no type of gambling.

No defamatory words must ever be said, nor should they insult each other or live in discord with each other, but let them be good to each other like brothers.

Contracts, business and labor All should carry out their task and labor with sincerity, without oaths, lies or other deceptions. Let them not defraud anyone in weights, samples and measures or any other way, and let them write down for themselves as well as for others only what is true, offering everyone the same treatment they would want for themselves.

Let them not sell merchandise under any false appearances, or mixing bad product with the good, or falsifying in any other way.

Let them not sell anything except for the just price, and let earnings be in proportion to the quality of the merchandise and the costs of production.

Even when a customer naively or mistakenly pays more than he owes, the employees must not take more than what is honest.

…

Putting these reminders into practice The masters and bosses should be the first to practice these reminders; and with their example, with words and every other solicitude let them bring everyone else around to observe them.

So everyone can remember, let these reminders be posted in the shop in a place where everyone can see and read them, and once a week let them be read in the presence of all, including the master, the boss and others of that rank.

Open your hearts to the Holy Spirit

Homily to the confirmands
Given in the Basilica of St. Simplician
Pentecost Monday
May 30, 1583

Beloved children, the Lord God by that marvelous charity with which he loves the world, marvelously desires to communicate his Holy Spirit to it. On account of that he worked and accomplished so many things, but especially this: he sent his only-begotten Son from Heaven to earth, his Son who, being among men, said, *I am come to cast fire on the earth; and what will I, but that it be kindled?* (Lk. 12:49). I ask you, why do you think he lived through the period of thirty-three years during which he was among men, endured so many labors, so many nights watching in prayer, so many torments, and in the end did not shrink from death itself, except in order that, ascending the heavens after consummating all the mysteries of our salvation, he might decree that marvelous sending of the Holy Spirit, whom we recall in this time, the sending by which he came down visibly upon the most holy apostles in tongues of fire. Of course God at that time communicated his Spirit to them in a certain marvelous and privileged way; but he never ceases, or ever has ceased, to pour him into the hearts of the faithful in various ways, especially those faithful who strive to sufficiently dispose themselves for this. There are indeed many opportune means to this end, but by far the most excellent of all are the most holy Sacraments. And among these, the most holy Sacrament of Chrismation has been instituted, whereby men are especially filled up with the most precious treasures of divine grace, and enriched in a wonderful way. The Lord has deigned to commit the administration and conferral of this Sacrament to us bishops, so the nobility of such ministry and the excellence of the gift would be most clear to all. Indeed other Sacraments have been committed to all priests, but this one he left to bishops alone to administer. For it was fitting that the minister of this Sacrament be a more perfect minister, since a man is brought to perfection by him. Therefore, what is our part in this and the part of all other bishops as well? Nothing other than this, namely that as Christ accomplished so many things (as we have said from the beginning) for the sake of this very mission, so we too should set ourselves most diligently to work, and employ all care and effort, so that all the faithful entrusted to us may zealously come hastening to receive this most excellent gift. That is the reason why we shall with the greatest solicitude take care that they do so; and for that reason, we have decided to minister this most holy

Sacrament not only in our metropolitan church (which has been the custom these last years), but also in ordinary churches. Therefore, by means of our ministry that most Holy Spirit comes to your homes, and to your churches, the Spirit who, not disdaining your hospitality, once descended upon the apostles with such a plenitude of all graces. Since therefore today has been especially designated for you, those of you who are to receive this celestial gift should make an effort to learn something about it, since ignorance would make you less disposed to approach it.

In the first place, therefore, take note of God's admirable providence and outstanding charity to the human race, by which he has provided all things necessary and useful for the continuation of corporal and temporal life, and likewise to an even greater extent for the spiritual life; for it is by his gift that we all came first to the light of day. Once born, we grow and turn out as men. He supplied us with several kinds of foods, by which we refresh our bodies. He created medicinal substances, so that if we fall sick, we might have the means to recover our pristine health. And God provided no less for the spirit than for the body, for in the Sacrament of Baptism we are reborn and regenerated. By the chrism of this day we are vitally strengthened and grow; and there is one single medicine for fighting off all illnesses, holy Penance. But now, how sweet is the food of souls, the Body and Blood of Christ, and likewise for all the other Sacraments. So, you all now see clearly to what end holy chrism was instituted, namely so that human beings grow up spiritually and get big and through the Holy Spirit turn out as men made perfect. This celestial gift has therefore been instituted as an increase of life.

Do you know what chrism confers? Pay attention, I beg you. By baptism a man is only regenerated; he is entirely similar to a little infant at the breast. But once confirmed by chrism, he is similar to a perfect and robust man. Infants are weak, do not know how to talk, are unable to walk, and unsuited for accomplishing any of the actions of a man. But when they have grown up, when they have turned out as men, O how they become fit to undertake all works, even the most difficult! Therefore, is it any wonder if those who have only been baptized are still weak, succumb to so many temptations, fall so easily, and slide into innumerable sins? It is by chrism, we must say, that people receive the strength whereby they run the path of God to the end, carry out the divine precepts, embrace the evangelical counsels, escape the demon, are able to mock this world and subdue their flesh. O how many dangers this life of ours is exposed to! How many temptations press upon us on all sides, so that it is in every way hard not to succumb to them! The amazingly crafty demon is continually upon us in a thousand ways;

the world aims its sights at nothing other than driving us into the abyss; our inviting enemy, our flesh, lies always in ambush within us. Therefore, in the midst of such difficulties and dangers, shall we resist this most holy sacrament, by which we receive strength against all these things? May it in no way be the case with us. With the grace of God we shall be capable of everything that is conferred by this gift.

But neither can I refrain, O my children, from bewailing the miseries and calamities of so many who are so blind that in forgetfulness of both their own and others' salvation, they have neither up to this point been confirmed with chrism themselves, though they are adults, nor make any sufficient effort to have their sons and daughters confirmed. What cruel fathers they are, both to themselves and their children. For those whom they must follow with the highest love, they nevertheless culpably deprive of this heavenly treasury and these infinite riches. The Holy Spirit stands at their door, knocks and wishes to enter and enrich them, but these people—and O what sorrow!—refuse to open the door of their heart to him. What an insult they cast upon the Holy Spirit! If some prince, as noble as he was rich, did not disdain your hospitality; and if moreover he manifested his love toward you all the more by wanting to enter your house and remain there with you, then what penalty and what torments would be too severe a punishment for you, if, in utter ingratitude and unworthiness toward the benevolence of so great a king, you not only did not want that, but also closed the door of your house to him and pushed him away from entering? Would you not be worthy of rejection from human society? The Most Holy Spirit, the third Person in God, one with the Father and the Son, in every way equal to them, intensely desires to enter your soul and is ready to fill it up with innumerable treasures—and there are people who afterward want to be called Christian, but keep God himself at a distance from their homes and the hearts of their sons and daughters? O what insult and injury they bring upon such a guest, and certainly not to be left unavenged!

In the Sacrament of Baptism, you have all been made and been consecrated the house, abode, and dwelling and temple of this Holy Spirit. He wishes to enter his house with a much greater and, in a way, royal splendor, unless you refuse. God grant there be no one among you so negligent and ignorant of his salvation, that what long ago happened to the horrible archheretic Novatus, should happen to him. As it is said in the Roman Catechism, Novatus fell into so many calamities especially on this account, that held down by a most grave and mortal illness, he neglected to receive the most holy Sacrament of

Confirmation.[7] Nor do I believe any such can be found among you; but in order that you may approach this gift more worthily and promptly, let us touch on a few things which will instruct you on the proper manner of preparing for it.

Certainly the first and most important thing to say is that since this Sacrament confers an increase of heavenly grace, the first kind of preparation for it is grace itself. It is not permitted to anyone to approach here unless he is in the state of divine grace, as you were able to understand by the reading of today's Gospel, when the Lord said, *If any one love me, he will keep my word, and my Father will love him, and we will come to him, and will make our abode with him* (Jn 14:23). The coming of the Lord requires the observance of the divine precepts; for grace itself is most powerful for the increase of grace, and a prior disposition thereto. Lost by sin, this grace is recovered by the most holy Sacrament of Penance. On account of this, and you confirmands were admonished on it yesterday in our name, the first thing is that no one approached without having confessed. And know that the more someone is in grace and has good works helping him, the more abundantly he will receive treasures and rich fruits.

Secondly, a certain special devotion and piety of soul is required. For just as you would not only strive most diligently to clear out and clean your whole house for a king or prince who was coming to you (to stay with the example previously mentioned), also to decorate it in every way you could, and to go forth to meet him outside the gate of your home, so with the divine guest, God himself, approaching you, not only should your conscience be cleared with the brooms of penitence, but your soul should be adorned with tapestries of devotion. You must go forth to meet him with the most ardent affection of mind. The gifts which he is coming to give you should be diligently examined, and innumerable thanks should be rendered to him for such charity in your regard. Look closely, I ask you, so I may finish in a few words, at the most blessed choir of apostles, which was able to obtain the plenitude of the Holy Spirit coming down on them in tongues of fire in

---

[7]St. Charles refers to an episode related by the ancient Church historian Eusebius and cited by the Catechism of the Council of Trent. Novatian (Novatus) was a Roman priest of the third century who set himself up as Antipope against Pope St. Cornelius in 251. There is some confusion between Novatian in Rome and a certain Novatus in Carthage in the patristic sources. The well-known Novatian became a schismatic over the question of the *Lapsi*, those Christians who had apostatized under persecution but afterward repented and sought readmission to the communion of the Church. Could they be readmitted? When they were readmitted in the various local Churches by the bishops, Novatian and other rigorists made their schism with the claim that this was wrong. According to Pope St. Cornelius, Novatian's errors were due in part because he had been baptized but not confirmed.

an unheard of and noble way. Many times Christ had promised to give them the Holy Spirit, to send them the Paraclete from Heaven, who would teach them all truth, who would continually stand by them. Take note of how they disposed themselves for that: awaiting this promise with the most ardent desire, and enclosed in the Upper Room for ten days continuously, they all persevered with one soul in their prayers. What do you think that unity of theirs signified, if not the charity and concord which are so necessary in your homes, so that all agree together in the Lord, the father with his children, the husband with his wife and vice-versa, and all persist in their devout prayers?

But since you are now standing here about to receive this Sacrament, consider well what the Spirit himself works within you through the external actions of the bishop. The bishop anoints your foreheads in these words: *I sign you with the sign of the Cross, and confirm you with the Chrism of salvation* (*Signo te signo Crucis, et confirm te Chrismate salutis*); but interiorly the Paraclete fills you and enriches you with his gifts, and makes you quite unlike the way you were before. For already at the beginning of this sermon you heard how much the confirmed differ from those who are only baptized. Therefore with how much reverence, and how much submission of soul, and how much heartfelt desire, and with what tears, must you not approach here. Indeed I am amazed, and I consider it utterly reprehensible that there are usually some who approach with so much commotion, that it is as if it were not necessary, for those about to receive the Spirit of peace, to be here with the greatest peace. For certain ones among you desire so much to be first and fear so much to be last, that you seem to think you must spend a long time, not a day or two days, but all time, in order to receive the Holy Spirit. Consider closely, I beg you, how many things merchants do, for the sake of the slightest profit, how far they proceed into distant regions, how many dangers they overlook. And you, in order to obtain such a great treasure, are terrified by a few hours, and approach the God of peace with a great commotion? Are you going to not keep the stores closed, if you are to be confirmed during a holiday? Be on guard that does not happen out of punishable ignorance of divine gifts. But let us bring this now to a close. Come forward, most beloved souls, open the door of your heart to the Spirit coming into them, prepare your houses; which if you cannot do because of your sickness and poverty, ask it from the Spirit himself with tears, on account of that charity by which he communicated himself to the whole world, so he may grant you to will and to be able to do it, and so he may fit out a home for himself, preparing his temple here by his celestial grace, making you share at last, by his help, in eternal glory. Amen.

Charles Borromeo

Imitating the Holy Family

Homily for the Sunday within the octave of the epiphany
Given in the Cathedral of Milan
January 8, 1584

Most beloved children, we have seen different kinds of people giving testimony to Christ our newly born Savior: the angels already announced him to the shepherds; a star newly appearing led the Magi Kings from the Orient to the manger; a little later most holy Simeon, filled with the Spirit and holding the Infant in his arms closely, said *Now do dismiss your servant, O Lord, according to your word in peace; Because my eyes have seen your salvation, Which you have prepared before the face of all peoples* (Lk. 2:29–31). Will Jesus the Redeemer remain always silent with everyone talking about him? Will he whom all creatures venerate with such notable testimonies allow himself to be perpetually hidden? All you who are listening should realize, it is not going to be that way at all! Rather, when the time foretold will come, he will show the light of his divinity by the rays of his preaching and his works and his miracles. O how he will manifest himself in the theater of the cross, what a window he will open in his breast, so that men will penetrate the intimate thoughts of his own heart! For this admirable manifestation, which he desires so much, he reserved that time when he would say, *With desire I have desired to eat this pasch with you* (Lk. 22:15), the time when the time of his Passion was already approaching, *And I have a baptism wherewith I am to be baptized: and how am I straitened until it be accomplished* (Lk. 12:50), as if to imply, "With what anguish and anxiety I am oppressed." But those times are very far away, O good Jesus. Are you therefore going to hide yourself until you are over thirty years old, and tolerate the fact that your brethren, whom you have approached to seek out, are held in so much darkness, you who have come into the world as the true light, to illumine every man (cf. Jn 1:9)? Be in good spirits, you children of men, because he desires to be known by you, more than you desire knowledge of him. He burns with love of you; already *you have wounded his heart with one of your eyes* (Song 4:9). Your miseries and calamities have now transfixed his soul. Nor will he allow you to lack knowledge of him for so long a time. Therefore behold, today, while still a boy, being exactly twelve years old, he begins little by little to suggest his divinity to men, while he sits in the Temple among the teachers of the law, by turns hearing and asking questions of them, while all marvel *at his wisdom and his answers* (Lk. 2:47). Most splendid indeed is the account written down in today's Gospel, and presented to us by Holy Mother Church to be opened up in detail. Going through it therefore, we will extract a few things from the text that will be most useful for the improvement of our lives.

Most beloved children, Christ was the true Sun of Justice, so it was impossible that he not shine before the whole world. But just as this visible sun, before it puts forth its rays entirely and sheds them over the whole earth, precedes them with the dawn, which is followed by the sun gradually shining stronger and stronger until it appears most splendid at midday, so the Son of God, before midday comes, at which time he will show his divinity and immense love toward us, gradually begins to shine today in his boyhood like the dawn *when he was twelve years old* (Lk. 2:42), as the evangelist Luke says. Indeed these words are full of mystical and moral considerations.

Earlier Luke had recounted that the parents of Christ were accustomed to go every year on the feast day to Jerusalem, and here he adds: *they going up into Jerusalem, according to the custom of the feast* (Lk. 2:42). From this we are taught first of all, with what assiduous and inviolable diligence we must observe pious and praiseworthy customs, and the established religious practices received and confirmed by long use. Furthermore, it is your principal duty, fathers, to explain them now and again to your children, to imbue them with these established practices, to point them toward and urge them to observe those ecclesiastical traditions and customs. It is not for you to investigate their causes out of curiosity; for example, to know why such and such a supplication is made on such and such a day, why certain ceremonies are employed at a fixed time, why certain fasts are to be done; but with simplicity and purity of heart, like the parents of Christ, to keep the customs, which are of such authority that the apostle Paul, prescribing that women are not to be present in church except with heads veiled, based himself on no other cause than that, when he said: *we have no such custom, nor the church of God* (1 Cor. 11:16). But what times, what customs! What kinds of customs are also kept now, and indeed inviolably? The ones the devil has brought in, which he has brought forth even until our times. Among Christians, the festivals of the Gentiles, I mean the bacchanalia, are in force, and which in these very days we are forced to hear and see with the greatest sorrow and not without tears. They run through the cities, and men run about like goats, offending God in a thousand ways, lamentably polluting their souls, not only within, but also outwardly putting on the ugliest masks and faces of demons. This is not the way to keep the most holy and laudable practices of the primitive Church, the practices of daily communion, freely professing the faith of Christ, assiduously frequenting churches and the like. What grief, what pain! Behold, my children, the customs which the parents of Christ observed.

And so three times a year they were held to come to the Temple (cf. Exod. 23:17, Deut. 16:16), except those for whom on account of too great a distance, it was enough to approach only once. But is not God everywhere? Does he not fill heaven and earth? Is he not to be adored everywhere, and is it not permitted to pour forth prayers to him in every place? Yes indeed, but the more opportune and helpful place for prayer is the church, about which it is said: *My house shall be called the house of prayer; but you have made it a den of thieves* (Mt. 21:13). Prayer carried out in places deputed for prayer has in some mysterious way a greater efficacy, a certain hidden energy. How much power is attached to those many blessings, consecrations, incensations and sprinklings by which churches are designated for prayer!

And most of all is the charity and fervor of those praying increased when many come together to pray in churches, and by their devotion and religious example motivate each other as it were and most vehemently to piety. This uniform and unanimous prayer can accomplish much with God, since he himself not only promised he would be in the midst of two or three gathered in his name, but also promised that if two of us agree on earth in prayer, their prayers will be heard (cf. Mt. 18:20, 19). After Solomon raised up this house to the Lord, to which the parents of Christ came in today's Gospel, for it was the celebrated Temple of Jerusalem, he obtained so many things from the Lord with that extended and most beautiful prayer: *That your eyes may be open upon this house night and day… and hear them in the place of your dwelling in heaven* (1 Kgs 8:29–30), and so much more that followed. By this prayer he implored divine power against enemies and against destitution, hunger and drought, not only for the children of Israel, but for aliens who had fled there. But how much more, and more easily, will all those things be obtained by those who approach this true temple, this sacred house of God, to make petition? This place does not hold and keep the stone tablets of the Law, nor the showbread, nor the rod of Aaron, nor the Ark of the Covenant. But present here on the throne of majesty, on that altar most holy, is the Son of God himself, God and man, whom countless thousands of angels surround. Here is that bread which descends from heaven. Here is the giver of the Gospel's law, who has not written it on wood or stone tablets, but on tablets of flesh, of the heart (cf. 2 Cor. 3:3). Here is that rod which flowered in the Virgin's womb. In sum this place contains the ark of divinity and treasure of all graces. Who, I ask, does not deeply feel, while praying in our churches, certain life-giving rays flowing from the sacred altar, illumining his mind and inflaming his heart? In the Old Testament the church of God was called the Propitiatory ("The Mercy Seat"). But ours is the true Propitiatory, in which is present him *who forgives all your iniquities: who heals all your diseases* (Ps. 102:3), he whom we are to approach with the greatest confidence and hope.[8]

Behold, therefore, how right and just it is to pray in churches, more than other places; for this reason the Lord commanded, though he is everywhere, that we should go to the temple when we decide to give ourselves to prayer. But note this: even though it is fitting for Christian people to be attached to each and every church, still, they should be attached most of all to the mother churches, that is the cathedrals, and to their parish churches, and go most often to them rather than others. For this is commanded by ancient decrees of sacred canons, which order that during the Mass[9] the people should be told that those who are not of the parish should rather go to their own churches. In their own churches, by order of the bishops, each grouping of people is taught and given whatever pertains to the spirit by its own parish priest, namely what it is necessary to pray for, what marriages are going to be celebrated, what sacred services are to be done for the deceased, and finally what days are feasts, which must be spent in a spirit of devotion. Those who do not attend their parish churches slowly go back to the natural state, spiritually, and are ignorant of all those things which it is most incumbent upon them to know, things to which they should attach the greatest importance. Do not say to yourself, O Christian, "If I do not go to vespers, I am not on that account guilty of sin." Certainly in this way a pernicious forgetfulness of divine things is imperceptibly brought in, and the heart of such people becomes a lamentable *land of forgetfulness* (Ps. 87:13). The path people do not frequently take slowly becomes impassible; the field that is not cultivated often and diligently does not take long to fill up with nettles, thorns and brambles. The same happens to that soul which only rarely goes to the church where he would otherwise be cultivated with the most sacred ceremonies, harmonies and psalms. These have the

---

[8]The Italian translator Carnaghi refers us to Chapters 25 and 37 of *Exodus* for "the propitiatory." St. Charles here commits a slip in the biblical details about the Propitiatory, but this does not detract from the validity of his overall typological approach to Scripture.

[9]We have translated the common phrase *intra Missarum sacra solemnia* with "during," on account of *intra,* although the meaning would seem to require "before" in this case.

greatest influence, especially on those whose spirits are more simple, so that Augustine, Doctor of the Church and a most holy bishop, admitted about himself that he was used to being affected and moved, now to tears, and now to devotion and piety, by what he saw and heard being done and sung in the churches. For in the first place, our human infirmity is helped by these external dispositions, by which little by little it is raised to the taste and knowledge of heavenly things. The same thing is seen in temporal affairs, for the decorations in the houses of kings, the many rugs embroidered and shining with jewels, and the silver and gold vessels, inspire in everyone the greatest honor and respect toward those very kings who otherwise would appear worthy of disdain.

But it was to males alone that the law gave this precept of going up to Jerusalem on the feast day. For the Lord was hinting at how unbecoming it is for women to be wandering about, frequently seen in public places, or running here and there through the streets, unless it be for some action bringing honor to God or help to souls, for in doing these actions no delay should be allowed. But women were not even obliged to go to the Temple. What, I ask, would you say, O Moses, most holy scribe of God, if you now looked upon our women going back and forth every day through public streets and piazzas, and also sinning and enticing others to sin, or worse, casting nets for souls at crossroads? That, O daughters, is not what our holy father Ambrose wrote concerning you. This rather is what you should be doing: to remain always at home or in churches, and to pass through the streets only for reasons of impelling necessity. The most holy Virgin and Mother of God, teacher and advocate of your sex, or rather the whole human race, she who, when going by divine directive to her cousin Elizabeth, to provide the services necessary to the pregnant woman, went *with haste* (Lk. 1:39).

But still we can ask, when the Virgin herself was not obligated by the law to go to Jerusalem for the celebration of that solemnity, but was free to do as she willed, that is either remain at home or go up there with her husband, why, I ask, did she even decide to be a companion on this journey? O most unhappy people, who choose to accomplish nothing unless you are compelled by necessity, or unless you would run the danger of mortal sin by omitting it! Learn from the Virgin, how pleasing to God are the cheerful and generous givers (cf. 2 Cor. 9:7). How much to be pitied is this coldness of yours! You therefore dare, most unhappy mortal, to treat with God in just as rigid a way? "I am not bound," you say, "except once a year, to receive the Sacraments of Penance and the Eucharist. I am not bound to perform this or that pious work." So because an order of God or the Church does not weigh upon you, for that reason you refuse to spend some time devoutly? Woe to you, if the Lord decided to deal with you within the limits of justice alone! Furthermore, by what law or duty to you is he bound to spare you who sin against him so often, and to wait for you until you repent? A servant who does nothing, except when his master commands, cannot be pleasing to his master. Because he is so generous in giving, as to practically waste everything he has, if I may put it that way, it is with a big heart, my children, that God is to be served because he deserves much greater services from us than we are able to show him. God had not commanded David to build a house for him, and yet he so ardently desired to do so (cf. 2 Sam. 7:1–2). He who is zealous for the divine honor does not weigh or measure things by so slight and paltry a standard; rather, when he has done whatever he was able to say, do or think up, he says, *We are unprofitable servants; we have done that which we ought to do* (Lk. 17:10).

Going up to the Temple, therefore, Joseph and Mary brought their dearly beloved son the Lord Jesus with them. This is the first duty of fathers and mothers of families, to bring their children to church, and not permit them to wander about through streets and squares. But, you will say, my son is still too young, he is not able to learn or understand the things taught or preached in church. That matters little. There will be no little fruit if he spends time in church; for if he does not, he will grow up more inclined to chatter idly with people who detest spiritual things. And let that not be an excuse to you, O father, if he has not yet come out of infancy. For the younger he is in age, the more it is your responsibility, as for a tender young sapling, that he grow straight up and that he absorb this good habit even with his mother's milk if that were possible. Although the child is indeed not yet capable of understanding the things treated in church, he nevertheless gets used to being frequently in them, and puts on this holy habit, so that if he retains it while growing up, he will more easily and promptly obey its commands. This is no meager result, brethren.

But why did the Lord Jesus come to the Temple at the age of twelve, not before, and not at a more advanced age? Our Savior wanted to reveal himself to the world, and he determined to observe a certain proportionate age for this. Our Lord at the first moment of his conception was full of wisdom and grace, and enjoyed the full use of reason; and because especially at the age of twelve, other children in general begin to use reason, and because he had had that most abundantly long before, he began to reveal it at the time it normally appears in others.[10] Even in this matter, he taught us that any Christian, when he first arrives at the age of sufficient maturity, is held to recognize God immediately with the first free act he conceives in his life. Indeed if we do not accomplish this act, we are stained with a lethal fault, my children, and if death then came upon us, we would be thrust down into the pains of Hell.[11] And yet, how few fathers strive to educate their children for this! Shall our life therefore be an affair of chance? If a statue or some earthen vessel could speak, then as soon as it received the elegance of its form, it would attend its painter or sculptor with some kind of pleasing homage. Man who is so noble, brought out of nothing to be according to God's image, the superior to all creatures, is it not his duty to turn toward his creator and to render thanks for so many gifts received, since on him the light of mind shines forth more clearly? And if he does not do this explicitly, let him accomplish it at least in desire, by good works, and by religion and devotion in his soul.[12]

Second part

Before proceeding further, now that you know you must frequently gather together in church, we also want you made aware of this: it was in the Old Law and always most pleasing to the Lord that men approaching the Temple should profess publically the supreme dominion of God by making some offering from their own goods. Therefore he commanded: *neither shall you appear before me empty* (Ex 34:20). He does not need our goods,

---

[10]Regarding the human knowledge of Christ, St. Charles' remarks express the common teaching on Christ's infused supernatural and prophetic knowledge (cf. St. Thomas Aquinas, *Summa Theologica*, III, qq. 9–12). The final paragraph of Borromeo's homily below will also shed more light on what he understands here.

[11]Cf. St. Thomas Aquinas, *Summa Theologiae*, I–II, q. 89, a. 6.

[12]An example of what the saint means here is found in the life of St. Josephine Bakhita. Raised as a child in Africa in animism, she could later recount her childhood natural perception of the world as God's, and her desire for the Revelation which would one day reach her.

> [Bakhita] would observe the sky at night, the sun in the morning, and all the other natural phenomena. Filled with wonder, she would ask herself, "Who could possibly be the master of these beautiful things? And I felt a great desire to see him, to know him, and to give him homage." ... Mother Josephine denied ever adoring idols ... "In the morning I watched the sun as it was born and in the evening as it set. And I thought that if it was beautiful, how much more beautiful must be the one who had made it."

> Roberto Italo Zanoni, *Bakhita: From Slave to Saint*, trans. Andrew Matt (San Francisco: Ignatius, 2013), 136–37.

but O supreme goodness of God! Although everything of ours is his, he nevertheless deigns to grant us a way of meriting. For this reason we have established that this most holy and most ancient custom of offerings should be restored in the churches.[13] Therefore, each of you in the future will offer something in your parish churches when you come to Mass. He who is rich will offer much, but he who is poor will bring forth what he can, so that in this way everyone will give testimony that he himself and everything he has is subject to the good pleasure of God.

The Lord Jesus thus came with his mother and Joseph to the solemnity, which lasted seven days; indeed they came from far away, fearing neither the tedium nor the difficulty nor the dangers of the way. How many aspects of this event are a reproach to our coldness and tepidity in spiritual matters! The divine Child, little and tender, hurries from the remote ends of Galilee to Jerusalem. Joseph, for fear of Archelaus, the son of Herod, who had attempted to destroy Christ in the crib, did not want to come to Jerusalem, but still, on this occasion no fear or terror entered his soul, and instead he paid no attention to all the dangers. In things pertaining to the honor of God, it is necessary to suffer some inconvenience. There are no dangers that should be greatly feared where the salvation of the soul is concerned; not for excessive heat and warmth, nor for a draft of wind should churches be deserted, sermons neglected, or the sacred schools of Christian doctrine abandoned. When worship of God is being offered, when it is an occasion for helping souls, there must be no danger that a man is unwilling to face readily and promptly. All dangers are to be endured willingly and with alacrity.

And having fulfilled the days, when they returned (Lk. 2:43). They remained there for seven whole days, during which that festival was celebrated. So what kind of Christians are they, who complain that the offices are too long, who, making an objection out of the late hour, flee the churches and the sermons? They certainly do not learn this from Christ, from the Virgin, from Joseph. Indeed for those who love God, divine things cannot be or seem too long. Here I cannot remain silent about one thing in particular, which ought to embarrass us most. In those regions which are beyond the mountains (to which in these recent days I had to go, out of obedience to the most holy Vicar of Christ), the inhabitants have to struggle with a very great lack of priests, and even though in many places they only have one, still, on festive days they do not dare to eat until Mass has been solemnly sung in their churches. The Mass is sung throughout

---

[13]St. Charles refers here to a decree of the Fourth Provincial Council.

this city in so many churches of religious and priests, in so many parishes, and yet so many people as soon as they have gotten up, hurry to hear some private Mass, so that afterward they can freely get to their feasts and drinking parties! But let us agree that the offices are long and that one must remain for hours in order to finish them. Is not the whole feast day the Lord's? Is not this whole day supposed to be passed in spiritual things, just like the other days of the week are used up for earthly things? Furthermore, any servile works whatsoever, that is selling, buying and business dealings are prohibited on feast days; not because these are intrinsically evil or to be condemned, but because these days must not be violated by these kind of activities. They are to be dedicated to God alone and passing time in devout works.

The child Jesus remained in Jerusalem; and his parents knew it not (Lk. 2:43). It could seem that little care was being taken for such a son, since neither parent had any knowledge of his being lost. Nevertheless blame for this is not to be ascribed to either of them, for the law provided that when they went to the Temple, men and women should not travel in mixed company, but since this was mitigated with infants or children, it was therefore licit for them to be together now with the father, now with the mother. Joseph, therefore, thought Jesus was with Mary, and Mary thought he was with her husband Joseph. But when they found each other, the son was nowhere to be found. O what was the sorrow of Mary at that moment and how great it was! She knew this Son was God and the Son of God; therefore, she feared that by her fault she had made herself unworthy of such a Son, for it is the habit of a delicate conscience to fear fault even when there is none. But once three days had passed, they finally found him whom they had been seeking everywhere. Truly it was not without a mystery that three days had elapsed, for this triduum was like a certain foretaste of that most bitter triduum, when your Son, O most holy Mother, was to remain three days in the tomb, torn away from your gaze. This sorrow announced beforehand that most atrocious one which was going to transfix your own soul. But the subsequent joy and exultation of Mary entirely conquered the bitterness of this sorrow when at last she found her dearly beloved Son, sought with so many tears. Indeed can anyone mentally conceive the kisses and embraces coming from the God-bearer now filled with joy? Her words were interrupted with crying for joy, even though within herself she was saying, "O my sweetest son, my life, my hope, my heart, and my entire good. *Now shall I die with joy, because I have seen your face* (Gen. 46:30). Do not ever again, I beg you, move my soul with such great sorrow, nor in the end transfix my breast with these swords; for I shall be unable to live if I have to suffer another so bitter affliction of soul." Nevertheless, O blessed Mother, you will suffer greater afflictions, and live; but with a life more bitter than a thousand deaths. You will see your most innocent Son in the hands of sinners and in such a bad state that you will seem to be looking at utter monstrosity rather than a man, because *there was no sightlines* in him (Isa. 53:2). You will see him most disgracefully affixed to the gibbet of the cross between thieves. You will see his most holy side transfixed with hard point of a lance; at length you will see the blood which he took from you pour forth, and yet you will not be able to die. O what sorrows remain for you, what torments!

So finally Mary in her affliction, sorrow and full of bitterness finds her most beloved Son. But where? It is not where mothers today find their sons—in piazzas, in marketplaces, in streets—is it? Certainly not; but *in the temple, sitting in the midst of the doctors, hearing them, and asking them questions* (Lk. 2:46). Where the worship of God takes place, there Christ is found. O young people of today, the Son of God teaches you where you ought to be spending time, where it is fitting for you to keep regular company, with what activities you should occupy your first years and spend your flowering youth.

And all that heard him were astonished at his wisdom and his answers (Lk. 2:47). Necessarily, the greatness and divinity of Christ was shining forth, since the Pharisees, so proud and arrogant, were seized with amazement. Not only did they find his knowledge admirable; they were stupefied.

And his mother said to him: Son, why have you done so to us? behold your father and I have sought you sorrowing (Lk. 2:48). Christ is not being reproved here, but with devout affection and trembling words the Blessed Mother expresses to her Son the magnitude of her sorrow, in order to inquire whether she had been at fault in anything, so as to be able to most diligently avoid it, whatever it may have been, in the future.

And he said to them: How is it that you sought me? did you not know, that I must be about my father's business? (Lk. 2:49). O you children, when it is question of the honor and service which must be given to God, let the flesh cede its rights, let blood cede, let father, and mother, and blood relatives cede: *We ought to obey God, rather than men* (Acts 5:29). A son should even walk over his father prostrate in the doorway, says Bernard. If God calls you to a more perfect state, but father or mother strive to call you back, let God go ahead and win. This answer of Christ is the most fitting shield we could have against all those things that in any way can separate us from divine and spiritual things. Does a daughter wish to enter a monastery and consecrate her virginity to God and the mother is saying no? Let the daughter say: *what is that to me and to you,* Mother (Jn 2:4)? *Did you not know, that I must be about my father's business?* Is there anyone who has conceived the desire in his soul to receive the Most Holy Eucharist, tomorrow or another day, or to undertake some other devout work, and many things stand in the way? All obstacles are to be repelled and cut away, so that the first place in us may be left for God alone.

And he went down with them, and came to Nazareth, and was subject to them (Lk. 2:51). When you obey God, my children, you must also be submissive to your parents. This adolescent girl often eats the Eucharistic food and makes herself pleasing to God by devout and religious works. She must not for all that become proud, but when she is at home, let her learn to get along with her parents and let her be humble enough for all labors, even the more lowly ones. More than that, she must herself set the example in this for her sisters and everyone in the household. Christ the Son of God was subject to a carpenter. Just try going about proudly now, and exempting yourself from the obedience that must be given to superiors and parents! What is that objection you are making? You have more learning under your belt than some of your superiors? Who was wiser? Joseph or Christ, *in whom are hid all the treasures of wisdom and knowledge* of God (Col. 2:3)? Who was more excellent for virtue and sanctity? Christ or Joseph? And still Christ is subject to Joseph. O miserable man, even if someone placed over you is in some way deficient, learn to revere him; and know that the Lord God will give him opportune light, by which he may be able to bear worthily the weight of rule laid upon him. Hear what the wise man teaches you in this matter: *Son, support the old age of your father, and grieve him not in his life; And if his understanding fail, have patience with him, and despise him not when you are in your strength* (Eccl. 3:14–15). For this reason, the angel commanding flight into Egypt appeared not to Mary, but to Joseph, whom she nevertheless so greatly surpassed, and this was because God, when enjoining an office of ruling on someone, is accustomed to provide him with apt helps for carrying it out.

Jesus therefore *advanced in wisdom, and age, and grace with God and men* (Lk. 2:52), because day by day he was manifesting himself more to men, not because the perfections in him which were infinite could be increased, but because he was growing also in experiential knowledge according to the measure of his age. This whole passage of the Gospel, dear hearers, was for a most full instruction for all of you. For all fathers, mothers and children, superiors and subjects, it was a brilliant mirror in which they could most easily see how to live their lives. Who among us could not be numbered among some of them? Therefore let parents and superiors imitate Joseph and Mary, let children and subjects imitate the Lord Jesus, so that where they have gone, we too may by following the same path one day arrive. Amen.

WORKS TRANSLATED

Acta Ecclesiae Mediolanensis
Joseph Anthony Sax, ed. *Sancti Caroli Borromei Homiliae*, volumes 1–5, Milan: Joseph Marellum, 1747–48.

Pursuing God's Interests, Not Ours (Sax, volume 5, 1–8).
Cultivating the Field Persistently (Sax, volume 5, 9–18).
Reforming Together (Sax, volume 5, 29–37).
Washing Feet as Christ Did (Sax, volume 1, Homilia II, 8–15).
God's Overwhelming Love in the Eucharist (Sax, volume 1, Homilia XXIV, 187–92).
Taste the Sweetness of the Lord (Sax, volume 1, Homilia XXV, 193–201).
Receiving This Sacrament Frequently, Worthily and Zealously (Sax, volume 1, Homilia XXVII, 215–24).
Uniting Heaven and Earth at the Altar (Sax, volume 1, Homilia XLI, 354–62).
Preaching the Word of God (*Acta Ecclesiae Mediolanensis*, part IV, columns 1207–48).
Will You Risk Your Life for the Flock? (Sax, volume 1, Homilia XI, 93–97).
A Face Humble and Free from Vanity (*Acta Ecclesiae Mediolanensis*, part VII, columns 612–18).
Come with the Right Intention (Sax, volume 4, Homilia CXXIV, 325–9).
Be Holy or Be Struck Down (Sax, volume 4, Homilia CXXV, 330–4).
Spiritual Deformity or Integrity? (Sax, volume 4, Homilia CXXVI, 335–9).
My Portion Is You, O Lord (Sax, volume 1, Homilia XIX, 149–51).
Priestly Anointing Reflected in a Virtuous Life (Sax, volume 1, Homilia XX, 152–4).
Seeking Greater Holiness (Sax, volume 3, Homilia XCI, 273–85).
Vigilant Shepherds (Sax, volume 3, Homilia XCII, 286–301).
You Are the Pattern of the Flock (*Acta Ecclesiae Mediolanensis*, part IV, columns 883–903).
Daily Christian Living (*Acta Ecclesiae Mediolanensis*, part VII, columns 644–69).
Open Your Hearts to the Holy Spirit (Sax, volume 1, Homilia XIV, 117–22).
Imitating the Holy Family (Sax, volume 3, Homilia XCV, 333–48).

BIBLIOGRAPHY

Books and Monographs

Alberigo, Giuseppe. *Karl Borromäus: geschichtliche Sensibilität und pastorales Engagement*. Münster: Aschendorff, 1995.

Bach, Hedwig. *Karl Borromäus: Leitbild für die Reform der Kirche nach dem Konzil von Trient*. Köln: Wienand, 1984.

Bascapé, Carlo. *Vita e opera di Carlo arcivescovo di Milano cardinale di S. Prassede*. Milan: Veneranda Fabbrica del Duomo, 1965. First published in 1592.

Bassi, Maria Piera, ed. *Itinerari di san Carlo Borromeo nella cartografia delle visite pastorali: Provincia di Milano*. Milan: Unicopli, 1985.

Biscottini, Paolo, ed. *Carlo e Federico: la luce dei Borromeo nella Milano spagnola*. Milan: Museo Diocesano, 2005.

Camenisch, Carl. *Carlo Borromeo und die Gegenreformation im Veltlin: mit besonderer Berücksichtigung der Landesschule in Sondrio*. 1901. Reprint, Whitefish: Kessinger Legacy Reprints, 2010.

Crivelli, Luigi. *San Carlo: l'uomo, il pastore, il santo*. Milan: Ancora, 2010.

Deroo, André. *Saint Charles Borromée: cardinal réformateur, docteur de la pastorale (1538–1584)*. Paris: Éditions Saint-Paul, 1963.

Giussano, Giovanni Pietro. *The Life of St. Charles Borromeo*, vols. 1–2 [translator not given]. London: Burns & Oats, 1884. First published in 1610. Reprint, London: Forgotten Books, 2015.

Headley, John M. and John B. Tomaro, eds. *San Carlo Borromeo: Catholic Reform and Ecclesiastical Politics in the Second Half of the Sixteenth Century*. Washington, DC: Folger Shakespeare Library, 1988.

Jedin, Hubert. *San Carlo Borromeo*. Rome: Istituto della Enciclopedia Italiana, 1971.

La Più Grande Riforma: San Carlo e la sua passione per l'uomo. Edited by the Priestly Fraternity of the Missionaries of Saint Charles Borromeo. Milan: Fraternità di San Carlo, 2005.

Majo, Angelo. *San Carlo Borromeo: vita e azione pastorale*. Milan: Edizioni San Paolo, 2004.

Muraoka, Anne H. *The Path of Humility: Caravaggio and Carlo Borromeo*. Renaissance and Baroque: Studies and Texts, vol. 34. New York: Peter Lang, 2015.

Navoni, Marco. *Carlo Borromeo: Profilo di un vescovo santo*. Milan: Centro Ambrosiano, 2010.

Orsenigo, Cesare. *Life of Saint Charles Borromeo*. Translated by Rudolf Kraus. St. Louis: B Herder, 1943.

Bibliography

Pistoni, Giuseppe. *Il sinodo nonantolano di S. Carlo Borromeo del 1565*. Modena: Mucci, 1986.

Rossi di Margnano, Federico A. *Carlo Borromeo: un uomo, una vita, un secolo*. Milan: Mondatori, 2010.

San Carlo Borromeo: La casa costruita sulla roccia. Edited by the Archdiocese of Milan and the Veneranda Biblioteca Ambrosiana. Bari: Pagina soc. Coop., 2011.

San Carlo Borromeo. Omelie sull'eucaristia e sul sacerdozio. Translated and annotated by Felice Carnaghi. Rome: Edizioni Paoline, 1984.

Sancti Caroli Borromaei. Orationes XII, ad ususm episcoporum in concilium oeacum. vaticanum II convenientium Pauli VI Pont. Max. iussu denuo editae. Rome: [no publisher given], 1963.

Stacpoole-Kenny, Louise Mary. *Saint Charles Borromeo: A Sketch of the Reforming Cardinal*, 1911. Reprint, Charleston: BiblioBazaar, 2009.

Sylvain, Charles. *Histoire de Saint Charles Borromée: cardinal, archevêque de Milan d'après sa correspondence et des documents inédits*. Bruges: Desclée de Brouwer, 1884.

Tettamanzi, Dionigi. *Dalla tua mano: San Carlo, un riformatore inattuale*. Milan: Rizzoli, 2010.

Thompson, Edward Healy. *The Life of St. Charles Borromeo*. New York: P.J. Kennedy & Sons, 1900.

Turchini, Angelo. *Monumenta borromaica II. Milano Inquisita. Inchieste di Carlo Borromeo sulla citta' e diocesi 1574–1584*. Cesena: Il Ponte Vecchio, 2010.

Turchini, Angelo and Nicola Raponi, eds. *Stampa, libri, e letture a Milano nell'età di Carlo Borromeo*. Milan: Vita e Pensiero, 1992.

Yeo, Margaret. *Reformer: Saint Charles Borromeo*. Milwaukee: Bruce Publishing Company, 1938. Reprint, Whitefish: Kessinger Publishing, 2010.

Zardin, Danilo. *Carlo Borromeo: cultura, santità, governo*. Milan: Vita e Pensiero, 2010.

———. *Riforma cattolica e resistenze nobiliari nella diocesi di Carlo Borromeo*. Milan: Jaca Book, 1983.

———. *S Carlo Borromeo ed il rinnovamento della vita religiosa dei laici: Due contributi per la storia delle confraternite nella diocesi di Milano*. Milan: Soc arte e storia, 1982.

Articles

Alberigo, Giuseppe. "Du Concile de Trente au tridentinisme," *Irénikon* 54.2 (1981): 192–210.

———. "La riforma dei principi." In *Il Concilio di Trento come crocevia della politica europea*, edited by Hubert Jedin and Paolo Prodi, 161–77. Bologna: Società editrice il Mulino, 1979.

Alexander, John. "Architectural Unity and Rhetoric: The Patronage of Carlo Borromeo," *Sacred Architecture* 15 (2009): 16–22.

Benedict XVI, Pope. Address to the Italian Embassy to the Holy See, December 13, 2008.

———. Angelus Address, November 4, 2007.

———. Message *Lumen caritatis* to Cardinal Dionigi Tettamanzi, Archbishop of Milan, on the occasion of the 400th anniversary of the canonization of St. Charles Borromeo, November 1, 2010.

Cattaneo, Enrico. "Il sinodo diocesano Milanese del 1564." In *Miscellanea Carlo Figini*, edited by G. Colombo, A. Rimoldi and A. Valsecchi, 273–80. Milan: Editrice La Scuola, 1964.

Forrestal, Alison. "Revisiting Sacred Propaganda: The Holy Bishop in the Seventeenth-Century Jansenist Quarrel," *Reformation and Renaissance Review* 6.1 (2004): 7–35.

González Novalín, José Luis. "San Carlos Borromeo y su relación con España: Nota Crítica," *Hispania sacra* 40.81 (1988): 193–204.

Góralski, Wojciech. "Il primo sinodo diocesano (1564) del card Carlo Borromeo." In *Cristianità ed Europa: miscellanea di studi in onore di Luigi Prosdocimi*, edited by Cesare Alzati, 729–42. Rome: Herder, 1994.

Huerga, Álvaro. "La irradiación de San Carlos Borromeo en España a principios del siglo XVII," *Hispania sacra* 40.81 (1988): 179–91.

Iserloh, Erwin. "Karl Borromäus (1538–1584): ein Heiliger der katholischen Reform im 16. Jahrhundert." In *Weisheit Gottes—Weisheit der Welt: Festschrift für Joseph Kardinal Ratzinger zum 60. Geburtstag*, edited by Walter Baier and Stephan Otto Horn, 889–900. Ottilien: EOS Verlag, 1987.

John Paul II, Pope St. Address at Borromeo College in Pavia, November 3, 1984. English translation: *L'Osservatore Romano (English Edition)*, December 3, 1984, 8.

———. General Audience, November 4, 1981. English translation: *L'Osservatore Romano (English Edition)*, November 9, 1981, 3.

———. Homily during the Mass in Arona, November 4, 1984. English translation: *L'Osservatore Romano (English Edition)*, December 24, 1984, 16–17.

———. Homily during the Mass in the piazza of the Cathedral in Milan, November 4, 1984. English translation: *L'Osservatore Romano (English Edition)*, December 24, 1984, 14–15.

Maselli, Domenico. "La lotta contro l'eresia a Milano dal 1568 al 1584 nel carteggio di S. Carlo Borromeo: note e documenti." In *Umanesimo e teologia tra '400 a '500*, edited by Memorie Dominicane, vol. 4, 289–343. Pistoia: Centro Riviste Padri Domenicani, 1973.

Pius X, Pope St. Encyclical Letter *Editae saepe*, May 26, 1910.

Prodi, Paolo. "Charles Borromée, archevêque de Milan, et la papauté," *Revue d'historie ecclésiastique* 62.2 (1967): 379–411.

Rimoldi, Antonio. "I laici nelle regole delle confraternite di S. Carlo Borromeo." In *Miscellanea Carlo Figini*, edited by G. Colombo, A. Rimoldi and A. Valsecchi, 281–303. Milan: Editrice La Scuola Cattolica, 1964.

Schofield, David. "Carlo Borromeo and the Dangers of Laywomen in Church." In *The Sensuous in the Counter Reformation Church*, edited by Marcia B. Hall and Tracey E. Cooper, 187–205. Cambridge: Cambridge University Press, 2013.

Bibliography

Smart, David H. "Charles Borromeo's *Instructiones fabricae et supellectilis ecclesiasticae*: Liturgical Space and Renewed Ecclesiology after the Council of Trent," *Studia liturgica* 27.2 (1997): 166–75.

Thurston, Herbert. *The Papal Eulogy of St. Charles Borromeo*, London: Catholic Truth Society, [1911].

Vodola, Max. "I Met Charles Borromeo … and He Brought Me to Vatican II," *Pacifica* 26.2 (2013): 171–83.

Wicks, Jared. "Tridentine Motivations of Pope John XXIII Before and During Vatican II," *Theological Studies* 75.4 (2014): 847–62.

Westervelt, Benjamin W. "The Prodigal Son at Santa Justina: The Homily in the Borromean Reform of Pastoral Preaching," *The Sixteenth Century Journal* 32.1 (2001): 109–26.

INDEX OF BIBLICAL REFERENCES

Index of Biblical References

30:2 174
33:16–17 75
33:16 77
44:10 117
44:14 107
44:17 34
46:8 128
48:11–12 134
48:13 52
49:16 87
61:1 59
67:24 31
68:2 174
69:2 174
76:10–11 163
79:6 32
79:15–16 32
87:13 195
102:3 195
105:35 138
118:57 115
140:4 43

Proverbs
6:9 138
20:10 146
24:30–31 137
31:19 151

Ecclesiastes
3:14–15 202
4:7–8 134

Song of Solomon
4:9 192

Wisdom
1:4 79

Sirach
18:23 125
19:27 126

Isaiah
1:6 108
1:11–15 100
5:13–14 70
6:8 152
12:3 77

21:12 101
24:2 128
29:8 134
33:11 142
35:3 40
38:15 120
40:30–31 149
45:14–15 55
51:1 70
52:5 129
52:11 104, 107
53:2 201
53:6 134
56:10–11 133
56:11–12 136

Jeremiah
1:10 36
5:30–31 135
5:31 136
6:13–14 135
11:15 76
16:16 140
17:14 174
31:21 119, 129
51:34 155

Ezekiel
3:16 29
13:18 136
36:26 164

Daniel
13:52 66

Hosea
7:11 128

Zechariah
13:7 108

Malachi
1:6 62
1:8 123
1:11 73
1:14 123
2:1–2 128
2:7 35, 132, 133

Index of Biblical References

GENERAL INDEX

General Index

General Index